We'Moon 2023
Gaia Rhythms for Womyn

Sunrise & Crescent Moon ▫ *Gloria Campuzano 2011*

SILVER LINING
42ND EDITION OF WE'MOON
published by
Mother Tongue Ink

We'Moon 2023: Gaia Rhythms for Womyn
Spiral, Sturdy Paperback Binding, Unbound & Spanish Editions
© Mother Tongue Ink 2022

Mother Tongue Ink
Estacada, OR 97023
All Correspondence:
P.O. Box 187, Wolf Creek, OR 97497
www.wemoon.ws

We'Moon Founder: Musawa, *Special Editor:* Bethroot Gwynn
We'Moonagers: Sue Burns, Barb Dickinson *Graphic Design:* Sequoia Watterson
We'Moon Creatrix/Editorial Team: Bethroot Gwynn, Sequoia Watterson, Sue
Burns, Leah Markman, Barb Dickinson *Production Coordinator:* Barb Dickinson
Production Assistant & Retail Sales: Leah Markman *Proofing:* EagleHawk,
Sandra Pastorius, Kathryn Henderson, Becky Bee, Amber Fragione
Promotion: Leah Markman, Sue Burns, Susie Schmidt, Barb Dickinson
Accounts Manager: Sue Burns *Order Fulfillment:* Susie Schmidt, Erin Ryon

This eco-audit applies to all We'Moon 2023 products:

Hansol Paper — Environmental Benefits Statement:

We'Moon 2023 is printed on Hansol paper using 60%
recycled content: 50% pre-consumer waste, 50% post-
consumer waste, with Solvent-free Soy and Vegetable Based
inks with VOC levels below 1%.
By using recycled fibers instead of virgin fibers, we saved:
116 fully grown trees
46,602 gallons of water
32 million BTUs of energy
2,747 pounds of solid waste
8,222 pounds of greenhouse gasses

As a moon calendar, this book is
reusable: every 19 years the moon
completes a metonic cycle, returning
to the same phase, sign and degree
of the zodiac.

We'Moon is
printed in South Korea
by Sung In Printing
America on recycled
paper using low VOC
soy-based inks.

Green America — APPROVED FOR PEOPLE AND PLANET

Order directly from Mother Tongue Ink
For more information see p. 233.
Retail: 877-693-6666 or 541-956-6052 Wholesale: 503-288-3588

We'Moon 2023 Datebooks: • $22.95
Spiral ISBN: 978-1-942775-38-6
Sturdy Paperback ISBN: 978-1-942775-39-3
Unbound ISBN: 978-1-942775-40-9
Spanish Edition ISBN: 978-1-942775-41-6
In the Spirit of We'Moon • $26.95
Paperback ISBN: 978-1-890931-75-9
Preacher Woman for the Goddess • $16
Paperback ISBN: 978-1-942775-12-6

The Last Wild Witch • $9.95
Paperback ISBN: 978-1-890931-94-0
Other We'Moon 2023 Products:
We'Moon on the Wall • $17.95
ISBN: 978-1-942775-42-3
Greeting Cards (6-Pack) • $13.95
ISBN: 978-1-942775-43-0
Organic Cotton Totes • $13 & $15
Cover Poster (11" x 17") • $10

2023

Chakra Flow
© Mandalamy Arts 2020

JANUARY

S	M	T	W	T	F	S
1	2	3	4	5	6	7
8	9	10	11	12	13	14
15	16	17	18	19	20	21
22	23	24	25	26	27	28
29	30	31				

FEBRUARY

S	M	T	W	T	F	S
			1	2	3	4
5	6	7	8	9	10	11
12	13	14	15	16	17	18
19	20	21	22	23	24	25
26	27	28				

MARCH

S	M	T	W	T	F	S
			1	2	3	4
5	6	7	8	9	10	11
12	13	14	15	16	17	18
19	20	21	22	23	24	25
26	27	28	29	30	31	

APRIL

S	M	T	W	T	F	S
						1
2	3	4	5	6	7	8
9	10	11	12	13	14	15
16	17	18	19	20	21	22
23	24	25	26	27	28	29
30						

MAY

S	M	T	W	T	F	S
	1	2	3	4	5	6
7	8	9	10	11	12	13
14	15	16	17	18	19	20
21	22	23	24	25	26	27
28	29	30	31			

JUNE

S	M	T	W	T	F	S
				1	2	3
4	5	6	7	8	9	10
11	12	13	14	15	16	17
18	19	20	21	22	23	24
25	26	27	28	29	30	

JULY

S	M	T	W	T	F	S
						1
2	3	4	5	6	7	8
9	10	11	12	13	14	15
16	17	18	19	20	21	22
23	24	25	26	27	28	29
30	31					

AUGUST

S	M	T	W	T	F	S
		1	2	3	4	5
6	7	8	9	10	11	12
13	14	15	16	17	18	19
20	21	22	23	24	25	26
27	28	29	30	31		

SEPTEMBER

S	M	T	W	T	F	S
					1	2
3	4	5	6	7	8	9
10	11	12	13	14	15	16
17	18	19	20	21	22	23
24	25	26	27	28	29	30

OCTOBER

S	M	T	W	T	F	S
1	2	3	4	5	6	7
8	9	10	11	12	13	14
15	16	17	18	19	20	21
22	23	24	25	26	27	28
29	30	31				

NOVEMBER

S	M	T	W	T	F	S
			1	2	3	4
5	6	7	8	9	10	11
12	13	14	15	16	17	18
19	20	21	22	23	24	25
26	27	28	29	30		

DECEMBER

S	M	T	W	T	F	S
					1	2
3	4	5	6	7	8	9
10	11	12	13	14	15	16
17	18	19	20	21	22	23
24	25	26	27	28	29	30
31						

⬤ = NEW MOON, PST/PDT

⬤ = FULL MOON, PST/PDT

Cover Notes

Ancient Angel © Cathy McClelland 2020

Ancient Angel meditates before the bowl of infinite possibilities and discoveries. She holds the space for us to enter into the darkness of the bowl, which calls the soul to explore uncharted horizons of the self and beyond. The magical crescent moon shines first light onto the portal of discovery. Stars sparkle with ancient wisdom. Labyrinths and spirals evoke the journey of going deep within, communing with the divine self and returning with new insights and deep memory. We are all the *Ancient Angel*, connected to the stars and the universe, always creating, exploring and recognizing the star beings that we are.

After the Storm © Jeanette M. French 2015

After the Storm is an original oil painting. The dark of the storm, with all its wild fury, has passed. The waves are still being tossed about, streaked with foam, as Mother Nature begins to settle into a new rhythm. The glow of the setting sun makes the waters sparkle, reminding us that the Light always returns, and Nature's rhythms are ever changing. She calls to us to ride the waves of change with Grace.

Dedication

Every year we donate a portion of our proceeds to an organization doing good work that resonates with our theme. This year we partner with Bring Back the Blue (BBB), an organization creating a Silver Lining by turning ocean trash into treasure.

Andrea Neal and Megan Havrda got the idea of BBB in 2009, during a scientific expedition. On this mission they understood that the task of cleaning the ocean could become a self-sustaining endeavor. A lifelong passion was born for Andre and Megan.

BBB creates sustainable and renewable economy solutions for people and the ocean. The organization aims to convert plastic removed from the ocean into money through the new industry "Mining for Plastic"—delivering on the promise to create jobs, generate up-cycled products, and incentivize people not to put plastic back into the ocean. In the process, companies are educated about plastic reduction and sustainable alternatives. BBB is a majority women-owned Benefit Corporation, and their current partners are also women-owned businesses.

To learn more about how BBB is creating positive change for our oceans and offsetting plastic consumption visit bringbacktheblue.blue

Leah Markman © Mother Tongue Ink 2022

Bodies of Water © Van Lefan 2020

TABLE OF CONTENTS

INTRODUCTION

Title Page 1
Copyright Info 2
Year at a Glance 2023 3
Cover Notes/Dedication............... 4
What is We'Moon? 6
How to Use This Book 7
Astro Overview 2023 8
Eclipses/Mercury Retrograde.......10
Sky Map 2023 11
Exploring Past Lives 12

Astro Year at a Glance Intro.......15
Observations in First Light........16
Dream Seeds..............................18
Year of the Rabbit.....................19
Introduction to the Holy Days ..20
The Wheel of the Year..............21
Finding Hope in the Fives..........22
Introduction to We'Moon 2023 ..23
Invocation 25

MOON CALENDAR: SILVER LINING

I   First Light........................ 27
II   Dare Hope 37
III   Ebb & Flow...................... 49
IV   Ceremony......................... 61
V   A Radiance of Love 73
VI   Listen. Muse Speaks 85
VII   New World....................... 97

VIII   Sacred Wild 109
IX   Ancestors........................ 121
X   Wax & Wane................... 131
XI   Passage........................... 145
XII   She Changes................... 157
XIII   Gifts & Promises............. 167

APPENDIX

We'Moon Evolution.................178
We'Moon Land 179
We'Moon Tarot........................180
Staff Appreciation....................181
We'Moon Ancestors 182
Contributor Bylines/Index 184
Errors/Corrections....................195
We'Moon Sky Talk...................196
Astrology Basics.......................198
Signs and Symbols at a Glance 201
Constellations of the Zodiac....202
Moon Transits 203

Know Yourself...........................204
Goddess Planets 205
Ephemeris 101 206
Planetary Ephemeris.................207
Asteroid Ephemeris 213
Month at a Glance Calendars ...214
2023 Lunar Phase Card...........226
Conventional Holidays 228
World Time Zones 229
Year at a Glance 2024...............230
Available from We'Moon 231
Become a We'Moon Contributor 234

WE'MOON 2023 FEATURE WRITERS:

We'Moon Wisdom: Musawa; **Astrologers:** Astrologer Six; Heather Roan Robbins; Sandra Pastorius; Gretchen Lawlor; Susan Levitt; Melissa Kae Mason, Mooncat!; Beate Metz; **Introduction to the Theme:** Bethroot Gwynn; **Holy Days:** Molly Remer; **Lunar Phase Card:** Susan Baylies; **Herbs:** Karen L. Culpepper; **Tarot:** Leah Markman.

WHAT IS *WE'MOON*? A HANDBOOK IN NATURAL CYCLES

We'Moon: Gaia Rhythms for Womyn is more than an appointment book: it's a way of life! We'Moon is a lunar calendar, a handbook in natural rhythms, and a collaboration of international womyn's cultures. Art and writing by wemoon from many lands give a glimpse of the great diversity and uniqueness of a world we create in our own images. We'Moon is about womyn's spirituality (spirit-reality). We share how we live our truths, what inspires us, and our connection with the whole Earth and all our relations.

Wemoon means "we of the moon." The Moon, whose cycles run in our blood, is the original womyn's calendar. We use the word "wemoon" to define ourselves by our primary relation to the cosmic flow, instead of defining ourselves in relation to men (as in woman or female). We'Moon is sacred space in which to explore and celebrate the diversity of she-ness on Earth. We come from many different ways of life. As wemoon, we share a common mother root. We'Moon is created by, for and about womyn: in our image.

We'Moon celebrates the practice of honoring the Earth/Moon/Sun as our inner circle of kin in the Universe. The Moon's phases reflect her dance with Sun and Earth, her closest relatives in the sky. Together these three heavenly bodies weave the web of light and dark into our lives. Astrology measures the cycle by relating the Sun, Moon and all other planets in our universe through the backdrop of star signs (the zodiac), helping us to tell time in the larger cycles of the universe. The holy days draw us into the larger solar cycle as the moon phases wash over our daily lives.

We'Moon is dedicated to amplifying the images and voices of wemoon from many perspectives and cultures. We invite all women to share their work with respect for both cultural integrity and creative inspiration. We are fully aware that we live in a racist patriarchal society. Its influences have permeated every aspect of society, including the very liberation movements committed to ending oppression. Feminism is no exception—historically and presently dominated by white women's priorities and experiences. We seek to counter these influences in our work. We do not knowingly publish oppressive content of any kind. Most of us in our staff group are lesbian or queer—we live outside the norm. At the same time, we are mostly womyn who benefit from white privilege. We seek to make We'Moon a safe and welcoming place for all wimmin, especially for women of color (WOC) and others marginalized by the mainstream. We are eager to publish more words and images depicting people of color, *created by* WOC. We encourage more WOC to submit their creative work to We'Moon for greater inclusion and visibility (see p. 234).

Musawa © Mother Tongue Ink 2019

How to Use This Book
Useful Information about We'Moon

Refer to the **Table of Contents** to find more detailed resources, including: World Time Zones, Planetary and Asteroid Ephemeris, Signs and Symbols, Year at a Glance, and Month at a Glance Calendars.

Time Zones are in Pacific Standard/Daylight Time with the adjustment for GMT and EDT given at the bottom of each datebook page.

The **names and day of the week and months** are in English with four additional language translations: Bengali, Spanish, Irish and Croation.

Moon Theme Pages mark the beginning of each moon cycle with a two-page spread near the new moon. Each page includes the dates of that Moon's new and full moon and solar ingress.

Susan Baylies' **Lunar Phase Card** features the moon phases for the entire year on pp. 226–227

There is a two-page **Holy Day** spread for all equinoxes, solstices and cross quarter days, from a Northern Hemisphere perspective. These include writings by a different feature writer each year.

Astro Overview gives a synopsis of astral occurrences throughout the year from one of our featured astrologers, Heather Roan Robins, on pp. 8–9.

Read the **Astrological Prediction** for your particular sign on the pages shown on the right —>

♒ p. 39
♓ p. 51
♈ p. 63
♉ p. 75
♊ p. 87
♋ p. 99
♌ p. 111
♍ p. 125
♎ p. 137
♏ p. 149
♐ p. 161
♑ p. 173

ASTROLOGICAL OVERVIEW: 2023

This year the planets ask us to engage in dynamic social change, and to create and nurture new circles, webs, and cohorts. But we need to humbly explore what that means before we jump in to action.

Structured and responsible Saturn starts the year in Aquarius and enters Pisces March 7. Transformative Pluto steps into Aquarius from March 23–June 11, then retrogrades back into Capricorn until February 2024. The new chapter of Pluto in Aquarius offers hope—but don't expect all sweetness and light.

Aquarius, the fixed air sign, offers an image of equals sitting in a circle, people holding hands and working together. Pluto takes 247 years around the zodiac and last walked through Aquarius 1778–1797, heralding an era for revolution—the abolition of monarchies and creation of democracies. Once again, we step into a few decades which could revolutionize how we gather, connect with, educate and govern our world.

Pluto in Aquarius calls us to make sure every voice is heard, every vote counted. But the wisdom of the people's mind depends on what they know, what questions they ask, and how the heart and mind connect. Crowd mentality can be unreliable and inaccurate. We are responsible for asking the tough questions, for educating ourselves and others in order to help the populace look deeper and keep minds and hearts connected. In 2023 it furthers us to come out of isolation, break out of our old groups, and retain our individual thinking. Now is the time to coalesce and collaborate in new communities.

Neptune stays in Pisces and encourages our spiritual practice, our empathy and intuition, but can make truth foggy and leave people clinging to spiritual philosophies without really questioning whether they are still beneficial, or if they are being used to hide from some uncomfortable truth.

Saturn joins Neptune in Pisces March 7, which can bring old wisdom, discipline, and practicality (Saturn) into our spiritual search (Neptune) and can help us control our personal and cultural addictions. Water problems will keep climate change urgency in the forefront.

The year may have a slow start with Mercury, Mars, and Uranus all retrograde, so let's use the first few weeks in January to review and prepare rather than push. Mars turns direct January 12, Mercury January 18, and Uranus January 22; then we're off and running. Expect a direct, feisty spell as Venus enters Aries February 19 and imbues emotional and artistic bravery; women take the lead as Venus conjuncts Jupiter in Aries around March 2. Speak up, but don't burn a bridge unless you mean to.

Get organized and deal with urgent short-term agendas through a Solar eclipse square Pluto on April 19, and as Mercury retrogrades April 21–May 14. Process emotions but stay future-focused and proactive. We cannot change the past, but we can influence the future.

History turns up the heat and calls us to live fully. Watch for creative actions and political grandstanding during the period begining May 20 when Mars enters Leo and opposes Pluto, until June 26, when Mars square Uranus. Venus and Mars conjunct in Leo through early July, which can bring romance and feed creative projects everywhere, or it can be an excuse to create personal drama. Look for the best possible way to share the heart and leave melodrama alone.

The stars bring our attention to our life's work as Mercury enters Virgo on July 28 and gives us a chance to get organized and collaborate. But before the momentum can take off, Mercury retrogrades August 23–September 15 and helps us take a deep breath and keep our future integrated with our past. Contemplate how to stay responsible to our vision and health while balancing that with our responsibilities to the collective.

We need to fight the good fight but not waste energy arguing as Mars squares Pluto October 8 then enters Scorpio October 11. A solar eclipse October 14 and lunar eclipse October 28 act as astrological acupuncture to shake up and clarify our emotions, and they call us to check for the extremes of codependency or selfishness so we can find a more balanced way forward. Through early November, a Mars-Pluto quintile encourages us to question old patterns of learning, training, or authority; we can go beyond our teachers but not throw away what they've taught us.

Heather Roan Robbins © Mother Tongue Ink 2022

Eclipses: 2023

Solar and Lunar Eclipses occur when the Earth, Sun and Moon align at the Moon's nodal axis, usually four times a year, during New and Full Moons, respectively. The South (past) and North (future) Nodes symbolize our evolutionary path. Eclipses catalyze destiny's calling. Use eclipse degrees in your birth chart to identify potential release points.

April 19: Total Solar Eclipse at 29° Aries obscures our view and our willpower flags. Use this down time to gain fresh notions of where to put your energy, and what's worth pursuing. The return of light offers promise.

May 5: Penumbral Lunar Eclipse at 14° Scorpio opens us up in revealing ways. Old emotional wounds may surface. Let the returning light bring closure, and embrace the healing of your heart anew.

October 14: Annular Solar Eclipse at 21° Libra reveals how other points of view expand our horizons. Give other viewpoints some space. In the returning light imagine the possibilities. Share the bounty.

October 28: Partial Lunar Eclipse at 5° Taurus stirs up our security needs. Look deeply for what's meaningful to you. Let the returning light expand your comfort zones. Invite support that feeds your sense of belonging.

Mercury Retrograde: 2023

Mercury, planetary muse and mentor of our mental and communicative lives, appears to reverse its course three or four times a year. We may experience less stress during these periods by taking the time to pause and go back over familiar territory and give second thoughts to dropped projects or miscommunications. Breakdowns can help us attend to the safety of mechanics and mobility. It's time to "recall the now" of the past and deal with underlying issues. Leave matters that lock in future commitments until Mercury goes direct.

Mercury has three retrograde periods this year in earth signs:

Dec. 29, 2022–Jan. 18, 2023: When Mercury retrogrades in Capricorn, prepare ground for the annual leap from 2022's edge to 2023's edge. Use caution. Feed the ancestors with your appreciations.

April 21–May 14: As Mercury retrogrades in Taurus, discard what is not working in your communications. Learn to articulate subterranean vocabularies that matter to you, and then speak your truth upgraded.

August 23–Sept. 15: During Mercury in Virgo's retrograde period, our healing journey may make some unexpected turns. Cultivate your inner healer, and divine the medicines you need for wellbeing to take hold.

Dec. 12–Jan. 1, 2024: Mercury in Capricorn retrogrades again at year's end, and highlights restructuring behind the scenes. Make the next steps on your holy path with determination. Unknown blessings may be on their way.

Sandra Pastorius © Mother Tongue Ink 2022

Sky Map 2023

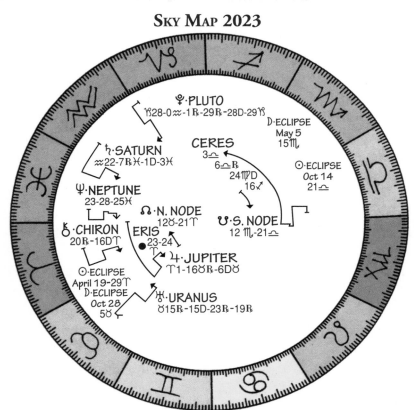

♀·PLUTO
Ⓨ28-0≈-1℞-29℞-28D-29Ⓨ

☾·ECLIPSE
May 5
15♏

ℏ·SATURN
≈22-7℞ℋ-1D-3ℋ

CERES
3♎
6♎℞
24♍D
16✶

☉·ECLIPSE
Oct 14
21♎

Ψ·NEPTUNE
23-28-25ℋ

☊·N. NODE
12♉-21♈

☋·S. NODE
12♏-21♎

♇·CHIRON
20℞-16Dℾ

ERIS
23-24
Ⓣ

♃·JUPITER
ℾ1-16℧℞-6D♉

☉·ECLIPSE
April 19-29ℾ
☾·ECLIPSE
Oct 28
5♉

♅·URANUS
♉15℞-15D-23℞-19℞

The Sky Map is an illustration to accompany the writings offered in
We'Moon 2023. It helps to gaze at this diagram when lost or overwhelmed
by the navigational challenges of being alive in these complicated days.

We'Moon is actually a wisdom school curriculum, created by a
faculty of brilliant, devoted writers, oracles, seers, pythias and sybils—
overseen by the Moon, the Sun and the Stars.

Every year for many years a group of women have gathered in the
woods to collect up all the We'Moon contributions into a big pot.
They cook it until the flavor of each offering begins to flirt with the
others. They stir out the bumps and tangles, then hang it all out to
dry. Then they spin and weave it all into a manual for the wisdom
school. This work is done in sacred ceremonial trance.

If you are reading this, Welcome! You have already begun the
wisdom school courses. They last for 13 Lunar Cycles, and are best
accomplished by studying this almanac daily, by using it, applying it
to your life. Thousands have gone before you; many repeat the courses
over and over—Students become teachers, teachers become ancestors,
ancestors become stars.

Gretchen Lawlor © Mother Tongue Ink 2022

Exploring Past Lives
To Resolve Present Life Challenges

Your astrological chart contains potent clues to past lives, shedding light on challenges you face in this life. Unresolved business can intrude and repeat, causing confusion/mayhem. Contracts, promises and old vows may continue to bind you. Significant relationships become flavored by other lives and settings, with people you have known before, over and over again.

What if you are being given another chance this time around? What if your astrology chart reveals something that tripped you up in a past incarnation? When you return, you take on another set of circumstances, often with the same familiar souls. You launch into another life to learn, make right, accept or forgive, release, resolve. Old scripts or ancestral traumas can be recognized—and released.

Where to begin? Start with your Moon. Your Moon sign describes where you instinctively feel at home. It's familiar, it comforts, it's your unconscious default response to life. Why? Because it's been a dominant component of at least one other life. Your Moon sign was probably your Sun sign in another life relevant to this one.

Water sign Moons (Cancer, Scorpio, Pisces) carry legacies of attunement and abilities in the subtle realms: magical witches, sorceresses and seers. Fire sign Moons (Aries, Leo, Sagittarius) carry legacies of boldness or grandness, magical leaders able to ignite and encourage others. Air sign Moons (Gemini, Libra, Aquarius) carry legacies of knowledge, magically using their silver tongues to illuminate and inspire. Earth sign Moons

Center of the Universe Cosmic Dark Goddess
© KT InfiniteArt 2018

(Taurus, Virgo, Capricorn) easily access a legacy of manifestation magic, rich with innate connections with plants, animals and the rhythms of nature.

If the Moon describes a familiar soul group—familiar terrain or perspectives carried forward from another life—the Nodes of the Moon add details about roles or specific experiences. The astrological house where your South Node is found (more so than the sign of the Node) points to where a challenge likely appeared, and where it might show up again in this incarnation.

The North Node, by house, suggests a way forward, an evolutionary reframing of the old story. Often, we vacillate back and forth between South and North nodes as we attempt to integrate past with future. Look there for clues about how to use old gifts in new lives, new ways.

Where to find your nodes? Most astrology birth charts show your North Node or True Node. Your South Node is always exactly opposite the North node on that 12-spoked diagram (ie. North Node at 17° Aries in the 7th house is always opposite South Node at 17° Libra, in the 1st house).

Claudia, a client with her Moon in Cancer and South Node in the 5th house, was asked about any permeating emotional trauma carried down from her female lineage; she recalled her mother and grandmother, both very sensitive souls, saying "I cannot live without my great love. I'd rather die than be abandoned." Both had been abandoned, and they never recovered.

Claudia was devoted to living her inherited deep passion and sensitivity in positive ways—especially in the way she raised her daughter. Echoes from her matriarchal line began showing up when her daughter (South Node in 5th house rules children) began to explore very different life choices, which Claudia experienced as rejection/abandonment—Claudia became dangerously ill.

Astrology helped her recognize the patterns at play, and her team of friends helped her see her daughter's situation in a larger more progressive context (all North Node in 11th house gifts). This introspection led to her own recovery as she realized her daughter was, in her own way, evolving the family story. She came back to life with a passion for causes associated with her daughter, and a devotion to pursue her own passions.

Look for unfinished business, lessons still to be learned that might be causing friction or pain in your life. Stay creatively alert to the recurring stories that play out in your life, and your ancestors'. The North Node shows where evolutionary growth can occur; the South Node is "what we push off from in the direction of growth" (Caroline Casey). You don't need to uncover the whole story—it is enough to capture glimpses, intimations, an essential theme, or pivotal memory. Try free word association; share your family stories. Watch for familiarity with a culture, a role, or a situation.

Often childhood interests stem from these ancient memories. As a young child I had an unusual fascination with Lascaux cave art. Exploring later through the lens of my Scorpio Moon, I realized with delight that I was recognizing and remembering ancient women shaman/oracles in ceremony, who no doubt help guide me today as a ceremonialist, oracle and shaman.

Be playful. Step outside your box. Entertain impossible fantasies—follow obsessions, especially those relating to particular cultures, characters and historical eras. Don't limit yourself to words—use art, listen to music, take a dance class from a culture or time you love. Use Halloween—when the veils between the lives are so very thin—to explore other characters, other roles. Release any old stories that hold you back, and reclaim ancestral strength and wisdom that can help you on your path today.

Gretchen Lawlor
© *Mother Tongue Ink 2022*

Soluna © *Mandalamy Arts 2017*

Astrological Year at a Glance Introduction

We start 2023 with the continued desire for stability and security. The North Node in Taurus symbolizes the power of being able to recognize the value of our material possessions. Taking stock of your silver linings is an invaluable practice that will serve you when negotiating with your desires. The beginning of the year may feel a bit sluggish and frustrating. Try not to dwell on what cannot be easily communicated; those words will come with time. Moving slowly does not symbolize idiocy or foolishness; careful speed is wise discernment of consequences. With Saturn in Aquarius for the remainder of the year, we may not be able to express ourselves as freely as we could previously. This energy will most heavily be felt early in the year until Saturn enters Pisces in March. Then, the collective will be called to bring their dreams to life. There is no success without hard work and a willingness to sacrifice. When our resolve is on building strong foundations, idealized realities can be brought to fruition.

This year will give us all plenty to think about; in certain scenarios we will not have prior life experience to inform our present-day actions. It's imperative that you are quick on your feet and willing to trust your instincts. Fluid intelligence is defined as our ability to adapt to situations that we are unfamiliar with. When Jupiter, planet of knowledge and wisdom enters Taurus, all the practical knowledge that was attained early in the year will be of use. In August, we will be required to leave our heads and settle any inkling of analysis paralysis—easier said than done. Part of the lesson from Saturn in Pisces is to learn how to get the help we need when our mind calls for it. As the year ends, reflect on the individual you have become this year. Refrain from getting stuck in shame over past mistakes—they happen and you're growing. You will find your balance when you're able to make peace with darkness and light; neither have an inherently good or bad connotation. Have a wonderful year.

Astrologer Six © Mother Tongue Ink 2022

≈ p. 39
♓ p. 51
♈ p. 63
♉ p. 75
♊ p. 87
♋ p. 99
♌ p. 111
♍ p. 125
♎ p. 137
♏ p. 149
♐ p. 161
♑ p. 173

To learn more about astrological influences for your sign, find your Sun and Rising signs in the pages noted to the right.

Observations in First Light:
Pluto enters Aquarius

In the Beginning,
we got dreamed up . . .

Creative Energy □ *Joan Zehnder 2001*

This year finds us on a precarious and profound edge of inner and outer discovery. From 2023 through 2043, Pluto, the planet of personal and collective power and transformation, enters the visionary sign of collective complexity and creativity: Aquarius. This occurrence represents a liberation from our limited human scope, and reflects a potent symbolic moment, as the firmament of the Aquarian Age—Era of the New Humanity— becomes illuminated.

We are in a corresponding era of powerful mirrored telescopes viewing the deepest reaches of the heavens, including the James Webb Space Telescope, the upcoming Nancy Grace Roman Space Telescope and the Extremely Large Telescope (ELT) in Chile, which, after taking in "first light," will bring into human vision images of the birthing of the very first stars, referred to as the Cosmic Dawn.

As this liberation of ancestral light breaches our darkness, how can we become bearers of light from these ancient skies? We may reflect on and from our inner world, surrounding ourselves with the metaphorical mirrors of our own human instrument, abiding in our Inner Observatory.

When we scan our personal horizons, we may evolve fresh perspectives of the world, within and without. In the domains of our meditations, dreaming states, or from the deep recall and emotion of our most intimate ponderings, lies the firmament from which we attune ourselves. Here we become witnesses of the first light of conscious awareness within ourselves. We may then observe and recognize first light dawning in others, in awe of the mutual awakenings that reveal our truest Being.

Pluto in Aquarius will be reflecting the growing pains of a New Humanity, with disrupting flows and patterns on the terrestrial plane for the next 20 years. The effects of the global pandemic that we are inheriting from Pluto's final flourish of the Capricorn transit

(2007–2023) leave us in a planetary healing crisis, with collective grief and dysfunction of sick, stuck, exploited and traumatized societies. Inherent in the wounded world are the seeds of healing and renewal. Pluto's energy compels us to clear our systems—be they immune, political, AI or global climate networks—by releasing built up pressures and accumulated poisons. These purges can reveal missing pieces that allow for a functional re-patterning and re-collectivizing of our human hive. Through new variants of hope, and a liberating radical empathy, we may grow in wisdom and agape love, turning the many reckonings we face into opportunities.

As revolutionary spirits surge, and the novel constellations of repair and innovation take shape, we stimulate the evolutionary intelligence required for broad social cultural adaptations that the Aquarian Age, and our shared common destiny ask of us.

The gifts contributed by each next generation of humanity may become a silver lining for our evolutionary unfolding. They express the unconscious drives and survival behaviors needed to shift focus and free up the potentials for our species to thrive. As more portals into space-time and mind-space come into view, what will these generations dream up for the New Humanity?

Aquarius: The Vision Bearers

We are the Vision Bearers,
Messengers in mind space.

Upon our shoulders rests
The vessel of Aquarius—
Pouring forth vibrations of change
With songs, finely tuned,
Carrying freedom's call.

A new vision ripples across
The collective mind—
Expectancy charging through the air!

We are the Vision Bearers,
Sowing seeds of time—
Into tomorrow's creation,
Only a thought away.

Sandra Pastorius © Mother Tongue Ink 2022

DREAM SEEDS

Way makers. Freedom fighters. Earth lovers. Change bringers. Come together as we honor the ancient webs of interconnectedness. We are generations and bloodlines and traumas and secrets and shadows and magic. Inhale renewed life into your dreams. Exhale ways of being that no longer serve. For our lives, we are thankful. The dawn of light is breaking.

Out of the darkness, our dream seeds are blooming. They have pushed through to the other side. By every means necessary, we fortified our seeds in the midst of the collective plague and pivot of the past few years. Speak into our community listening. What is your gaze set on? What is the world that you are dreaming up on this continuum, for the sake of generations forward and backward? May the flame of spirit within us continue to guide us and open the way.

We pay homage to the ancestors with our herb bundles of rosemary for remembrance and periwinkle for resilience. We honor you. We remember you. We thank you for every way that you have made. We call in your continued favor, protection and brilliance. We will fearlessly carry our individual and collective liberation work forward. Bless our dreams created from our biggest imaginations. Firmly root us in your wisdom so that we may actualize a lived experience of vitality, joy, justice and victory.

We call in the energy of grace, curiosity and open paths. May every dream be realized. Our plancestors will create a community infusion that will fortify our synergy. We call in nettles to nourish us; lemon balm to lift us to higher heights; tulsi to sustain our spirits; rose to remind us of the beauty and thorns of our journeys; and calendula to heal our wounds and help us see clearly. May we answer the call of

service, community care, collective collaboration, and destinies that make our hearts sing.

A return to light. A return to life. A living of life to its fullest capacity. Focus on your freedom NOW. We are the ones that made it.

Karen L. Culpepper © Mother Tongue Ink 2022

New Life Rose *© Alexa Sunshine Rose 2009*

THE YEAR OF THE RABBIT: 2023

Hare ¤ *Robin Lea Quinlivan 2017*

Chinese New Year is the second new Moon after Winter Solstice, when the new Moon and Sun are conjunct in Aquarius. The year of the Rabbit begins on January 21 in 2023 (January 22 in China). In Chinese mythology, Rabbit is a symbol of longevity, imaged as an alchemist and shaman who lives on the Moon with the Moon Goddess Chang'e.

Rabbit year can be a time of peace, calm, and healing after the dynamic Tiger year. Rabbits are gentle, peaceful souls who excel in the arts, so during Rabbit year, enjoy living an artistic life in the beauty you create and share with others. Fine arts and crafts, good food, and a lovely home are appreciated. Money can be made and spent easily. Globally, anticipate political compromise and diplomatic peace making.

Wemoon born in Rabbit years (1927, 1939, 1951, 1963, 1975, 1987, 1999, 2011, 2023) are friendly, sensitive, even-tempered, well-mannered, amiable, and naturally artistic. Rabbit's harmonizing energy and diplomatic ability makes her welcome in social circles. Rabbit is keenly perceptive and can sense danger in any situation. She quickly takes action to protect herself whenever a predator approaches. Rabbit is not a fighter; she would rather flee than confront conflicts. She's content to enjoy the peace and quiet of the charmed circle she creates. When it comes to affairs of the heart, Rabbit wemoon are extremely romantic, and enjoy the finer things in life. Rabbits are most compatible with another Rabbit, Sheep, or Pig. Dog is also compatible.

Of the five Taoist elements Fire, Earth, Metal, Water, and Wood, 2023 is the year of the Water Rabbit. Water adds depth of feelings, intuition, strong emotions, empathy, and kindness. Water is the most feminine of the five elements, and therefore is considered very *yin*. Femininity is not considered weak; on the contrary, Water is the most powerful element. It can move around any obstacle without losing its essential nature. Over time, Water can dissolve the hardest mountains. In Chinese medicine, Water rules the kidneys and bladder, so take care of your urinary system. Feng shui focus is on the bathroom to make yours a healing sanctuary this year. Rabbit correlates to the Western sign Pisces.

Susan Levitt © Mother Tongue Ink 2022

Promise of Spring © *Lindy Kehoe 2020*

Introduction to the Holy Days

We often discover the wheel of the year reflected within our own inner lives. In late fall, we may feel bountiful and abundant, with a rich harvest of offerings to share. In winter, we may feel like retreating into our caves, drawing inside to incubate and make plans. In spring, we may be ready to emerge again, bursting with enthusiasm and planting seeds of new ideas. In summer, after witnessing the thriving and blooming, we can see what is growing well and what needs to be pruned away. And, then, we re-turn and find fall has come again.

This year, we seek silver linings, emerging from the shadows with moonlight in our eyes and roses in our hands, looking for the good that still dwells among us, the heart that beats beneath the skin of the world. We have come carrying seeds of possibility, legacies of longing, with our own power looped loosely across our hips and shining in our bones.

Sometimes we stand here, in fear. Sometimes, in joy. Sometimes we stand not knowing how we will ever figure it all out. Sometimes we remember we don't have to.

We hear the call, the howl, the song, and we gather from around the globe, meeting in spirit across the miles, remembering that our most reliable sacred text is the one we write each day, bone by bone, shard by shard, side by side.

Remember that your attention is your most powerful and precious prayer, your most potent act of resistance in a culture of distraction. Re-collect it, call it in to your center, press it into your heart and let it soak beneath your skin, softening your edges and opening your eyes. Once we re-home our attention within our bodies and bones, we can then extend outward with care and compassion, reaching out to others in their joys and concerns, sorrows and fears, to lend a genuine hand. We make prayers of witnessing, of justice and awakening. We make prayers of presence, where we find ourselves each day.

Molly Remer © Mother Tongue Ink 2022

The Wheel of the Year: Holy Days

The seasonal cycle of the year is created by the Earth's annual orbit around the Sun. Solstices are the extreme points as Earth's axis tilts toward or away from the sun—when days and nights are longest or shortest. On equinoxes, days and nights are equal in all parts of the world. Four cross-quarter days roughly mark the midpoints in between solstices and equinoxes. We commemorate these natural turning points in the Earth's cycle. Seasonal celebrations of most cultures cluster around these same natural turning points:

February 2, Imbolc/Mid-Winter: celebration, prophecy, purification, initiation—Candlemas (Christian), New Year (Tibetan, Chinese, Iroquois), Tu Bi-Shevat (Jewish). Goddess Festivals: Brighid, (Celtic), Yemanja (Brazilian).

March 20, Equinox/Spring: rebirth, fertility, eggs—Passover (Jewish), Easter (Christian). Goddess Festivals: Eostare, Ostara, Oestre (German), Astarte (Semite), Persephone (Greek), Flora (Roman), Norooz/New Years Day (Persian).

May 1, Beltane/Mid-Spring: planting, fertility, sexuality—May Day (Euro-American), Walpurgisnacht/Valborg (German and Scandinavian), Root Festival (Yakima), Ching Ming (Chinese), Whitsuntide (Dutch). Goddess Festivals: Aphrodite (Greek), Venus (Roman), Lada (Slavic).

June 21, Solstice/Summer: sun, fire festivals—Niman Kachina (Hopi), Tirgan (Persian). Goddess Festivals: Isis (Egyptian), Litha (N. African), Yellow Corn Mother (Taino), Ishtar (Babylonian), Hestia (Greek), Sunna (Norse).

August 2, Lammas/Mid-Summer: first harvest, breaking bread, abundance—Green Corn Ceremony (Creek), Sundance (Lakota). Goddess Festivals: Corn Mother (Hopi), Amaterasu (Japanese), Hatshepsut's Day (Egyptian), Ziva (Ukraine), Habondia (Celtic).

September 22, Equinox/Fall: gather and store, ripeness—Mabon (Euro-American), Mehregan (Persian), Sukkoth (Jewish). Goddess Festivals: Tari · Pennu (Bengali), Old Woman Who Never Dies (Mandan), Chicomecoatl (Aztec), Black Bean Mother (Taino), Epona (Roman), Demeter (Greek).

October 31, Samhain/Mid-Fall: underworld journey, ancestor spirits—Hallowmas/Halloween (Euro-American), All Souls Day (Christian). Goddess Festivals: Baba Yaga (Russia), Inanna (Sumer), Hecate (Greek).

December 21, Solstice/Winter: returning of the light—Kwanzaa (African-American), Soyal (Hopi), Jul (Scandinavian), Cassave/Dreaming (Taino), Chanukah (Jewish), Christmas (Christian), Festival of Hummingbirds (Quecha), Shabeh Yalda/Birth Night (Persian). Goddess Festivals: Freya (Norse), Lucia (Italy, Sweden), Sarasvati (India).

* Note: Traditional pagan Celtic / Northern European, Jewish and Muslim holy days start earlier than the customary Native / North American ones—they are seen to begin in the embryonic dark phase: e.g., at sunset, the night before the holy day—and the seasons are seen to start on the Cross Quarter days before the Solstices and Equinoxes. In North America, these cardinal points on the wheel of the year are seen to initiate the beginning of each season.

© *Mother Tongue Ink 2003 Sources:* The Grandmother of Time *by Z. Budapest, 1989;* Celestially Auspicious Occasions *by Donna Henes, 1996 &* Songs of Bleeding *by Spider, 1992*

The Gift © *Diane Norrie 2016*

FINDING HOPE IN THE FIVES

In every suit in Tarot throughout the Minor Arcana lives the dreaded Five of Cups, Swords, Pentacles, and Wands. Traditionally the Fives bring conflict, doubt, disharmony, disappointment, and loss. Do not turn away from the storm—shadow may seep into your reading but steel your nerves to face the approaching turbulence and meet it with strength. Light captured on the edges of shadow often appears brighter and effervescent. Look for the silver lining.

When Five lands in your lap, take a moment and try to step back. Every challenge is an opportunity to change a pattern or try a new tactic. Five of Swords foretells of competition, conflict, and deception. Let this card direct you away from confrontation towards diplomacy. Five of Pentacles represents loss, lack or isolation—allow this card to challenge your poverty mentality. Five of Wands signifies disharmony, stress, and short-term difficulties. Follow through with perseverance and ingenuity when the Five of Wands confronts you with frustration and obstacles. Five of Cups portends disappointment, regret, pessimism: your expectations did not turn out as you may have liked. Let Five of Cups lead you into a gratitude practice with reminders that a loss at this moment may mean abundance and opportunity later.

Oppression, poverty, jealousy, pessimism, and power dynamics are often revealed here. Fives may bring these shadow issues to light; don't let them drag you into darkness. They are here to remind us to stay in control and remember our resilience in the face of frustration and strife. Use them as a sign to invigorate your journey, to support and strengthen the initiatives and services that exist to combat inequality in our communities.

Gratitude, ingenuity, adaptability, and creativity are all tools that lie hidden on the bright edges of these dark clouds. Five is a fight for balance, but also calls up perseverance and intense courage. Once the meaning is grasped solidly in all five fingers, you can start rebuilding the world.

Leah Markman © Mother Tongue Ink 2022

Introduction to We'Moon 2023: Silver Lining

Prepare yourself to be surprised, delighted, shaken, challenged, inspired when you enter the pages of *We'Moon 2023*. Be ready.

This datebook is a stunning weave of art and writing from women offering radiant wisdom, passionate earth-devotion, love miracles, inventive joy—alarm and outcry!

Against All Odds: that's the irony of a *Silver Lining* theme.

As we cycle from *The Magical Dark* (*We'Moon 2022*), there at the edge of night sky is a young crescent moon, a curl of promise, a hook on which to hang our imaginations. And so the spark of new light guides us through the thirteen moons of 2023. Our titles for the Moon theme "chapters" wrap metaphor around our journey through the days: First Light, Dare Hope, A Radiance of Love, New World, Sacred Wild, Gifts and Promises—to name several.

Praise and Exaltation. How dare we speak with sanguine voices, however, at this time of peril to earth and all her life forms!

It is a daily discipline to choose
how much of the world's darkness we touch and why.
We could be incandescent with righteous rage
every second of every minute of every hour...
But sworn enemy of joy we can't take Ecocide with us
on every walk even though it whines and scratches at the door.

(Debra Hall, p.65).

Yet, opportunity astounds us, challenge compels our resilience. These writers and artists are seers. With tools of paint and cadence, they peer beneath the obvious to unearth buried lessons—for this time/for all time. "Not getting lost is not the goal/ The goal is to allow this lost-ness/ To ripen you..." (Alexa Iya Soro, p.156).

The crescent, the silver sliver, the moon-boat winds its way through weeks and months of this year, sending its odd-angled illuminations into community life, individual heart-space, onto the world stage. Listen to this mooniness: "Mass kindness erupts/on every continent forcing people/into their neighbors' houses for dinner/and to care for each other's children/...Community gardens and renewable energy become international law..." (Stephanie A. Sellers, p. 96).

Transformation. The magnificent affirmation of Change which the moon shows us every month of days. The clarion call is clear: We Can Do This! This mending of the broken, this fierce insistence on loving repair among peoples and for the sake of earthscapes and creatures!

The moon herself, seen or unseen, is a Grand Actor in earth's drama. Moon pulls on our global waters, her weight dancing a duet every day with tides in and out, creating home for countless sea creatures. Moon III, *Ebb & Flow*, celebrates as well the waters that rush from land to shore, the ones that fall—Goddess willing! —from the sky with sustenance for birds and bats, wolves and frogs, bears and butterflies.

And as the moon orb circles earth orb, so do the seasons—Mother Sun's gift to the circle-dancing earth, summer to winter, seeds to harvest, blossom to fruit. We honor seasonal Holy Days (Equinoxes, Solstices, and Cross Quarter Days) with exquisite writings by Molly Remer. She invites us to pray, dance, sob, count on magic. She invites us to Stop. Open to gratitude. To wonder. "We persist in mending the web...mixing...with the golden seeds of possibility and the flares of inspiration, touching this moment of now." (Molly Remer, p. 151).

As with the moon, so with us: we wax, we wane. A cluster of our 2023 moon themes give focus to our human trajectory: life cycles, ancestors, death. Maiden, Mother, Crone archetypes invite acceptance of our life stages. How sweetly women speak here of mother-love's adoration for the child—who has so much to teach. What spiky wisdom comes from the old ones! And the Very Old Ones, the Ancestors, hover and instruct and bless—from a variety of cultures, voices of universal love.

And what does the moon show us of Death? She waxes, she wanes, she comes again. Do we come again?

off we fly, souls regenerated,
onward to the next great arc of sky, the
next beautiful unfurling. our eyes are flecked with
nova and starstuff. we are made for this journey.

(*excerpt ¤ marna scooter 2020*, p. 131)
Bethroot Gwynn © Mother Tongue Ink 2022

Ah, crescent wonder! Smiling arc of light
Sliding down the western sky
Sliver of radiant promise: More is on the way!
Tomorrow You will curl up onto the eastern heaven—
Fatter, brighter. Ever laughing.
Baby Moon, grinning to Begin. Calling out "Next!"
Arawa   Diana   Yemanja
Moon Maiden rising
Juna   Artemis   Selene
Moon Mama, cuddling our hopes   cradling our growth
Sickle at the ready   protecting, just in case
Moon Goddess on the edge
edging darkness with Your sharp horn
dig clear unearth   bow to the fragile sprout
the fleeting chance   the unlikely miracle
the grace to start over

Nightgazers!   Behold: Mother of Rebirth
All Praise: Child of Again
We summon the world to smile back
Look up!   Dare hope.
Keep Watch!

Be Luminous, Skydancers

Be luminous, skydancers,
Undulate in the sparkle-wise shimmy
of the ululating moon

Resplendent in her draped bounty,
you are the systers of mystery:
her silver sheen is your horn of plenty

Sip from this eternal silvery spoon
a cosmic elixir of regeneration
to sustain you in earth-whirling magics

Solidarity is a kind of light
shimmering through you

You were carved in careful crescents
from the bones of moon
and blessed by ancient priestesses
for this time and tune

Your third eye is a rune to speak to future ones
about how to fly through this portal
of challenge and possibility
with the grit and grace of starstuff
and the wings of heron and loon

Specked with sparks of moonlight,
croon justice into cracking open the egg

of tomorrow with the fierce beak of clear intention
and faster-than-soon

◻ *marna scooter 2021*

I. FIRST LIGHT

Moon I: December 23, 2022–January 21, 2023

Sun in ♑ Capricorn Dec. 21; New Moon in ♑ Capricorn Dec. 23; Full Moon in ♋ Cancer Jan. 6

The Rites of Passage
© *Tessa Mythos 2016*

December 2022

Mí na Nollag

Dawning of a New Earth

─── ꍈꍈꍈ Dé Luain ───

♏

Monday
19

♀□♃	8:23 am
♀⊼♂	9:37 am
♂⚹♃	2:38 pm
☽⚹♀	5:21 pm
☽☍♅	10:33 pm

─── ♂♂♂ Dé Máirt ───

♏
♐

Tuesday
20

☽⚹♅	3:58 am
♃→♈	6:32 am
☽□♄	8:41 am
☽△♆	11:01 am
☽⚹♇	6:45 pm v/c
☽→♐	11:12 pm
☽△♃	11:19 pm

─── ☿☿☿ Dé Céadaoin ───

♐

Wednesday
21

☉→♑	1:48 pm
☉□♃	4:50 pm
☽☍♂	5:48 pm

Winter Solstice

☉ → ♑

Sun in ♑ Capricorn 1:48 pm PST

─── ♃♃♃ Dé Ardaoin ───

♐
♑

Thursday
22

♀△♅	1:48 am
☽⚹♄	10:19 am
☽□♆	12:16 pm v/c
☽→♑	11:49 pm

─── ♀♀♀ Dé Haoine ───

♑

Friday
23

☽□♃	12:13 am
♃D	12:40 am
☉☌☽	2:17 am

New Moon in ♑ Capricorn 2:17 am PST

ALL ASPECTS IN PACIFIC STANDARD TIME; ADD 3 HOURS FOR EST; ADD 8 HOURS FOR GMT

Fragments

Hold tightly onto a sliver, just a
Little sliver is all one needs.

A sliver of hope,
Of love, of luck, of faith,
Of life, but quite often only possessing
A thin sliver of me.

Notice a sliver is at times an illusion;
a deluge of darkness hiding
What is whole.

And slowly; fragment, by fragment,
by fragment, see Her light
Reveal what has always been
a completely bared and luminous
Soul.

¤ *Erin Guntis 2021*

ᚺᚺᚺ Dé Sathairn

♑
♒

Saturday
24

☽△♅ 12:02 am
☽PrG 12:22 am
☽☌♀ 4:16 am
☽☌♉ 11:32 am
☽⚹♆ 11:48 am

☿⚹♆ 5:16 pm
☽☌♇ 7:11 pm v/c
☽→♒ 11:14 pm
☽⚹♃ 11:56 pm

☉☉☉ Dé Domhnaigh

♒

Sunday
25

☽△♂ 3:34 pm
☽□♅ 11:35 pm

MOON I

Dec. '22–Jan. '23
diciembre / enero

Monday
26

☽♂♄ 10:19 am v/c
☽→⯑ 11:34 pm

Tuesday
27

☉⚹☽ 9:23 am
☽□♂ 3:54 pm

Wednesday
28

♀⚹♆ 12:32 am
☽⚹♅ 1:02 am
☽♂♆ 2:05 pm
☽⚹♀ 3:25 pm
☽⚹☿ 4:43 pm
☽⚹♇ 10:20 pm v/c

Thursday
29

☿R 1:31 am
☽→♈ 2:36 am
☽♂♃ 4:11 am
☿♂♀ 5:58 am
☉□☽ 5:20 pm
☽⚹♂ 7:17 pm

Waxing Half Moon in ♈ Aries 5:20 pm PST

Friday
30

☉⚻♂ 3:21 pm
☽⚹♄ 6:52 pm
☽□♅ 10:00 pm

Silver Boat

Compressed to a month, our story
of 13.8 billion years,
finds us here at the silver sliver;
the dark of the moon so recent,
we haven't yet noticed the change.
Who will look up?
Who will board the silver boat?

This phase of the human story
is a virgin path
that's never been crafted before.
We can ride the growing light.
We are the ones who can look up,
we can board the silver boat.

We Cultivate Hope
© Katie Ree 2021

I hear our descendants calling through time,
asking us to turn
toward the crescent hope,
entreating us to embark and evolve.
Will we look up?
Will we board the silver boat?

© Susa Silvermarie 2021

ᚼᚼᚼ sábado

♈
♉

Saturday
31

☽□♀   2:59 am
☽□♇   4:44 am v/c
☽→♉   9:08 am
♀♂♇   9:25 pm

☉☉☉ domingo

♉

Sunday
1

January

☉△☽   5:42 am
☽♂♅   1:52 pm
☿⚹♆   10:42 pm

January
sijećanj

Moon
They say she's less powerful than the sun,
but she has her own gravity.
See how her silent tug pulls oceans.
excerpt © Rachel Creager Ireland 2018

☽☽☽ ponedjeljak

♉ ♊

Monday 2

☽□♄ 4:15 am
☽△☿ 4:30 am
☽⚹♆ 4:53 am
☉□⚷ 8:02 am
☽△♇ 2:16 pm v/c
♀→♒ 6:09 pm
☽→♊ 6:44 pm
☽△♀ 6:48 pm
☽⚹♃ 9:37 pm

♂♂♂ utorak

♊

Tuesday 3

☽☌♂ 11:47 am

☿☿☿ srijeda

♊

Wednesday 4

♀⚹♃ 1:08 am
☽△♄ 3:54 pm
☽□♆ 4:07 pm v/c

♃♃♃ četvrtak

♊ ♋

Thursday 5

☽→♋ 6:15 am
☉△♅ 8:43 am
☽□♃ 9:50 am

♀♀♀ petak

♋

Friday 6

☽⚹♅ 12:30 pm
☉☍☽ 3:08 pm
☽☍☿ 5:36 pm

Full Moon in ♋ Cancer 3:08 pm PST

All aspects in Pacific Standard Time; add 3 hours for EST; add 8 hours for GMT

**Hecate Rides the
New Moon**
◻ *Diana Denslow 2021*

Luminosity

She is the crescent moon, the bow,
  rising and setting in perfect arcs,
    hooking the great mantle of darkness,
      pulling it across the listless sky.

excerpt © Megan Welti 2013

───── ♄♄♄ subota ─────

♋
♌

Saturday

7

☽△♆ 4:30 am
☉♂♉ 4:57 am
☽☍♇ 2:23 pm v/c
☽→♌ 6:40 pm
☽△♃ 11:00 pm

───── ☉☉☉ nedjelja ─────

♌

Sunday

8

☿PrH 12:34 am
☽ApG 1:20 am
☽☍♀ 8:52 am
☽⚹♂ 11:19 am
☿△♅ 3:23 pm

January
Poush

© Jakki Moore 2015

Starry Night

☽☽☽ sombar

♌

Monday
9

☽□♅ 1:02 am
♀△♂ 7:22 am
☽☍♄ 5:52 pm v/c

♂♂♂ mongolbar

♌
♍

Tuesday
10

☽→♍ 7:15 am
☽□♂ 11:36 pm

☿☿☿ budhbar

♍

Wednesday
11

☿□♃ 12:49 am
☽△☿ 6:58 am
☽△♅ 1:17 pm

♃♃♃ brihospotibar

♍
♎

Thursday
12

☉△☽ 3:07 am
☽☍♆ 5:21 am
♀⚹♃ 10:46 am
♂D 12:56 pm
☽△♇ 3:06 pm v/c
☽→♎ 6:56 pm

♀♀♀ sukrobar

♎

Friday
13

☽☍♃ 12:33 am
☉⚹♆ 6:11 am
☽△♂ 10:46 am
☽□♅ 1:55 pm
☽△♀ 9:58 pm

ALL ASPECTS IN PACIFIC STANDARD TIME; ADD 3 HOURS FOR EST; ADD 8 HOURS FOR GMT

Silver Lining

The first sign of the Moon Mother—
a sliver of light against Night's dark and infinite backdrop.

One eye of the sleeping Wild Woman peeks open as if to say.
"I am still here. You didn't forget about me, did you?"

Down on Earth a flurry of action begins.
"O Divine Mother, O Beloved One,
of course we did not forget about you;
see all the work we've been doing?"

Meanwhile, the wise women, the ones who know Her rhythms,
who feel Her as their very own Self,
quietly continue the work that they never for a moment let up.

Steady in their faith, they know Her Presence
whether visible or not.

"So lovely to see you again Great Mother," they whisper
as they continue their ever-important work of
planting, tending, loving, singing, dancing, and weaving
Her liquid silver light into every thread of existence.

© Johanna Elise 2021

———————— ꑫꑫꑫ sonibar ————————

♎

Saturday
14

☽△♄ 4:47 pm
♀□♅ 5:22 pm
☉□☽ 6:10 pm

———————— ⊙⊙⊙ robibar ————————

Waning Half Moon in ♎ Libra 6:10 pm PST

♎
♏

Sunday
15

☽□♇ 12:39 am v/c
☽→♏ 4:08 am
☽⚹♉ 7:47 pm

Nectar

we are unprotected
here in the mottled world,
where darkness veins the light
and everything we love
is on its way to becoming
everything we lose,

>ceaseless metamorphosis
>turns inside us and around us
>until we're dizzy with the frenzy
>of this being here,
>embodied.

Meanwhile, outside
the hummingbird
skims the air
with her piston
of desire
Her clear want for nectar
breaks my doubtful heart
open

>I remember something
>from when I was still just light
>When I was looking
>into this world
>from the one outside of it,
>looking down, listening,

I remember hearing laughter
and wanting that new nectar,
yes, even with so much being ripped
from us, yes, even with all the pain of endings

>I remember: the world is what I wanted.

Emily Kedar 2021

II. DARE HOPE

Moon II: January 21–February 19

Sun in ♒ Aquarius Jan. 20; New Moon in ♒ Aquarius Jan. 21; Full Moon in ♌ Leo Feb. 5

Hummingbird © Tamara Phillips 2016

January
Mí Eanair

Distant

───── ☽☽☽ Dé Luain ─────

♏︎

Monday
16

☽☌♅	7:17 am
☽□♀	11:09 am
☽△♆	9:47 pm
☿⚹♂	10:30 pm
☽□♄	11:27 pm

───── ♂♂♂ Dé Máirt ─────

♏︎
♐︎

Tuesday
17

☉⚹☽	4:35 am
☽⚹♇	6:27 am v/c
☽→♐︎	9:33 am
☽△♃	3:41 pm
☽☍♂	11:39 pm

───── ☿☿☿ Dé Céadaoin ─────

♐︎

Wednesday
18

♅D	5:12 am
☉☌♇	6:44 am
☽⚹♀	7:05 pm

───── ♃♃♃ Dé Ardaoin ─────

♐︎
♑︎

Thursday
19

☽□♆	12:17 am
☽⚹♄	2:08 am v/c
☽→♑︎	11:11 am
☽□♃	5:29 pm

───── ♀♀♀ Dé Haoine ─────

♑︎

Friday
20

☉→♒︎	12:29 am
☽☌♅	12:30 am
☽△♅	10:54 am
☿⚹♂	5:04 pm
♇ApH	7:19 pm

☉→♒︎

Sun in ♒︎ Aquarius 12:29 am PST

ALL ASPECTS IN PACIFIC STANDARD TIME; ADD 3 HOURS FOR EST; ADD 8 HOURS FOR GMT

2023 Year at a Glance for ≈ Aquarius (Jan. 20–Feb. 18)

Aquarius, be brave when it comes to sharing your talents with others. When you speak up and let the world around you know what you care about, opportunities will soon follow. Because of negative experiences in the past and momentary upsets, you may be scared to take a chance on yourself. People can be very judgmental, and because of that you have learned to be reserved and hold your tongue. Despite judgmental eyes and careless whispers, challenge yourself to be fully and authentically yourself. There will always be someone who has something negative to say about you, no matter how spectacular you are. Do not internalize harsh words and criticism that is not constructive, especially if it keeps you from expressing yourself. The world around you will benefit from what you have to offer; your essence is a blessing. Towards the end of the year, your beliefs and value systems may also be challenged. Be kind to yourself. This year, influences in the universe will aid your creativity if you're willing to leave your comfort zone. Allow space for safety and serenity; it is in moments of peace that we are able to clear our minds and ground ourselves. Once you have achieved your center, be willing to be bold. The most helpful lesson that you will learn this year is that failure is temporary and giving up is permanent. Be your own best friend this year by not giving up on your dreams. They are what make you unique.

Astrologer Six © Mother Tongue Ink 2022

ᚻᚻᚻ Dé Sathairn

♑	
≈	

Saturday
21

☽⚹♆ 12:01 am
☽♂♇ 7:52 am v/c
☽→≈ 10:29 am

☉♂☽ 12:53 pm
☽PrG 1:09 pm
☽⚹♃ 5:08 pm

Lunar Imbolc

New Moon in ≈ Aquarius 12:53 pm PST

☉☉☉ Dé Domhnaigh

≈	

Sunday
22

☽△♂ 12:02 am
☽□♅ 9:49 am
♀♂♄ 2:13 pm
♅D 2:59 pm

January
enero

© *Mojgan Abolhassani 2010*

Light Workers

 ☽☽☽ lunes

 ≈
♓

Monday
23

☽☌♄ 1:24 am
☽☌♀ 2:19 am v/c
☽→♓ 9:36 am
☽□♂ 11:56 pm

♂♂♂ martes

♓

Tuesday
24

☽⚹♅ 1:59 am
☽⚹♅ 9:43 am
☉⚹♃ 5:30 pm
☽☌♆ 11:42 pm

☿☿☿ miércoles

♓
♈

Wednesday
25

☽⚹♇ 8:11 am v/c
☽→♈ 10:48 am
☽☌♃ 7:18 pm
☉⚹☽ 8:59 pm

♃♃♃ jueves

♈

Thursday
26

☽⚹♂ 2:40 am
☽□♅ 7:08 am
♀→♓ 6:33 pm

♀♀♀ viernes

♈
♉

Friday
27

♅□♫ 2:42 am
☽⚹♄ 7:13 am
☽□♇ 1:01 pm v/c
☽→♉ 3:42 pm
☽⚹♀ 5:56 pm

ALL ASPECTS IN PACIFIC STANDARD TIME; ADD 3 HOURS FOR EST; ADD 8 HOURS FOR GMT

Poem 22

This is the place where we do not measure time in seconds; we measure time in lessons. The day you learned to tie your shoes. The day you learned to pray for your enemies. All this knowing and growth, the tree rings of my soul. The day we learned that this mere fragile body, electrified by a complex of light, is indeed as resilient as the earth who grows and dies and grows and grows and dies and dies and is born again and grows to see the sun rise again. And again. And again. The cyclic mass extinction of hope. Longest, darkest nights followed by afternoons broken open by laughter. A flame bent by the wind.

This is the vibrant land of danger and bravery where we can only ever discover that we are breathtaking, risk-taking miracles equipped with razor-tipped faith and an insatiable appetite for growth and grace, whatever it takes.

This is the place where we measure time in lessons, every flesh wound a blessing—chaos compelling us towards a lasting order, fortified by wisdom and knowing—where everything begins with forgiveness and ends in love for that is all there is.

This is where you will be born.

This is where you will die.

This is where you will be born.

This is where you will learn to fly.

excerpt © Lyla June 2018

ħħħ sábado

 ♉

Saturday
28

⊙□☽ 7:19 am
☽△♉ 5:44 pm
☽♂♅ 7:37 pm

Waxing Half Moon in ♉ Taurus 7:19 am PST

◉◉◉ domingo

♉

Sunday
29

☽✶♆ 12:02 pm
☽□♄ 4:03 pm
⊙△♂ 5:45 pm

♉△♅ 6:16 pm
☽△♇ 9:52 pm v/c

January / February
sijećanj / veljača

☽☽☽ ponedjeljak

♉ ♊

Monday 30

☽→♊ 12:35 am
☽□♀ 9:24 am
☽⚹♃ 12:01 pm
☽☌♂ 8:27 pm
☉△☽ 10:24 pm

♂♂♂ utorak

♊

Tuesday 31

☽□♆ 11:21 pm

☿☿☿ srijeda

♊ ♋

Wednesday 1

February

☽△♄ 3:58 am v/c
☉⚹⚷ 11:26 am
☽→♋ 12:11 pm

♃♃♃ četvrtak

♋

Thursday 2

Imbolc

☽□♃ 12:55 am
☽△♀ 4:15 am
☽⚹♅ 6:27 pm

♀♀♀ petak

♋

Friday 3

☽☍☿ 4:09 am
☽△♆ 12:02 pm
☉□♅ 6:50 pm
☽☍♇ 10:19 pm v/c

All aspects in Pacific Standard Time; add 3 hours for EST; add 8 hours for GMT

Imbolc

Here we are in seed time, dream time, looking for the cracks of light that tell us to stretch out and grow. We are invited to consider this possibility: What if there is nothing wrong? What if there is no too slow? What if we live a miracle every single day, and we don't have to earn it?

As the first shoots of tentative growth begin to lift, and we sense the beginning sparks of possibility, of new ways of being, we may feel the itch to create a lengthy to-do list for a new year. Resist and sit, curled and waiting. Uncover what is enough. Not in the sense of playing too small, but the kind of enough that allows our hearts to expand and our shoulders to loosen, that allows creativity to blaze and joy to bloom, the kind of enough that opens space in our lives to hold ourselves and our seed dreams. Darkness and silence can hold both the sparks of our dreams and the embers of our hopes. We are our own seeds of promise.

Molly Remer © Mother Tongue Ink 2022

Alive Heart © Sigita Mockute (Psigidelia) 2021

The Nature of Risk

What courage, each year, has the tree
to once again birth her leaves,
her pink cherry blossoms or delicate dogwood petals,
knowing in days, weeks or months,
they will wither and fall to the ground.
So, too, the crocus or tulip,
who struggles through the frozen ground,
regardless the chance of Spring snowfall.
Even if warmed, her flower's glory will be
short-lived.
What freedom to show up, generously share,
sure of one's value to Earth.
Oh, to be like that,
to bloom without fear,
not clinging to longevity,
nor demanding guarantee,
but offer our best without expectation.

▢ Patricia Soper 2017

Petal Pirouette © *Serena Supplee 2004*

Esperanza ⌘ *Koco Collab 2021*

♋︎
♌︎

Saturday
4

☽→♌︎ 12:48 am
☽ApG 12:56 am
☽△♃ 2:34 pm
♀□♂ 7:29 pm
☽⚹♂ 11:35 pm

♌︎

Sunday
5

☽□♅ 7:08 am
☉☍☽ 10:28 am

Full Moon in ♌︎ Leo 10:28 am PST

February
Magh

© Elizabeth Diamond Gabriel 2020

Bedtime Moon

---))) sombar ---

♌
♍

Monday
6

) ☍ ♄ 6:15 am v/c
☿ ⚹ ♆ 10:26 am
) → ♍ 1:14 pm

--- ♂♂♂ mongolbar ---

♍

Tuesday
7

) □ ♂ 1:05 pm
) ☍ ♀ 7:01 pm
) △ ♅ 7:16 pm
♀ ⚹ ♅ 9:29 pm

--- ☿☿☿ budhbar ---

♍

Wednesday
8

) ☍ ♆ 12:40 pm
) △ ☿ 6:30 pm
) △ ♇ 10:40 pm v/c

--- ♃♃♃ brihospotibar ---

♍
♎

Thursday
9

) → ♎ 12:46 am
) ☍ ♃ 4:02 pm

--- ♀♀♀ sukrobar ---

♎

Friday
10

) △ ♂ 1:25 am
☿ ☌ ♇ 9:16 am
☉ △) 7:38 pm

ALL ASPECTS IN PACIFIC STANDARD TIME; ADD 3 HOURS FOR EST; ADD 8 HOURS FOR GMT

Mother's Love

society steeped in chaos
record temperatures on the earth's surface
species with uncertain futures
lineages of wisdom keepers disappearing
smoke and flame engulf the landscape
yet somehow in your eyes
I see the innocence of humanity
I find all galaxies in your gaze
absolute purity met with absolute presence
immaculate wonder and mystery in your skin
a wilderness of tender territory
your angelic honesty
in your presence
my heart lives in a vast expanse of fertile forests
I remember that all will decay,
again and again
and everyone I love,
including us
will die yet
I know in the deepest parts of me
this love will transcend all fear

¤ *Tasha Zigerelli 2020*

— ᚻᚻᚻ sonibar —

Saturday
11

☿→♒	3:22 am	♂⚹⚷	10:02 am
☽△♄	5:07 am	☽→♏	10:34 am
☽□♇	8:41 am v/c	☽□☿	11:27 am

— ☉☉☉ robibar —

Sunday
12

☽☍♅ 2:42 pm

Blessing for a River at its Source

Dear River, may you fulfill all your promises.

May you quench the thirst of deer and coyotes, people and beetles. May you raise forests upon your banks, feed swamps where beavers cocoon you. May you flow undirected, undammed. May you deepen with trout, with otters, with snails and with salmon, with kingfisher dreams and water-strider footprints. May you nurse fat tadpoles in your pockets, and may you renew every land.

May lovers and poets rejoice alongside you. May the weary bathe in you and rise up refreshed. May your sound be each person's story. May you be comfort, may you be faith. May you wash away the sorrow of cities while remaining ever pure. May you be a gathering place, may you be worshipped, and may your worshippers care for your body and pick you clean of what does not belong to you. May their children find and lose treasures in your crumpling eddies, splash in your shallows and daydream in your depths, find salamanders beneath your stones and then release them gently right back where they found them.

May the love of you make us holy. May you be peace. May you give the gifts you long to give, and may those gifts be honored. May you be held sacred, everywhere you go.

And because you are a river, may you flow onward and outward and downward, without ever pausing to say, *These things are not possible.*

Because you are a river, and you have no fear of falling. Because you are that thread unbreakable, the chain of water between sky and sea. Because you can only go down, toward that only center, and nothing, ultimately, can ever stop you.

Dear River, just go and go, and be our freedom. Dear River, be our forgiveness, Dear River,

Be.

¤ *Mindi Meltz 2021*

Prayers for Turtle Island
© *Dana Wheeles 2020*

III. EBB & FLOW

Moon III: February 19–March 21

Sun in ♓ Pisces February 18; New Moon in ♓ Pisces February 19; Full Moon in ♍ Virgo March 7

Yemaya © Amy Haderer-Swagman 2010

February
Mí Feabhra

Monday
13

☽△♀ 2:16 am
☽△Ψ 6:48 am
☉□☽ 8:01 am
☽□♄ 12:53 pm
☽✶♇ 3:52 pm v/c
☽→♐ 5:31 pm

Wise Fish

□ Shauna Crandall 2015

Waning Half Moon in ♏ Scorpio 8:01 am PST

Tuesday
14

☽✶♅ 12:39 am
☽△♃ 8:56 am
☽☍♂ 6:06 pm

Wednesday
15

♀☌Ψ 4:25 am
☽□Ψ 11:06 am
☽□♀ 11:43 am
☉✶☽ 4:03 pm
☽✶♄ 5:06 pm v/c
☽→♑ 8:59 pm

Thursday
16

♄ApH 4:04 am
☉☌♄ 8:48 am
☽□♃ 12:10 pm
☽△♅ 9:55 pm

Friday
17

☽✶Ψ 12:16 pm
☽✶♀ 5:06 pm
☿✶♃ 6:13 pm
☽☌♇ 8:18 pm v/c
☽→♒ 9:34 pm

ALL ASPECTS IN PACIFIC STANDARD TIME; ADD 3 HOURS FOR EST; ADD 8 HOURS FOR GMT

2023 Year at a Glance for ♓ Pisces (Feb. 18–March 20)

Hard work comes with rewards; make sure to set aside time to appreciate your gains. Last year you cultivated a stronger sense of personal values. You are the type of person who pays attention and picks up on the diverse narratives that swirl around the world. Thankfully, this observant nature will prove to be your blessing during 2023. After paying attention and being mindful, you will begin to pick up on the appropriate times to speak up and express your truth. Being a trendsetter and a leader can be exhausting, so be fair to yourself when working to be a change maker within society. Trust that there are people in your corner who believe in you and will support ideas you bring to the table. You offer an abundance of wisdom and have faithful allies who are willing to take risks with you. The most detrimental thing you can do this year is to lead a life driven by fear. Bravery is not an easy exercise; it requires relentlessness, and the willingness to believe that the impossible is possible. As the year nears its end, you will begin accumulating experiences that encourage you to learn by trial and error. Don't become your own worst enemy by replaying moments of failure and disappointment, Pisces. Trust that everyone knows what it feels like to fall short of their goals. Your willingness to keep trying, despite your feelings of doubt, is what will bring you the most meaningful rewards.

Astrologer Six © Mother Tongue Ink 2022

------------------------- ♄♄♄ Dé Sathairn -------------------------

≈

Saturday
18

☽✶♃ 12:51 pm
☉→♓ 2:34 pm
☽♂♉ 2:35 pm
☽□♅ 9:41 pm
☽△♂ 10:01 pm

☉→♓

Sun in ♓ Pisces 2:34 pm PST

-------------------- ☉☉☉ Dé Domhnaigh --------------------

≈
♓

Sunday
19

☽PrG 1:01 am
♀✶♇ 9:04 am
☽♂♄ 6:00 pm v/c

☽→♓ 8:56 pm
☉♂☽ 11:06 pm
♀→♈ 11:55 pm

New Moon in ♓ Pisces 11:06 pm PST

February
febrero

Spring Rain
the air was thick with the smell of
dust becoming mud becoming
creek becoming river
becoming ocean.
excerpt ¤ Geneva Toland 2020

──── ☽☽☽ lunes ────

Monday
20

☿⚹♆ 8:59 am
☽⚹♅ 9:20 pm
☽□♂ 10:44 pm

──── ♂♂♂ martes ────

Tuesday
21

☽♂♆ 11:52 am
♀□♅ 2:22 pm
☽⚹♇ 8:05 pm v/c
☽→♈ 9:14 pm

──── ☿☿☿ miércoles ────

Wednesday
22

☽♂♀ 1:26 am
☿△♂ 12:14 pm
☽♂♃ 2:48 pm

──── ♃♃♃ jueves ────

Thursday
23

☽⚹♂ 1:44 am
☽⚹☿ 3:03 am
☽⚹♄ 10:06 pm
☽□♇ 11:22 pm v/c

──── ♀♀♀ viernes ────

Friday
24

☽→♉ 12:29 am
☉⚹☽ 11:02 am

ALL ASPECTS IN PACIFIC STANDARD TIME; ADD 3 HOURS FOR EST; ADD 8 HOURS FOR GMT

Deep Waters ¤ *Morgen Maier 2018*

♉

Saturday
25

☽☌♅ 4:24 am
☽□♀ 4:16 pm
☽⚹♆ 9:15 pm

♉
♊

Sunday
26

☽□♄ 5:45 am
☽△♇ 6:42 am v/c
☽→♊ 7:48 am

February / March

veljača / ožujak ───── ⅮⅮⅮ ponedjeljak ────────────────────

♊

Monday
27

⊙□☽ 12:05 am
☽⚹♀ 12:24 am
☽⚹♃ 6:08 am
☽♂♂ 8:20 pm

───────────── ♂♂♂ utorak ───────────── Waxing Half Moon in ♊ Gemini 12:05 am PST

♊
♋

Tuesday
28

☽□♆ 7:46 am
☽△♅ 11:27 am
☽△♄ 5:07 pm v/c
☽→♋ 6:40 pm

───────────── ☿☿☿ srijeda ─────────────

♋

Wednesday
1

March

⊙△☽ 5:10 pm
☽□♀ 6:50 pm
☽□♃ 7:04 pm
♀♂♃ 9:36 pm

───────────── ♃♃♃ četvrtak ─────────────

♋

Thursday
2

☽⚹♅ 2:03 am
☿♂♄ 6:34 am
☿→♓ 2:52 pm
☽△♆ 8:23 pm

───────────── ♀♀♀ petak ─────────────

♋
♌

Friday
3

☽☍♇ 6:22 am v/c
☽→♌ 7:16 am
♀♂♅ 9:48 am
☽ApG 10:03 am

───
ALL ASPECTS IN PACIFIC STANDARD TIME; ADD 3 HOURS FOR EST; ADD 8 HOURS FOR GMT

Canoe

The waxing crescent casts a tiny canoe on the water. She is empty, enlivened by breezy waves. I swim out into the midnight lake and climb within her nacre. I take up a paddle painted with images of fish and birds. She carries me into a perfect shadow. Mayflies or snowflakes in starlight surround us. I face fear and joy in equal measure, my honest life. And in a minute or a month, when I return to shore, all that needs to heal lies behind me in a wake. And she sails off toward wholeness carrying the weight of my dreams.

© Joanne M. Clarkson 2021

Soul Journey © Eefje Jansen 2021

ᚼᚼᚼ subota

♌

Saturday

4

☽△♃ 8:56 am
☽△♀ 2:28 pm
☽□♅ 2:53 pm

☉☉☉ nedjelja

♌
♍

Sunday

5

☽⚹♂ 1:26 am
☽☍♄ 7:18 pm v/c
☽→♍ 7:38 pm

March
Falgun

Brighdelynne Stewart 2003

Circles of Love

♍

Monday
6

☉⚹♅ 5:42 am
☽☌☿ 8:32 am

♍

Tuesday
7

☽△♅ 2:51 am
☉☍☽ 4:40 am
♄→♓ 5:34 am
☽□♂ 3:06 pm
☽☍♆ 8:39 pm

Full Moon in ♍ Virgo 4:40 am PST

♍
♎

Wednesday
8

☽△♇ 6:07 am v/c
☽→♎ 6:44 am

♎

Thursday
9

☽☍♃ 9:27 am

♎
♏

Friday
10

☽☍♀ 1:06 am
☽△♂ 3:00 am
☽□♇ 3:36 pm v/c
☽→♏ 4:06 pm
☽△♄ 4:51 pm
☿ApH 5:14 pm

ALL ASPECTS IN PACIFIC STANDARD TIME; ADD 3 HOURS FOR EST; ADD 8 HOURS FOR GMT

Celestial Whale © Heidi Van Impe 2017

Quick, Silver!

Tides swell in places I have never seen,
pounding shores I've never touched,
yet somehow the same moon moistens me.
Ms. Moon, is your eye there glaring
solely to expose our restless longing,
or in silent silver sorrow do you
weep the wasting of magnetic light?
You who pull whole seas to sleeping
shores, startling slumbered mussels,
hoping to show lost lonely starfish
the urgent merging way towards divinity.

© Terri Watrous Berry 2021

———————— ♄♄♄ sonibar ————————

♏ **Saturday**
11

♀⚹♂ 7:05 am
☿⚹♅ 1:04 pm
☽☍♅ 9:42 pm
♃♂♆ 10:52 pm
☽△♅ 11:07 pm

———————— ☉☉ robibar ————————

♏ **Sunday**
12

☉△☽ 9:32 am
☽△♆ 3:18 pm
☽⚹♇ 11:58 pm v/c

Daylight Saving Time Begins 2:00 am PST

March
Mí Márta

♏︎
♐︎

Monday
13

☽→♐︎ 12:21 am
☽□♄ 1:33 am

Nourish

□ Jiling Lin 2019

━━━ ♂♂♂ Dé Máirt ━━━

♐︎

Tuesday
14

☽△♃ 2:56 am
☽□♅ 2:38 pm
♂□♆ 4:39 pm
☉□☽ 7:08 pm
☽□♆ 8:38 pm
☽☍♂ 8:45 pm

━━━ ☿☿☿ Dé Céadaoin ━━━   Waning Half Moon in ♐︎ Sagittarius 7:08 pm PDT

♐︎
♑︎

Wednesday
15

☽△♀ 1:50 am v/c
☽→♑︎ 5:05 am
☽✶♄ 6:41 am
☉♂♆ 4:39 pm

━━━ ♃♃♃ Dé Ardaoin ━━━

♑︎

Thursday
16

☽□♃ 7:17 am
☽△♅ 8:21 am
♅♂♆ 10:13 am
☉□♂ 11:09 am
♀□♇ 12:58 pm

♆ApH 2:01 pm
♀→♉ 3:34 pm
☿□♂ 9:48 pm
☽✶♆ 11:26 pm

━━━ ♀♀♀ Dé Haoine ━━━

♑︎
♒︎

Friday
17

☽✶♅ 1:27 am
☉✶☽ 1:37 am
☉♂♅ 3:44 am
☽♂♇ 7:13 am v/c
☽→♒︎ 7:25 am
☽□♀ 8:50 am
♀✶♄ 3:25 pm

ALL ASPECTS IN PACIFIC DAYLIGHT TIME; ADD 3 HOURS FOR EDT; ADD 7 HOURS FOR GMT

Rain Water

After days of rain
>> fresh streams declaim from the forest
>>> and the trees are laughing.

Yet there is humility, as water
>> chuckles out onto the shore rocks
>>> and their adaptable acorn barnacles.

While other places, whole countries, crack and crumble,
>> somehow, here, a quenching drench
>>> falling, flowing, flooding to the sea.

The air filled with soothing sound,
>> the tide and miraculous mergansers supplied
>>> with fresh water.
>>>> Rain water.

It rests atop the saline
so they can bathe their feathers.
A system designed for them, for their benefit,
>> and for a planet, and for a planet's benefit.
A wren perched on swaying salal
>> sings its discovery of new water.
>>> Rain water. Tasting
>>>> like the scent of trees.

□ *Christine Lowther 2020*

ᚅᚅᚅ Dé Sathairn

≈

Saturday
18

☽✳♃ 9:27 am
☽□♅ 9:50 am
☿✳♇ 8:24 pm
☿→♈ 9:24 pm

☉☉☉ Dé Domhnaigh

≈
♓

Sunday
19

☽△♂ 3:33 am v/c
☽→♓ 8:12 am
☽PrG 8:16 am
☽♂♄ 10:28 am
☽✳♀ 1:54 pm

MOON III   59

Council of Renewal

Lay an offering of time at your own feet.
Collect some kindling of shoulds and constraints
and construct a pyre on which to burn your shame.
Watch it ignite and drift away into smoke
and return to the flowers.
Gather up some reeds of satisfaction and delight
and weave together a blessing basket
strong enough to hold both dreams and action.
Lift your fingers to your brow and trace a crescent moon there
as slow as night.
Kiss your palms and lay them upon your belly.
Whisper everything you need to hear
and listen for what you've forgotten.
Call your spirit back from all the places it has wandered,
invite your fragments to unite
and watch them shine
in a sacred council of renewal
in your own front yard.
Watch for birds.
Trust the singing in your skin.
Lift your hands to the sky and call your name into the wind.
Cloak yourself with restoration,
crown yourself with grace,
lay your beads of courage around your neck.
Bow your head in understanding
as the petals drop
around your feet
and the honey drips
between your fingers.
Initiate yourself,
here, now
and free.

March
marzo

♓

Monday
20

☽✶♅ 10:33 am
☉✶♇ 1:12 pm
☉→♈ 2:24 pm

Spring Equinox

☉→♈

Sun in ♈ Aries 2:24 pm PDT

♓
♈

Tuesday
21

☽♂♆ 1:20 am
☽□♂ 5:54 am
☽✶♇ 8:58 am v/c
☽→♈ 9:01 am
☉♂☽ 10:23 am
☽♂♉ 6:34 pm

New Moon in ♈ Aries 10:23 am PDT

♈

Wednesday
22

☽♂♃ 1:17 pm

♈
♉

Thursday
23

♇→♒ 5:13 am
☽✶♂ 10:13 am v/c
☽→♉ 11:42 am
☽□♇ 11:42 am
☽✶♄ 2:57 pm

♉

Friday
24

☽♂♀ 3:31 am
☽♂♅ 4:51 pm

2023 Year at a Glance for ♈ Aries (March 20–April 20)

For you, this year is all about accepting new information. Guess what, my dear Aries: you do not know it all. There is still plenty more to see and an abundance of experiences to be had. As your fiery and fresh energy likes it, you will be spending this new year diving into the great unknown. Are you ready to dive into new experiences and take some embarrassing risks? Of course you are; you know that you're not the type to dwell on foolish moments. Think fresh mind, uncharted territory. You will benefit from developing a sense of courage, even if much of your bravery is falsified in the beginning. Keep in mind that you have made it this far, which means that in time you'll be able to make it even farther. Try not to turn your head in disgust when met with people whose lifestyle differs from your own. In fact, you will benefit from taking the time to appreciate what makes them unique. Let the differences of others teach you about yourself and the world around you. This year there may be a significant change in your finances, so spend with a mindset of manifestation. As the year progresses, your experiences will teach you how to utilize what you bring to the table. Have faith in yourself and mind your subconscious desires; often it is mindless habits and a need for escapism that lead to your undoing. As you will learn early in the year, there must be limits to who you allow into your life.

Astrologer Six © Mother Tongue Ink 2022

It's Spring Again © KT InfiniteArt 2021

────── ♄♄♄ sábado ──────

♉
♊

Saturday
25

♂→♋ 4:45 am
♂☌♇ 6:34 am
☽✶♆ 9:19 am v/c

☽→♊ 5:41 pm
☽△♇ 5:46 pm
☽□♄ 9:38 pm

────── ☉☉☉ domingo ──────

♊

Sunday
26

☉✶☽ 4:03 am
♉☌♇ 11:58 am

Spring Equinox

Spring is ripe with new beginnings and coiled possibilities. We hear strains of magic and strands of mystery, calling us to set forth, paying attention to the small, soft mysteries and wild magics of just where we are. There is a quickening inside you, and we are called to the riverside, bearing witness to the birthwaters of spring. Streams once tamed now leap their banks, charge with fury across colonized lands, charting new routes and refusing to stay inside boundaries. Our tears flood and join the rushing water, striking out to sea; inexorable is the call, fathomless is the need. With all our strength we cry out—to ancestral memory, to lifebeat rushing through our veins, to waters of the original womb. May we quench this thirst with tinctures of patience, action, reverence, and justice. We dip our hands into the cool current and anoint our bellies. As we touch wet fingers to our bodies, we hear distant whale songs, this waterway connected to the next to the next to the next, each future of each being entwined in ripples, bubbles, and waves.

Molly Remer © Mother Tongue Ink 2022

Earth Prayer: Benediction © Kay Kemp 2020

The Wrapping Ceremony

Our minds have fingers
there is so much they can touch
Our hearts plump or shock
from the impact
of what they choose.
Some days they are happy dogs
running on ahead
to sniff out the day's best
bees smooring
to the next nectar-fest.
Sometimes they are all
fingers and thumbs
and have to double back.
It is a daily discipline to choose
how much of the world's darkness we touch and why.
We could be incandescent with righteous rage
every second of every minute of every hour.
Our collective grief could raise the sea level overnight.
But sworn enemy of joy we can't take Ecocide with us
on every walk even though it whines and scratches at the door.
It is joy too we are here to spend. It is celebration and active reverence
that give us energy, the courage to make our most difference.
So, we actively seek out the silver linings. We write ourselves
into a poem that turns out to be a wrapping ceremony.
It cocoons us in sand-washed silk and the feathers of Snow geese.
The ancestors feed us raw heather-honey from their fingers
and take the trouble from our minds.
We discover we are in the arms of a she-bear
in a shelter round as a Mongolian yurt draped with heavy tapestries
of every being we have ever loved, human and furred.
Wolves howl their songs across the tundra
to each other and to us.
A snake in the corner waits to shed its skin with us.
We have never felt so held.

Passage Between Worlds
© LorrieArt 2019

¤ *Debra Hall 2021*

March / April
ožujak / travanj

♊

Monday
27

ⅅ⚹♉ 12:39 am
ⅅ⚹♃ 3:57 am
ⅅ□♆ 6:39 pm v/c
☿♂♃ 11:50 pm

♊
♋

Tuesday
28

ⅅ→♋ 3:22 am
ⅅ♂♂ 6:19 am
ⅅ△♄ 8:03 am
☉□ⅅ 7:32 pm

Waxing Half Moon in ♋ Cancer 7:32 pm PDT

♋

Wednesday
29

ⅅ⚹♀ 9:50 am
ⅅ⚹♅ 12:40 pm
ⅅ□♃ 4:34 pm
ⅅ□☿ 11:30 pm

♋
♌

Thursday
30

ⅅ△♆ 6:45 am v/c
♂△♄ 12:03 pm
♀♂♅ 3:26 pm
ⅅ→♌ 3:31 pm
ⅅ☍♇ 3:46 pm

♌

Friday
31

ⅅApG 4:17 am
☉△ⅅ 1:29 pm

ALL ASPECTS IN PACIFIC DAYLIGHT TIME; ADD 3 HOURS FOR EDT; ADD 7 HOURS FOR GMT

The Witch in Spring

Witch Apothecary ▢ *Anne Jewett 2020*

You spy emerging mugwort leaves, pale and soft as they catch drops of rain, each as round as the moon curving outward into the sky.

All the ingredients for magic are here:

the small overlooked things
fire inside of your breath
cool spring air

and that feeling at the back of your throat when someone can see right through you. With spring arrives the memory that mugwort's spell is to make you transparent—She can see the wildness under your skin, the power flowing through your blood. You welcome her back from her underground journey through winter, saying:
Come, let us tend to the shimmering veil, let us dance as the light of stars pulls us from one corner of the sky to another; together we will summon the rain and call down the moon.

© Haley Neddermann 2021

─────── ♄♄♄ subota ───────

♌ Saturday

☽ 1   April

☽□♅ 1:30 am
☽□♀ 5:06 am
☽△♃ 6:25 am
☽△♄ 11:03 pm v/c

─────── ☉☉☉ nedjelja ───────

♌   Sunday
♍   2

☽→♍ 3:57 am
☽☍♄ 9:44 am
☽✳♂ 12:07 pm

April
Choitro

♍

Monday
3

☿→♉ 9:22 am
♉□♇ 11:55 am
☽△♅ 1:28 pm
☽△♀ 11:04 pm

♍
♎

Tuesday
4

☽☍♆ 6:50 am v/c
☽→♎ 2:51 pm
☽△♇ 3:13 pm

♎

Wednesday
5

☽□♂ 1:11 am
☿⚹♄ 9:21 am
☉☌⚷ 3:18 pm
⚸ApH 9:08 pm
☉☍☽ 9:34 pm

Full Moon in ♎ Libra 9:34 pm PDT

♎
♏

Thursday
6

☽☍♃ 5:43 am v/c
☽→♏ 11:29 pm
☽□♇ 11:54 pm

♏

Friday
7

☽△♄ 5:44 am
☽☍♉ 10:53 am
♀⚹♆ 10:58 am
☽△♂ 11:42 am
☿⚹♂ 11:28 pm

ALL ASPECTS IN PACIFIC DAYLIGHT TIME; ADD 3 HOURS FOR EDT; ADD 7 HOURS FOR GMT

Women Living Alone

when the world is coming apart
women living alone
are ready to rumble.
dance party in the kitchen by night
spa bliss in the bath by day
revolution in the neighborhood
rapture in our own beds
plenty of time to do nothing.
we aren't waiting for anyone
and can spin all night
without guilt or pressure.
when a cosmic call rings out
we grab our own forms of magic
soar through sky and glade
far above flesh-born expectations
where few dare to fly,
and when the misinformed
see only our solitude
we just smile and say with a wink
"Come, be one of us."

¤ *Stephanie A. Sellers 2021*

Stardust
¤ *D. Woodring–Portrait Priestess 2020*

♏ **Saturday**
♉

☽☌♅ 6:55 am
☽△♆ 10:50 pm

♏ **Sunday**
♐ 9

☽☌♀ 2:09 am v/c
☽→♐ 5:56 am
☽⚹♇ 6:23 am
☽☐♄ 12:21 pm

April
Mí Aibreán

——— ⅅⅅⅅ Dé Luain ———

♐

Monday
10

☉△☽ 6:48 pm
☽△♃ 7:55 pm
♀→♊ 9:47 pm

Spark
We emerge from ancient oak groves
And from under the arms
Of shadowy willow branches.
Our voices grow stronger as we
Chant and conjure, and spark
In pewter moonlight.
excerpt ▢ Tonya J. Cunningham 2021

——— ♂♂♂ Dé Máirt ———

♐
♑

Tuesday
11

♀△♇ 3:14 am
☽□♆ 3:48 am v/c
☽→♑ 10:33 am
☉♂♃ 3:07 pm
☽⚹♄ 5:08 pm

——— ☿☿☿ Dé Céadaoin ———

♑

Wednesday
12

☽☍♂ 2:03 am
☽△♅ 6:35 am
☽△♅ 4:24 pm

——— ♃♃♃ Dé Ardaoin ———

♑
♒

Thursday
13

☽□♃ 12:19 am
☉□☽ 2:11 am
☽⚹♆ 7:14 am v/c
♃ApH 7:34 am
☽→♒ 1:42 pm
☽♂♇ 2:11 pm
☽△♀ 7:23 pm

Waning Half Moon in ♑ Capricorn 2:11 am PDT

——— ♀♀♀ Dé Haoine ———

♒

Friday
14

♀□♄ 9:38 am
☽□☿ 12:16 pm
☽□♅ 7:07 pm

Clann © Brigidina 2011

ᚻᚻᚻ Dé Sathairn ───────────

≈
♓

Saturday
15

☽✶♃ 3:36 am
☉✶☽ 8:16 am v/c
☽→♓ 3:57 pm
☽PrG 7:18 pm
☽♂♄ 10:57 pm

───── ☉☉☉ Dé Domhnaigh ─────────

♓

Sunday
16

☽□♀ 1:58 am
☽△♂ 10:48 am
☽✶♅ 4:24 pm
☽✶♅ 9:25 pm

Aching to Connect

In the depths
of a global trance of fear,
we ache to connect.
We create a sanity circle,
asking ourselves:
*What reality do I wish
to broadcast, broadcast, broadcast?*

We depathologize our language.
We lift each other
to a vision beyond polarities.
We optimize our self-talk.
We hear each other declare:
*I am part of making
a global consciousness of love.*

Aching to connect,
we remedy the fear.
We release it, release it,
breathing it out. Not once,
but every single time it rises.
With our presence, together,
we make the space for Change.
© *Susa Silvermarie 2021*

Reflecting © *Jakki Moore 2021*

V. A RADIANCE OF LOVE

Moon V: April 19–May 19

New Moon in ♈ Aries April 19; Sun in ♉ Taurus April 20; Full Moon in ♏ Scorpio May 5

April
abril

———— ⅅⅅⅅ lunes ————

Monday
17

♓
♈

☽♂♆ 11:57 am v/c
☽→♈ 6:09 pm
☽⚹♇ 6:41 pm

———— ♂♂♂ martes ————

Tuesday
18

♈

☽⚹♀ 8:46 am
☽□♂ 3:16 pm

———— ☿☿☿ miércoles ————

Wednesday
19

♈
♉

☽♂♃ 10:27 am
☉♂☽ 9:12 pm v/c
☽→♉ 9:30 pm
☽□♇ 10:04 pm

New Moon in ♈ Aries 9:12 pm PDT
Total Solar Eclipse 9:16 pm PDT

———— ♃♃♃ jueves ————

Thursday
20

♉

☉→♉ 1:13 am
☽⚹♄ 5:30 am
☉□♇ 9:27 am
☽⚹♂ 9:36 pm

☉→♉

Sun in Taurus 1:13 am PDT

———— ♀♀♀ viernes ————

Friday
21

♉

☽♂☿ 1:05 am
☿R 1:35 am
☽♂♅ 5:09 am
☽⚹♆ 8:41 pm v/c

*Eclipse visible in SE Asia, E Indies, Pacific & Indian Oceans, Australia, Phillippines, New Zealand

2023 Year at a Glance for ♉ Taurus (April 20–May 21)

No one wants to be a deer in headlights—being immobilized by dangerous experiences seems ridiculous. When in situations that could be detrimental to our health, our logical minds want to believe that we would do something to change our circumstances. Thankfully for you, this year will bring forth a multitude of moments which will challenge you to trust your gut. Life is one of the best teachers. Like children, we are ignorant of what we do not know, and it takes a willingness to have new experiences to increase our intellect. At the beginning of the year, your mission is to deepen your understanding of your subconscious drives. Keeping a dream diary will help you better understand your intuition. Write down your thoughts when you wake up or risk losing significant information. This year, your purpose is to better understand what you bring to the world. What qualities and talents do you have that make you shine extra bright? Pay close attention to the chills that collect on your spine and any occasional moments of realization—It is then when your intuition is speaking to you the loudest. Once the year reaches Libra season, your quest will shift from subconscious to conscious self-discovery. Your imagination will be challenged as the year ends. Knowledge is power, and your ability to mind your mind, body, and spirit will provide you with the most essential strength that a human can have.

Astrologer Six © Mother Tongue Ink 2022

ℏℏℏ sábado

♉
♊   **Saturday**
22

☽→♊ 3:11 am
☽△♇ 3:49 am
☽□♄ 12:00 pm

To See *© Eefje Jansen 2021*

☉☉☉ domingo

♊   **Sunday**
23

☽☌♀ 5:43 am
☿⚹♂ 8:19 pm

April

travanj

DDD ponedjeljak -

♊
♋

Monday
24

☽✶♃ 1:48 am
☽□♆ 5:15 am v/c
☽→♋ 11:58 am
☉✶☽ 9:10 pm
☽△♄ 9:40 pm

The Hunter © *Janey Brims 2017*

♂♂♂ utorak

♋

Tuesday
25

☉✶♄ 3:48 am
☽✶♅ 4:47 pm
♀✶♇ 4:50 pm
☽♂♂ 8:08 pm
☽✶♅ 11:45 pm

☿☿☿ srijeda

♋
♌

Wednesday
26

☽□♃ 2:09 pm
☽△♆ 4:41 pm v/c
☽→♌ 11:30 pm

♄♄♄ četvrtak

♌

Thursday
27

☽☍♇ 12:13 am
♂□♇ 6:34 am
☉□☽ 2:20 pm
☽ApG 11:38 pm

Waxing Half Moon in ♌ Leo 2:20 pm PDT

♀♀♀ petak

♌

Friday
28

☽□♅ 2:44 am
☽□♅ 12:26 pm
☽✶♀ 4:42 pm

ALL ASPECTS IN PACIFIC DAYLIGHT TIME; add 3 hours for EDT; add 7 hours for GMT

How to Hug an Aspen Tree
While Surrounded by Wildfires

Press your pounding drum heart right into her bark
let your breasts fall to either side, baring the bone there to her skin

Breathe her in, down to your toes
Exhale across her body so she recognizes your essence
In Heartbeat. In Breath.

Hold on tight   Ask forgiveness
Offer up your gratitude   For shade shelter oxygen beauty
Say help me.   Say Thank you.

Still holding tight, Listen
Widen your gaze to the forest surrounding you both
Let it all happen, receive. Feel all their essences flow into your heart
Your beautiful, aching heart

Let the song of the morning pour into you, and Sing   Sing

When you're ready to move on, you will know
Your hands, chest, and cheeks will be covered with aspen dust
Don't brush it off   Keep singing.

Leave the aspen grove covered as a kabuki dancer in white powder.

◻ Oak Chezar 2020

ħħħ subota

♌
♍

Saturday
29

☽△♃ 3:53 am v/c
☽→♍ 11:59 am
♂⚹♅ 1:04 pm
☽☍♄ 10:41 pm

☉☉☉ nedjelja

♍

Sunday
30

☉△☽ 7:59 am
☽△♅ 12:05 pm

May
Boishakh

♍︎
♎︎

Monday
1

Beltane

☽△♅ 12:38 am
☽✶♂ 2:08 am
♁R 10:09 am
☽□♀ 10:31 am

☉♂♉ 4:27 pm
☽☍♆ 4:53 pm v/c
☽→♎︎ 11:09 pm
☽△♁ 11:51 pm

♎︎

Tuesday
2

No Exact Aspects

♎︎

Wednesday
3

☽□♂ 2:10 pm

♎︎
♏︎

Thursday
4

☽△♀ 12:54 am
☽☍♃ 2:17 am v/c
☿PrH 6:58 am
☽→♏︎ 7:32 am

☽□♁ 8:12 am
♀□♆ 10:40 am
☽△♄ 5:53 pm
♀✶♃ 9:03 pm

♏︎

Friday
5

Lunar Beltane

☽☍♉ 12:15 am
☉☍☽ 10:34 am
☽☍♅ 5:13 pm
☽△♂ 10:51 pm

Penumbral Lunar Eclipse 10:22 am PDT
Full Moon in ♏︎ Scorpio 10:34 am PDT

---

*Eclipse visible in Asia, Africa, Australia, Pacific & Indian Oceans, Eastern Europe

Beltane

As we dance in the meadow, flowers wreathed around our heads, drumbeats in our ears, we sense the trembling web, many fine threads entwined with yours and mine. We send out love to the threatened biodiversity of our beloved earth, the waning butterflies, and the amphibians warning us through thin skins to change our ways. Now is not the time for apathy or regret, not the time for keening in sorrow. It is time for swift feet and gentle fingers. Time for cracked open hearts and wild tears. Time for delight and determination to twine back together, eyes open to where we are and what can still be done.

We begin—like the crow daring to peck away at what confines us, cracking out of the shell, persistent in our knowing. We begin like the snake, feeling the tightness that no longer suits us, stretching beyond our edges until we shed our shape and become reborn. We begin with a smile, with tears, with blood and possibilities, we begin by listening to the whispers of our inherent capacity to rise.

Molly Remer © Mother Tongue Ink 2022

Michif Horse Women © Leah Marie Dorion 2012

The Grand Experiment

What if love really were enough,
if somehow this were the last
grand experiment conducted
by the world-renowned scientist
herself, Madame Love? What if
she gave her own life testing
the tiny patterns only she has
been trained to see?
What if she were in the
internet and popped up
like an ad to get your data
but instead she stole
your heart, and you put
down the phone, closed
the laptop, and cried.
Yes, when that happens,
you know your heart
has been hacked by the
world's greatest girl coder
And the fire you feel
when another day is just
another day and shit
is still real and real

messy and no amount
of deep cleaning and
Marie Kondo-ing will
make it go away?
Love is there, too,
stoking the fire with
you. She makes a great
pyre. She says throw
it all in, the hunger and
fear, the anger and injustice,
the compassion and grief,
the need to do do do do
something anything
now that your compulsion
to flee shop run has been
taken from you, and
the bonfire is great, and
the flames can be seen
from outer space, but
even more importantly,
they can be seen right
here. And here and here
and here . . .

excerpt ¤ Cassie Premo Steele 2020

Genesis Mandala © Elspeth McLean 2012

Beauty in Bold ¤ *Tara deForest Hansen 2019*

♏
♐

Saturday
6

☽△♆ 7:38 am v/c
☽→♐ 1:04 pm
☽✶♇ 1:41 pm
☽□♄ 11:12 pm

♐

Sunday
7

♀→♋ 7:24 am
♀⚹♇ 3:10 pm

May
Mí Bealtaine

A Radiance of Love
This is the greatest act of power
I have come to know:
To be an activist of joy
A beacon of grace
A radiance of love
excerpt © Nell Aurelia 2021

───── ☽☽☽ Dé Luain ─────

♐
♑

Monday
8

☽□♆ 11:22 am
☽△♃ 1:28 pm v/c
☽→♑ 4:33 pm
☽☍♀ 7:20 pm

───── ♂♂♂ Dé Máirt ─────

♑

Tuesday
9

☽⚹♄ 2:38 am
☽△♅ 4:28 am
☉♂♅ 12:56 pm
♅ApH 8:36 pm

───── ☿☿☿ Dé Céadaoin ─────

♑
♒

Wednesday
10

☽△♅ 12:32 am
☉△☽ 1:20 am
☽☍♂ 9:38 am
☽⚹♆ 2:03 pm

☽□♃ 4:52 pm v/c
☽→♒ 7:05 pm
☽♂♇ 7:40 pm
☽PrG 10:08 pm

───── ♃♃♃ Dé Ardaoin ─────

♒

Thursday
11

☽□♅ 5:45 am

───── ♀♀♀ Dé Haoine ─────

♒
♓

Friday
12

☿⚹♄ 1:40 am
☽□♅ 3:12 am
☉□☽ 7:28 am
☿⚹♀ 7:44 pm
☽⚹♃ 8:15 pm v/c
☽→♓ 9:39 pm
♀△♄ 11:57 pm

Waning Half Moon in ♒ Aquarius 7:28 am PDT

ALL ASPECTS IN PACIFIC DAYLIGHT TIME; ADD 3 HOURS FOR EDT; ADD 7 HOURS FOR GMT

I Dare You

I dare you—awe me out of my hallway
of safe dreams and away from my map for how to live them
take me to the precipice with toes kissing the air on their soles
unzip me with gentle delight in what you see that I am, with seal skin
stretched out on the rock
I dare you—shatter my normalcy with a volcanic sky at dusk
and wake me up in moonshadow dusting my skin
I dare you—slip under my fences and try on the dark,
eyes adjusting to unfamiliar shapes until you dare light your torch
illuminating the underworld
I dare you—dance with the monsters you find in the closet
and pour tea with the crab who lives in the cave
I dare you—wrap my naked body
in breath warmed with passion and longing
until I crawl out of my own skin
with butterfly wings breaking the fog with flight
I dare you—wake me up
sing me alive and speak my name in syllables and kisses
until I am completely unwrapped & reborn
I dare you—see what happens
just, don't forget
my seal skin is mine,
and I will return

¤ Monika Denise 2020

―――――――――――― ᚻᚻᚻ Dé Sathairn ―――――――――――――

♓

Saturday
13

☽⚹♅ 7:43 am
☽☌♄ 8:12 am
☽△♀ 8:50 am

―――――――――――― ☉☉☉ Dé Domhnaigh ―――――――――――――

♓

Sunday
14

☽⚹♅ 6:22 am
☉⚹☽ 2:17 pm
☽△♂ 7:30 pm
☽☌♆ 7:56 pm v/c
☿D 8:17 pm

I Work for Earth

not because animals and plants
don't have voices,
but because we don't listen,

I compose letters
and books
with paints and poems—

not because they don't have voices
but because roots need soils,

and all of us have roots—
        animals and plants, you and me—
(*my* roots need *this* soil)

and we don't listen,
        or so I hear,
            but I am painting
                and writing
                    and hoping.

Oh, the power of hope.
        of the word—
the power of paints and poems and hearts.
                  ¤ *lisa kemmerer 2021*

Passing Around Moon Light Energy from the Same Fleece
© Sandy Bot-Miller 2016

May
mayo

Frida Kahlo ¤ *Corinne "Bee Bop" Trujillo 2020*

♓
♈

Monday
15

☽→♈ 12:56 am
☽⚹♇ 1:29 am
♂△♆ 6:44 am
☽□♀ 4:41 pm

♈

Tuesday
16

♃→♉ 10:20 am

♈
♉

Wednesday
17

☽□♂ 2:10 am v/c
☽→♉ 5:27 am
☽♂♃ 5:47 am
☽□♇ 6:00 am
☽♂♉ 4:27 pm
☽⚹♄ 4:57 pm
♃□♇ 6:11 pm

♉

Thursday
18

☉⚹♆ 1:59 am
☽⚹♀ 2:18 am
☽♂♅ 4:28 pm
☿⚹♄ 11:37 pm

♉
♊

Friday
19

☽⚹♆ 6:39 am
☉♂☽ 8:53 am
☽⚹♂ 10:51 am v/c
☽→♊ 11:48 am
☽△♇ 12:20 pm
☽□♄ 11:58 pm

New Moon in ♉ Taurus 8:53 am PDT

ALL ASPECTS IN PACIFIC DAYLIGHT TIME; ADD 3 HOURS FOR EDT; ADD 7 HOURS FOR GMT

2023 Year at a Glance for ♊ Gemini (May 21–June 21)

Are you ready to make some new friends? Of course you are! Don't overthink the process of putting yourself out there, Gemini. This year is giving you the opportunity to expand your network; all you must do is be willing to communicate. Since your planetary ruler is Mercury, that should be no problem for you. The key to this year is to not overextend yourself. You are human, flesh and bones, sweat and tears, feelings and emotions. It is important that you honor the energetic exchange that occurs when you open your mouth and share your thoughts. You must respect yourself by recognizing when to stop and rest to avoid burnout. Join virtual groups, connect with religious, activist, or spiritual communities, stay in touch with friends—these are practical strategies to connect with others that will prove beneficial as the year progresses. In order to stay focused, it will be extremely helpful to keep your goals in mind. As we age it can be harder to let ourselves dream. Life, responsibilities, and mortality have a way of clouding our imagination. Take stock of your superpowers and limitations. With a clear sense of self you can allow yourself the room to practically dream. What are small goals that you would like to accomplish within one year? The act of manifesting is a long process; however, that does not mean it's not possible. Confidence will open doors, and opportunities will fall on your lap when you carry yourself with a high sense of self-esteem.

The Healer, Side #2
© *Verlena Lisa Johnson 2021*

Astrologer Six © Mother Tongue Ink 2022

───────── ♄♄♄ sábado ─────────

♊

Saturday
20

♂→♌ 8:31 am
♂☍♇ 8:12 pm

───────── ☉☉☉ domingo ─────────

♊
♋

Sunday
21

☉→♊ 12:09 am
☉△♇ 6:58 am
☽□♆ 3:12 pm v/c

☽→♋ 8:28 pm
☽✳♃ 10:54 pm
☉✳♂10:56 pm

☉→♊

Sun in ♊ Gemini 12:09 am PDT

May
svibanj

Monday
22

☽△♄ 9:24 am
☽⚹☿ 12:07 pm
♂□♃ 10:13 pm

Tuesday
23

☽♂♀ 5:45 am
☽⚹♅ 11:07 am

Wednesday
24

☽△♆ 2:12 am v/c
☽→♌ 7:35 am
☽☍♇ 8:04 am
☽□♃ 11:13 am
☽♂♂ 12:21 pm
☉⚹☽ 2:31 pm
♀□♃ 4:39 pm

Thursday
25

☽□☿ 3:11 am
☽ApG 6:30 pm
☽□♅ 11:38 pm v/c

Friday
26

♀⚹♅ 12:37 am
☽→♍ 8:05 pm

When She Dances

She is peacock feather and cockatiel
She is honey dripping from the comb
She is water buffalo planting her feet
She is the whole forest swaying

She is the spiral pulse of smoke
She is the wave that ambushes the shore
She is glacier thundering into the bay
She is the whole forest falling

She is the quiver deep in the frog's throat
She is pollen rising like mist
She is candle flame over water
She is the whole forest singing

© *Jennifer Highland 2015*

***Dancing with
the Wind***
© *Karen Russo 2014*

ᚻᚻᚻ subota

♍ Saturday
27

☽△♃ 12:53 am
☉□☽ 8:22 am
☽☌♄ 9:53 am
☽△♅ 8:07 pm

Waxing Half Moon in ♍ Virgo 8:22 am PDT

◉◉◉ nedjelja

♍ Sunday
28

☉□♄ 3:46 am
☽△♅ 12:12 pm
☽⚹♀ 5:19 pm

May / June

Boishakh / Joishtho

Let the Wild Woman Sing
Open yourself wide
The creative flame
Whispers at your heart
Listen, listen
excerpt © Helen Smith 2017

〉〉〉 sombar

♍︎
♎︎

Monday
29

☽ ☍ ♆ 2:46 am v/c
☽ → ♎︎ 7:50 am
☽ △ ♇ 8:12 am
☽ ✶ ♂ 6:21 pm

♂♂♂ mongolbar

♎︎

Tuesday
30

☉ △ ☽ 12:38 am

☿☿☿ budhbar

♎︎
♏︎

Wednesday
31

☽ □ ♀ 7:53 am v/c
☽ → ♏︎ 4:45 pm
☽ □ ♇ 5:02 pm
☽ ☍ ♃ 11:03 pm

♃♃♃ brihospotibar

♏︎
◯

Thursday
1

June

☽ □ ♂ 5:11 am
☽ △ ♄ 5:29 am
♂ ⚹ ♄ 12:31 pm
☽ ☍ ☿ 11:52 pm

♀♀♀ sukrobar

♏︎
♐︎
◯

Friday
2

☽ ☍ ♅ 5:10 am
♀ △ ♆ 3:42 pm
☽ △ ♆ 5:42 pm
☽ △ ♀ 5:51 pm v/c
☽ → ♐︎ 10:03 pm
☽ ✶ ♇ 10:16 pm

ALL ASPECTS IN PACIFIC DAYLIGHT TIME; ADD 3 HOURS FOR EDT; ADD 7 HOURS FOR GMT

Faith © *Natasza Zurek 2020*

♐

Saturday
3

☽□ħ 10:07 am
☽△♂ 11:59 am
☉☍☽ 8:42 pm

Full Moon in ♐ Sagittarius 8:42 pm PDT

♐

Sunday
4

☿♂♅ 12:49 pm
☽□♆ 8:24 pm v/c

June
Mí Meitheamh

▷▷▷ Dé Luain

Monday
5

♐
♑

☽→♑ 12:31 am
♀→♌ 6:46 am
☽△♃ 7:44 am
♀☌♇ 9:05 am
☽✶♄ 12:11 pm

Suddenly the sky
gives us a broken dish moon
half of her enough
¤ Katya Sabaroff Taylor 2009

♂♂♂ Dé Máirt

Tuesday
6

♑

☽△♅ 10:10 am
☽△♄ 2:34 pm
☽PrG 4:17 pm
☽✶♆ 9:39 pm v/c

☿☿☿ Dé Céadaoin

Wednesday
7

♑
♒

☽→♒ 1:41 am
☽☌♇ 1:48 am
☽☍♀ 4:39 am
☽□♃ 9:34 am
☽☍♂ 7:11 pm

♃♃♃ Dé Ardaoin

Thursday
8

♒

☉△☽ 6:29 am
☽□♅ 11:37 am
☽□♄ 9:24 pm v/c

♀♀♀ Dé Haoine

Friday
9

♒
♓

☽→♓ 3:14 am
☽✶♃ 12:02 pm
♄✶♆ 2:14 pm
☽☌♄ 3:15 pm

ALL ASPECTS IN PACIFIC DAYLIGHT TIME; ADD 3 HOURS FOR EDT; ADD 7 HOURS FOR GMT

Clay and Silver

Potter's daughter, I grew up learning the wheel,
      insignia of Earth. My palms became tools
         of both friction and caress.
We formed cups and bowls, plates and teapots.

We searched riverbanks, digging for the perfect
malleability of sand and clay.
We studied which fields made the best use of sun.
We prized water, coming to understand
the sacred nature of her balance.

My mother taught me that not all spheres
      are equal. There is an art to the circle.
We timed our craftsmanship to the moon's
      revelation. We could shape
         a useful mug or dish
when she was waning or full.

But our best vases, our thinnest, strongest rims,
occurred under the delicate, waxing crescent,
that perfect curve when silver holds the future
of both itself and the world.

© Joanne M. Clarkson 2021

ᚻᚻᚻ Dé Sathairn

♓

Saturday
10

☉✱♄ 12:06 am
☉□☽ 12:31 pm
☽✱♅ 2:21 pm

☉☉☉ Dé Domhnaigh   Waning Half Moon in ♓ Pisces 12:31 pm PDT

♓
♈

Sunday
11

☽☌♆ 2:09 am
♇→♑ 2:47 am
☿△♇ 3:26 am
☿→♊ 3:26 am
☽✱♇ 6:20 am v/c

☽→♈ 6:20 am
☽✱♅ 6:43 am
♀□♃ 8:39 am
☽△♀ 4:40 pm

June
junio

Sit down and listen!
Lower your pen for the
moon muse transmission.
Thought into word,
word into action.
Me and the cosmic
ignite the blaze passion.
© Angela Bigler 2021

--- ☽☽☽ lunes ---

♈

Monday
12

☽△♂ 5:35 am
☉⚹☽ 8:59 pm

--- ♂♂♂ martes ---

♈
♉

Tuesday
13

♀⚻♄ 2:59 am
☽□♇ 11:27 am v/c
☽→♉ 11:31 am
☽♂♃ 10:40 pm

--- ☿☿☿ miércoles ---

♉

Wednesday
14

☽⚹♄ 12:36 am
☽□♀ 2:08 am
☽□♂ 2:15 pm

--- ♃♃♃ jueves ---

♉
♊

Thursday
15

☽♂♅ 1:55 am
☿□♄ 9:09 am
☽⚹♆ 2:19 pm
☽△♇ 6:36 pm v/c
☽→♊ 6:45 pm

--- ♀♀♀ viernes ---

♊

Friday
16

☽□♄ 8:20 am
☽♂☿ 12:12 pm
☽⚹♀ 1:57 pm

ALL ASPECTS IN PACIFIC DAYLIGHT TIME; ADD 3 HOURS FOR EDT; ADD 7 HOURS FOR GMT

Courting the Muse

How do you court the muse?
She calls through each phase of the moon
In her crescent smile,
fullness, waning, and silver lining
Goddess of the night
Waters rise
Unexpectedly she visits
Demands your full presence
At once
Drop everything
Before she goes
She leaves with the moonlight
If you missed her, she will come again

Be ready

¤ Sophia Faria 2021

She Lives by the Cycles
© Anna McKay 2021

ħħħ sábado

♊

Saturday
17

☽⚹♂ 1:14 am
☿⚹♀ 8:29 am
ħR 10:27 am
☉♂☽ 9:37 pm
☽□♉ 11:24 pm v/c

☉☉☉ domingo

New Moon in ♊ Gemini 9:37 pm PDT

♊
♋

Sunday
18

☽→♋ 3:58 am
☽⚹♃ 5:45 pm
☽△ħ 6:00 pm
☉□♆ 8:54 pm

Pandemonium of Peace

Now showing: Planetary Apocalypse!
only one woman can save us
before it's too late:
You.
the plot: Mass kindness erupts
on every continent forcing people
into their neighbors' homes for dinner
and to care for each others' children.
On a revenge mission for violations against Earth
our lone-wolf Super Hera straps on a bandolier
of graphite pencils and clips of acrylics
to command legal writs for equity.
Community gardens and renewable energy
become international law creating
a total global healing surge that robs
humans of the power to learn hate
because they never see it, worse,
Veteran Mothers ratchet up the stakes
by infiltrating the known world at every level
and building human bonds between
gangs of artists and the cynical
sending the miserly into studios to beg
for crayons, finger paints, and
the right to lie on the floor in a suit and draw.
Coalitions for the Prevention of Isolation, Fear, and Hunger
outlaw suffering and the wrathful are sentenced
by the Grand Wizards of Goodness
to months of gardening and caring for animals.
To ensure this world lasts in perpetuity
our Super Hera (You), the key to saving
Life as We Have Never Known and Only Imagined It
becomes an Outlaw of Armageddon
on her completely possible mission of Love
she was born ready to accept.

◻ *Stephanie A. Sellers 2021*

June
lipanj

Oregon Sunrise © Betty LaDuke 2011

♋

Monday
19

♃⚹♄ 8:53 am
☽⚹♅ 9:33 pm

♋
♌

Tuesday
20

☽△♆ 10:24 am
☽⚼♇ 2:43 pm v/c
☽→♌ 3:04 pm

♌

Wednesday
21

Summer Solstice

⊙⚼♇ 3:20 am
☽□♃ 6:14 am
⊙→♋ 7:58 am
☿⚹♂ 8:23 am
☿⚹♄ 6:42 pm
☽♂♀ 8:08 pm

⊙→♋

Sun in ♋ Cancer 7:58 am PDT

♌

Thursday
22

☽♂♂ 5:41 am
☽⚹☿ 8:51 am
☽□♅ 10:01 am v/c
☽ApG 11:34 am
♂△♄ 8:52 pm

♌
♍

Friday
23

☽→♍ 3:35 am
⊙⚹☽ 7:24 am
☽♂♄ 6:07 pm
☽△♃ 7:53 pm

ALL ASPECTS IN PACIFIC DAYLIGHT TIME; ADD 3 HOURS FOR EDT; ADD 7 HOURS FOR GMT

2023 Year at a Glance for ♋ Cancer (June 21–July 22)

You are familiar with the process of transformation and understand that it rarely comes easily. It is a long and often complicated journey involving setbacks, mountains to summit, and occasional disappointments. Dear Cancer, if change came without disruption, then how would we recognize it? Through occasional stressors and random obstacles, our wits are tested, and we are challenged to grow. Rest assured that you deserve the fruits of your labor. This year is challenging you to emerge from your cocoon. Grant yourself permission to take it slow as you go through the re-orientation process; you are meant to evolve at your own pace. Try not to get too comfortable; the universe will provide you with experiences that force personal development. Leaving your comfort zone and entering the unknown is never easy; it can be terrifying and difficult, and does not come without risks. Try not to overthink your decisions and trust that you have what it takes to discern how to move forward. Through your social network, you will find opportunities that come with ease. You are magnetically attracted to prosperous possibilities.

This year allows you to shine within your career, if you're willing to put energy into it. Be clear on what you wish to happen: it is through focus that we can actualize our potential. By the end of this year, you will have grown a more insightful understanding of yourself and your values.

Astrologer Six © Mother Tongue Ink 2022

Worthy □ *D. Woodring–*
Portrait Priestess 2021

ħħħ subota

♍

Saturday
24

☽△♅ 10:53 pm

☉☉☉ nedjelja

♍
♎

Sunday
25

☽□♉ 10:25 am
☽☍♆ 11:20 am
☽△♇ 3:24 pm v/c
♉□♆ 3:36 pm
☽→♎ 3:57 pm

Pneuma © Marnie Recker 2020

Summer Solstice

As we gather round the sacred fire of summer's peak, hands joined, the ribbon of time may fold and suddenly we see many things at once: those from history who were burned, their stories lost, their wisdom silenced. Those who are currently persecuted, their voices crying out if only we will take time to look and listen. The steadily warming planet and how little time we have left to slow the burning. The wildfires that sweep across the land howling at us to pay attention, to act, to change our course. Let us spread our arms out under this great wide sky and let the magic of being alive fill us with fire. Let us lift our arms to the sun and be restored and renewed by the heart of passion, the heat of longing, the warmth of pleasure. As the streaming light of purposeful joy replenishes our hearts, may we allow the wild magic of this time and space to restore our knowing that today is still fertile with possibility to do good work and to rejoice.

Molly Remer © Mother Tongue Ink 2022

Fearless

I want you
Untamed
You are needed now
Your truths swelling to spill over all contrived and man-made banks
Flooding across vast, fertile soils in which small seeds seek moisture

You quench them

Unleashing a torrent of unstoppable new green growth
Deep, deep into the month of June
I ask only you expand the honesty of your clear eyes
Courageously creating connection and community
Unafraid beneath bright and lengthening light

Brave one
Reveal now your red, raw,
ragged heart
Kept quiet and controlled
Too long under lock and key

Now is the time!
To cut cracks in concrete
To collapse and crumble it
Down, down
Into the soft, warm
earth of you

For we are all made new
In the raging rapids
Of your undamned love

And this is not the end
But only the beginning
The first fragile shoots
Of a new world
In which we are
Feet to earth
Fearless

¤ *Janis Dyck 2018*

Standing Tree
¤ *Diana Denslow 2000*

)))) sombar ───────────────────

♎

Monday
26

⊙□☽ 12:50 am
♂□♅ 2:23 am
☿⊼♇ 2:07 pm
☿→♋ 5:24 pm

───────── ♂♂♂ mongolbar ───────── Waxing Half Moon in ♎ Libra 12:50 am PDT

♎

Tuesday
27

☽⚹♀ 3:56 am
☽⚹♂ 11:25 am

──────────── ☿☿☿ budhbar ────────────────

♎
♏

Wednesday
28

☽□♇ 1:19 am v/c
☽→♏ 1:55 am
☽△☿ 8:32 am
⊙△☽ 2:49 pm
☽△♄ 3:06 pm
☽☍♃ 6:28 pm
⊙△♄ 6:42 pm ──────── ♃♃♃ brihospotibar ──────────

♏

Thursday
29

♀△♇ 1:41 am
☽□♀ 2:32 pm
☽☍♅ 5:22 pm
☽□♂ 9:05 pm
☿△♄ 11:23 pm

──────────── ♀♀♀ sukrobar ────────────

♏
♐

Friday
30

☽△♆ 3:58 am
☽⚹♇ 7:20 am v/c
☽→♐ 7:59 am
♆R 2:07 pm
☽□♄ 8:08 pm
⊙♂☿ 10:06 pm

───────────────────────────────────

ALL ASPECTS IN PACIFIC DAYLIGHT TIME; ADD 3 HOURS FOR EDT; ADD 7 HOURS FOR GMT

Risk's Wisdom

Open your hands
what do you see?
These lines trace
the way home
through a labyrinth
of longing.

Flight of Fancy *© Gretchen Butler 2021*

Risk is the daughter
of Desire and of Will
born of the moon, she knows
the sting of leaving,
the stomach knots that come
with edge walking,
the held breath
right before taking flight,
the softness it takes
to shapeshift, change.

She knows loss is necessary,
she knows empty hands
mean possibility,
she knows how to curl her toes
over that beckoning edge
and jump!

◻ Emily Kedar 2021

───────── ╰╰╰ sonibar ─────────

♐ ◑ **Saturday**
1

July

♉⚹♃ 12:10 am
☉⚹♃ 3:26 am
☽△♀ 8:21 pm

───────── ☉☉☉ robibar ─────────

♐ ◐ **Sunday**
♑ **2**

☽△♂ 2:18 am
☽□♆ 6:33 am v/c
♀□♅ 7:33 am

☿ApH 7:59 am
☽→♑ 10:20 am
☽⚹♄ 9:43 pm

July
Mí Iúil

The Moon is a belly
may what nourishes wax
may what starves us wane
till no belly, no heart
ever goes hungry again
¤ L. Sixfingers 2021

————))) Dé Luain ————

♑

Monday
3

☽△♃ 2:02 am
☉☍☽ 4:38 am
☽☍♅ 9:50 am
☽△♅ 9:30 pm

———— ♂♂♂ Dé Máirt ————

Full Moon in ♑ Capricorn 4:38 am PDT

♑
♒

Tuesday
4

☽⚹♆ 6:49 am
☽♂♇ 9:45 am v/c
☽→♒ 10:30 am
☽PrG 3:38 pm

———— ☿☿☿ Dé Céadaoin ————

♒

Wednesday
5

☽□♃ 2:28 am
☿□♃ 9:28 pm
☽□♅ 9:30 pm

———— ♃♃♃ Dé Ardaoin ————

♒
♓

Thursday
6

☽☍♀ 12:37 am
☽☍♂ 6:42 am v/c
♂⚻♆ 8:47 am
☽→♓ 10:32 am
☽♂♄ 9:47 pm
☿⚹♅ 9:54 pm

———— ♀♀♀ Dé Haoine ————

♓

Friday
7

☽⚹♃ 3:28 am
☉△☽ 11:48 am
☽⚹♅ 10:48 pm

Earth's Medicine © *Lani Kai Weis 2018*

♓
♈

Saturday
8

☽△♅ 2:55 am
☽☌♆ 8:22 am
☽⚹♇ 11:22 am v/c
☽→♈ 12:19 pm

♈

Sunday
9

♂⚹♇ 5:54 am
☿△♆ 4:57 pm
☉□☽ 6:48 pm

Waning Half Moon in ♈ Aries 6:48 pm PDT

MOON VII   105

July
julio

♈
♉

Monday
10

♂→♍ 4:40 am
☽△♀ 9:34 am
☿ℰ♇ 1:48 pm
☽□♇ 3:49 pm

☽□♅ 4:11 pm v/c
☽→♉ 4:55 pm
☽△♂ 5:31 pm
☿→♌ 9:11 pm

Twin Flame
© *Meridian Azura 2016*

──── ♂♂♂ martes ────

♉

Tuesday
11

☽⚹♄ 5:11 am
☽♂♃ 1:04 pm

──── ☿☿☿ miércoles ────

♉

Wednesday
12

☉□♅ 5:06 am
☉⚹☽ 5:30 am
☽♂♅ 9:42 am
☽□♀ 6:24 pm
☽⚹♆ 7:59 pm
☽△♇ 11:11 pm v/c

──── ♃♃♃ jueves ────

♉
♊

Thursday
13

☽→♊ 12:26 am
☽□♂ 3:51 am
☽⚹☿ 9:40 am
☽□♄ 1:06 pm

──── ♀♀♀ viernes ────

♊

Friday
14

☿⚻♄ 8:17 am
☉⚹♅ 4:02 pm

Invitation from the Bats

The day you feel sad to see the sun rise, come in with us to a cave the Earth made when the Earth was a child. Hook your feet to the roof of this womb. Be rooted in dreams we've dreamed right here, little ape, for fifty million years into stone, warmed by ancestors. We furred and hot-winged ghosts invite you: Drop your foolish head. Let go, go dark, while the sun out there rises, then falls, and the busy ones strive, and climax, and dissipate as men do, while we hang still in the dripping, ringing, listening place, and wait for the waking of Night.

Then we'll turn to each other's sharp faces, stretch our hands wide, fingers long, to grasp the Moon's Air for we—though warm, though we snuggle our children, too, we do!—we also are angels, tumbling into night as if wings could be made from the inner tissue of a heart, into stars, into the great dark artwork that remains of the day made of echo: Listen. It was the same day it ever was, since the beginning. But when you speak it out loud into night, into that star-painting, the world, you repaint it, unique, with your listening, with your voice—You call out your longing, and hear the shapes of your answers. At last, at last, you know where you are!

And when the dawn comes echoing back, at last, you'll know what it means because—Remember? Echolocation. We taught you how to pray.

◻ Mindi Meltz 2021

ᕁᕁᕁ sábado

♊
♋

Saturday
15

☽⚹♀	5:27 am	♀⚻♆	11:43 am
☽□♆	5:35 am v/c	☽⚹♂	4:48 pm
☽→♋	10:13 am	☽△♄	11:06 pm

☉☉☉ domingo

♋

Sunday
16

☽⚹♃	9:22 am

Under the Moon

Don't mind me,
I'm out getting lost
under the moon,
watching bats wheel
and vultures go to bed
and listening
to whippoorwills and starsong.
Don't seek me,
I'm dancing with sunset,
studying the shapes
of clouds and leaves,
serenading violets
and waltzing with wild
berries. Don't try to tell me
what to do
or ask me when the taxes
are due
I'm busy slipping between shadows
and under raindrops
and finding out where the river flows.
Don't worry about me
I'm dialoguing with crows
and dandelions,
watching butterflies dance
and remembering the witching
that was lost
when we stopped looking for the moon
and forgot to listen to flowers.
Don't call me back,
I'm uncovering magic
and remembering dreams,
following secrets laid down
by moss and mushroom
and tracking down wisdom
in holy books of bark and stone.

VIII. SACRED WILD

Moon VIII: July 17–August 16

New Moon in ♋ Cancer July 17; Sun in ♌ Leo July 22; Full Moon in ♒ Aquarius August 1

Night Goddess © Janet Newton 2020

July
srpanj

Monday
17

♋
♌

☿□♃	5:49 am
Ɒ⚹♅	6:21 am
☉♂Ɒ	11:32 am
Ɒ△♆	4:52 pm
Ɒ⚻♇	8:06 pm v/c
Ɒ→♌	9:39 pm

© Sierra Lonepine Briano 2018

Gazing Upward
New Moon in ♋ Cancer 11:32 am PDT

Tuesday
18

♌

| Ɒ□♃ | 10:02 pm |

Wednesday
19

♌

Ɒ♂☿	4:23 am
♇PrH	6:40 am
Ɒ□♅	6:51 pm
ƊApG	11:56 pm

Thursday
20

♌
♍

☉△♆	6:06 am
Ɒ♂♀	7:08 am v/c
Ɒ→♍	10:13 am
♂⚻♄	1:39 pm
Ɒ⚻♄	11:02 pm
Ɒ♂♂	11:36 pm

Friday
21

♍

Ɒ△♃	11:30 am
☉⚻♇	8:52 pm
☿△♇	11:57 pm

ALL ASPECTS IN PACIFIC DAYLIGHT TIME; ADD 3 HOURS FOR EDT; ADD 7 HOURS FOR GMT

2023 Year at a Glance for ♌ Leo (July 22–Aug 23)

Your relationships will get you far, Leo. It may feel difficult to maintain close friendships, especially because people can fall jealous of you when you take center stage. Your inner circle is privileged to have VIP access to your life experiences. Be patient with those you hold dear; they do not have the same access to opportunity as you do. Keep your eyes open and be willing to learn about the unique stories and narratives that those around you must share. As you develop a deeper understanding of why your close friends are the way they are, you can better understand how to utilize your unique assets to their advantage. Your light will shine brighter when joined by other stars—do not mistake a united front as a distraction from your glow. This year places priority on your ability to cultivate how you want to be perceived by the world around you. Spend this year identifying aspects of your personality that you wish to release or develop. Treat yourself with compassion during this period of transformation. This year will be met with moments that can encourage feelings of self-pity, and it is important that you not fall into traps of martyrdom. Patience and perseverance are key. Breathe through your moments of frustration and accompany each breath with a mantra. Having a clear sense of what you want and the willingness to integrate it into your daily life will help you actualize your desires.

Astrologer Six © Mother Tongue Ink 2022

ካካካ subota

Saturday
22

☽△♅ 7:48 am
☽☍♆ 5:59 pm
♀R 6:33 pm
☉→♌ 6:50 pm

☽△♇ 9:06 pm v/c
☽→♎ 10:54 pm
☉✶☽ 11:15 pm

Sun in ♌ Leo 6:50 pm PDT

⊙⊙⊙ nedjelja

Sunday
23

♃R 3:51 am
☿□♅ 2:39 pm

July
Asharh

Monday
24

☽✶☿ 11:39 pm

Tuesday
25

☽✶♀ 7:00 am
☽□♇ 8:05 am v/c
☽→♏ 9:55 am
☉□☽ 3:07 pm
☽△♄ 9:27 pm

Waxing Half Moon in ♏ Scorpio 3:07 pm PDT

Wednesday
26

☽✶♂ 4:31 am
☽☍♃ 10:38 am
☿☌♆ 8:59 pm

Thursday
27

☽☍♅ 4:10 am
☿☌♀ 8:16 am
☽△♆ 12:56 pm
☽□♀ 2:06 pm

☽□♅ 2:53 pm
☽✶♇ 3:36 pm v/c
☽→♐ 5:24 pm
☿☌♇ 9:24 pm

Friday
28

☉△☽ 2:22 am
☽□♄ 3:51 am
☽□♂ 1:09 pm
☿→♍ 2:31 pm
☉☌♄ 10:37 pm

A Promise to Rare Birds

Night Parrot, Damar Flycatcher
we thought you were gone
forever, not just in hiding.
Jamaican Petrel, Nightjar, Curlew
for ten generations we remembered
strained our eyes skyward
prayed for evidence
of your existence.
Red-throated Lorikeet,
Cozumel Thrasher
was that you we heard?
Turquoise-throated Puffleg,
Sinu Parakeet, is that your flash
of colored feathers in our lens?
Birds of a sacred second chance:
Hear us! 200 years ago
conquerors painted your portraits
like you were ornaments
then razed your homes.
We have planted and prosecuted
and now keep watch for your return.

□ Stephanie A. Sellers 2021

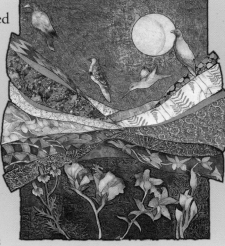

Path With Heart
□ *Patricia Wyatt 2015*

───── ᚼᚼᚼ sonibar ─────

♐
♑   **Saturday**
29

☽□♆   4:32 pm
☽△♀   4:51 pm v/c
☽→♑   8:44 pm
☽△♅   11:55 pm

───── ☉☉☉ robibar ─────

♑   **Sunday**
30

☽⚹♄   6:15 am
♀⚻♆   9:25 am
☽△♂   5:18 pm
☽△♃   6:51 pm

July / August

Mí Iúil / Mí Lúnasa

─── ☽☽☽ Dé Luain ───

♑
≈

Monday
31

☽△♅ 9:29 am
☽✶♆ 4:55 pm
☽☌♇ 7:13 pm v/c
☽→≈ 8:58 pm

─── ♂♂♂ Dé Máirt ───

≈

Tuesday
1

Lunar Lammas

☉☍☽ 11:32 am
♂△♃ 1:44 pm
☽□♃ 6:38 pm
☿☍♄ 7:18 pm
☽PrG 10:44 pm

Full Moon in ≈ Aquarius 11:32 am PDT

─── ☿☿☿ Dé Céadaoin ───

≈
♓

Wednesday
2

Lammas

☽□♅ 8:44 am
☽☍♀ 2:15 pm v/c
☽→♓ 8:05 pm

─── ♃♃♃ Dé Ardaoin ───

♓

Thursday
3

☽☌♄ 4:52 am
☽☍♅ 8:03 am
☽✶♃ 6:19 pm
☽☍♂ 8:15 pm

─── ♀♀♀ Dé Haoine ───

♓
♈

Friday
4

☽✶♅ 8:35 am
☽☌♆ 4:00 pm
☽✶♇ 6:21 pm v/c
☽→♈ 8:19 pm

ALL ASPECTS IN PACIFIC DAYLIGHT TIME; ADD 3 HOURS FOR EDT; ADD 7 HOURS FOR GMT

Lammas

There is a cauldron's call sounding in the late summer days inviting us to deepen and renew, wisps of steam rising and bubbles of possibility breaking the surface. The pot is on, the flavors are melding, our lives are coming to a boil. Remembering our task to re-call the fragments of our attention under a silver moon, reminded of what it means to truly care, we allow the cries of the world to touch our weary hearts, where they might yet take root and bear fruit.

While we watch what grows and thrives and ebbs and fades right where we are, a baby sea turtle is cradled in the gentle hands of a volunteer as it remembers how to follow the moon. A patch of coral is finding a new foothold on a reef gone gray. Everywhere, crows are calling in a wild, mad chorus that seems to circle the world, harsh and magic all in one call. Something becomes unlocked, unloosed in our still tender hearts and lifts off howling in gratitude for what it needs to thrive.

Molly Remer © Mother Tongue Ink 2022

The Magic Cauldron © Pam Taylor Photography 2019

My Harvest is New Intentions

Offering © *Joy Brady 2004*

On the day to mark
early harvest,
I carry dried clods
in a satchel.
My dream stick
falls to earth,
Dry hasps of mugwort
in six foot lengths
A kind of broken cane
between dimensions.

I carry clods of dust
from the remnants of
kin-action from work
that doesn't serve me

Buck up, and priestess power,
Everything is not broken. In fact, nothing is.

This is the early harvest, a kind of
intrinsic liberation
I am willing to try something else, to be something else.

I grate the clods in my pocket into fine silt
bless it
mix it with the dried leaves of dreams
allow the green-lit air
    (a kind of breath from across the sweet, bird-turning mist)
to gently moisten this in a pot of soul-seeds.

I plant these fresh intentions:
presence as sufficiency.

My harvest is new intentions.

◻ *marna scooter 2020*

Harvest

Five days darkened by heavy rains—
the swollen river pulses,
the temperature slips under,
the clouds sag with their weight in water.
I want to eat the roots of the world:
potatoes, carrots, parsnips.
I want the taste of things
that spent their entire lives in the dark
and became strong anyway.
The house itself
leans in towards the smells that fill it
with the rusty colors of warmth
and the full roundness of spice.
The day paints itself
in a pallet of greys around me,
but here, in the kitchen,
I am as hearty and alive
as the honeyed summer sun,
in love with the damp earth
and the nourishment
she yields.

© Megan Welti 2013

---------------------- ꜧꜧꜧ Dé Sathairn ----------------------

♈   Saturday
          5

☉△☽ 6:40 pm

---------------------- ☉☉☉ Dé Domhnaigh ----------------------

♈   Sunday
♉   6

☽△♀ 1:35 pm
☉□♃ 5:03 pm
☽□♇ 9:12 pm v/c
☽→♉ 11:24 pm

August
agosto

♉

Monday
7

☽✶♄ 8:46 am
☽△☿ 10:09 pm

♉

Tuesday
8

☽♂♃ 1:11 am
☉□☽ 3:28 am
☽△♂ 7:46 am
☽♂♅ 4:50 pm
☽□♀ 5:20 pm

Waning Half Moon in ♉ Taurus 3:28 am PDT

♉
♊

Wednesday
9

☽✶♆ 1:00 am
☽△♇ 3:38 am v/c
♀□♅ 4:08 am
☽→♊ 6:05 am
☽□♄ 3:45 pm
☿△♃ 5:47 pm

♊

Thursday
10

☽□♉ 11:02 am
☉✶☽ 4:37 pm
☽□♂ 7:28 pm
☽✶♀ 11:52 pm

♊
♋

Friday
11

♂⚼♇ 5:11 am
☽□♆ 10:27 am v/c
☽→♋ 3:52 pm

Dive © *Moss Wildwing 2014*

Closing the Circle

Crescent moon cavorts
among clouds
silver as a salmon's scale,
lithe as fish that bend and arc,
thrusting heavenward
to clear a cataract,
sharp silhouettes
leaping across blue days,
starlit nights,
redrawn a thousand ways
by Haida, Tlingit,
Mi'kmaq, Muckleshoot,
and Kwakwaka'wakw.

Moon's sea creature,
subject
to mother tides
and currents
till leaving home,
gives itself away,
curling mouth to tail,
struggles upstream
returning itself
to source,
choosing renewal
for all the relations.

© *Christine Irving 2021*

ħħħ sábado

♋ Saturday
12

D△ħ   1:37 am
⊙△⚷ 11:12 am
D⚹♃   9:06 pm

⊙⊙⊙ domingo

♋ Sunday
13

D⚹♅   2:25 am   D⚹♂   9:56 am
⊙♂♀   4:15 am   D⚹♅   1:30 pm
♀PrH   8:15 am   D△♆   9:57 pm

You Were Born

You were born at the dark of the Moon
eyes gazing up at the stars
unknown to the world
sheltered amongst the Redwoods
      in the heart of a city

You were born during strange times
but our grandmothers saw this coming
         and their grandmothers
            and their grandmothers

So under the slightest light
of a crescent glimmer
they birthed
    and mended
        and dreamed up
            what it might be
            that we would need
            to transform and
            be transformed
            by these strange and
            heartbreaking and
            hopeful times

Luna de solsticio 4
© Annika Gemlau aSombrasDelSur 2020

And you were born
at the dark of the Moon
but there was a murmuration
of grandmothers there
pulling back the veil of night
so that a crescent light
could guide you home
so that weathered hands
could hold the shape of you
so that their wisdom
      might glimmer
        upon your brow
      □ L. Sixfingers 2021

IX. ANCESTORS

Moon IX: August 16–September 14

New Moon in ♌ Leo August 16; Sun in ♍ Virgo August 23; Full Moon in ♓ Pisces August 30

Remembering ◻ *Emma Abel 2020*

August
kolovoz

Dear One
Know
you are your grandmother
woven
into another form.
excerpt © Sabina Jones 2017

——— ☽☽☽ ponedjeljak ———

♋︎
♌︎

Monday
14

☽☍♇ 12:46 am v/c
☽→♌︎ 3:36 am
♀△♄ 7:55 am

——— ♂♂♂ utorak ———

♌︎

Tuesday
15

☽□♃ 9:44 am
☽♂♀ 5:44 pm
☉□♅ 7:34 pm

——— ☿☿☿ srijeda ———

♌︎
♍︎

Wednesday
16

☽□♅ 2:04 am
☉♂☽ 2:38 am v/c
☽ApG 4:54 am
♂△♅ 6:53 am
☿⊼♄ 11:02 am
☽→♍︎ 4:14 pm

——— ♃♃♃ četvrtak ———

New Moon in ♌︎ Leo 2:38 am PDT

♍︎

Thursday
17

☽☍♄ 1:32 am
☽△♃ 10:48 pm

——— ♀♀♀ petak ———

♍︎

Friday
18

☽♂♅ 10:09 am
☽△♅ 2:51 pm
☽♂♂ 5:57 pm
☽☍♆ 11:01 pm

The Art of Satin

My grandmother the seamstress stitched the sheen within. Her craft: to shelter women in wool, coat for weather, cloak of worship, armor woven for warmth. She sewed the lining last, from fabric meant to waltz, woman-skin

Mending Cave *© Dorrie Joy 2019*

borrowed from a mirror's glimmer. She kept her satins on a separate shelf in a closet with only one key. As a child, when I entered this space, I felt myself illuminated, seen and beloved by my goddess grandmother and all the goddesses before her, an unbreakable thread spun from moonglow. And although I became nurse not seamstress, I understood that every task carries its own touch of satin, kindness fastened underneath and within.

© Joanne M. Clarkson 2021

───── ♄♄♄ subota ─────

♍
♎

Saturday
19

☾△♇ 1:51 am v/c
☾→♎ 4:53 am

───── ☉☉☉ nedjelja ─────

♎

Sunday
20

☉☍♅ 12:40 am
☾✶♀ 1:07 pm

August
Srabon

Temple Sisters
Sometimes I can hear them
temple sisters from days gone by,
quick footfalls on worn steps,
councils called at twilight
excerpt © Molly Remer 2021

—— ☽☽☽ sombar ——

Monday
21

☉⚼♇ 11:07 am
☽□♇ 1:19 pm
☉⚹☽ 1:31 pm v/c
☽→♏ 4:22 pm

—— ♂♂♂ mongolbar ——

Tuesday
22

☽△♄ 12:32 am
♀□♃ 5:16 am
♂⚼♆ 1:34 pm
☽□♀ 9:10 pm
☽⚼♃ 9:48 pm

—— ☿☿☿ budhbar ——

Wednesday
23

☉→♍ 2:01 am
☽⚹☿ 10:03 am
☽⚼♅ 12:19 pm
☿R 12:59 pm
☽△♆ 7:33 pm
☽⚹♂ 9:09 pm
☽⚹♇ 10:10 pm v/c

☉→♍

Sun in ♍ Virgo 2:01 am PDT

—— ♃♃♃ brihospotibar ——

Thursday
24

☽→♐ 1:07 am
☉□☽ 2:57 am
☽□♄ 8:29 am
♂△♇ 5:23 pm

Waxing Half Moon in ♐ Sagittarius 2:57 am PDT

—— ♀♀♀ sukrobar ——

Friday
25

☽△♀ 2:26 am
☽□☿ 3:43 pm

ALL ASPECTS IN PACIFIC DAYLIGHT TIME; ADD 3 HOURS FOR EDT; ADD 7 HOURS FOR GMT

2023 Year at a Glance for ♍ Virgo (Aug. 23–Sept. 22)

The beginning of the year is forcing you into a period of growth, Virgo. You are not meant to stay the same: as much as you may want to have a stable foundation, there is always room for mutability. Familiarity may call your name, and with its cries you will be likely to fall into old habits. Try to push past outdated coping mechanisms, especially if they are not to your benefit. Be willing to throw yourself into newness—you will find that excitement is likely to follow. Trust in your capabilities and knowledge; it will make a world of difference as you brave the nebulous realm of the unrevealed. Change is an inescapable aspect of nature. The mantra for this year is: if you have made it this far, then you're capable and able to keep going. This does not undermine how fear is a normal response to uncharted territory; in fact you should honor what makes you feel apprehensive. As the year continues you will find that after transformation follows a thirst for knowledge. Growing is a painful and exhausting experience, one that can leave you feeling mentally depleted. Make time for rest and idle-mindedness when you can; cognitive overload is a surefire way of stunting creativity. When you feel fully charged and capable of taking on more, you'll find that the information you need will be provided. Rest assured that even though the answers will not be spoon fed to you, the ability to find the solutions is carried within your utility belt.

Astrologer Six © Mother Tongue Ink 2022

Poetic Justice ▫ *Viandara 2021*

ᚻᚻᚻ ᛋonibar

♐
♑

Saturday
26

☽□♆ 12:49 am
☽□♂ 4:56 am v/c
☽→♑ 6:05 am
☉△☽ 11:38 am
☽⚹♄ 12:39 pm

☉☉ robibar

♑

Sunday
27

☉☌♄ 1:28 am
♄PrH 4:50 am
♂→♎ 6:20 am

☽△♃ 7:57 am
☽△♅ 5:00 pm
☽△♅ 8:22 pm

August / September
Mí Lúnasa / Mí Meán Fomhair

Dancing Among the Stars

─────))) Dé Luain ─────

♑
≈

Monday
28

☽⚹♆ 2:29 am
☽☌♇ 4:49 am v/c
☽→≈ 7:31 am
☽△♂ 8:39 am
♅R   7:38 pm

───── ♂♂♂ Dé Máirt ─────

≈

Tuesday
29

☽☍♀ 3:56 am
☽□♃ 8:11 am
☽□♅ 8:04 pm v/c

───── ☿☿☿ Dé Céadaoin ─────

≈
♓

Wednesday
30

☽→♓ 6:56 am
☽PrG 9:00 am
☽☌♄ 12:33 pm
☿⊼♇ 4:56 pm
☉☍☽ 6:35 pm

Full Moon in ♓ Pisces 6:35 pm PDT

───── ♃♃♃ Dé Ardaoin ─────

♓

Thursday
31

☽⚹♃ 7:25 am
☽☍♅ 12:28 pm
☽⚹♅ 7:20 pm

───── ♀♀♀ Dé Haoine ─────

♓
♈

Friday
1

September

☽☌♆   1:13 am
☽⚹♇   3:36 am v/c
☽→♈   6:25 am
☽☍♂ 11:50 am
♂⊼♄   2:01 pm

Didn't You Always Guess

Starseeded, oh yeah. Didn't you always guess it?
We were denizens elsewhere. Didn't you always
somewhere in your dreaming want to make friends
with sky relatives?

Owning up, coming back to the larger family
zoops you to where you can settle your mettle,
trust your purpose, alight in life as you never have.
Finding out how big

you really are, makes room for flaws,
laughs at "mistakes." It's all alive, connected, we're all
relation. You're here out of love for the big We.
They told me to tell you.

© *Susa Silvermarie 2021*

Transcendence © *Julia Jenkins Art 2017*

ᚻᚻᚻ Dé Sathairn

♈ ☽ **Saturday**
2

☽△♀ 2:19 am

☉☉☉ Dé Domhnaigh

♈ ☽ **Sunday**
♉   **3**

☽□♇ 4:57 am v/c
☽→♉ 8:00 am
☿PrH 8:06 am
☽⚹♄ 1:36 pm
♀D   6:20 pm

September

septiembre

♉ ## Monday
4

☿△♃ 3:29 am
☉△☽ 4:12 am
☽□♀ 5:08 am
♃R 7:11 am
☽△♅ 10:35 am
☽♂♃ 11:06 am

Menopause Ancestor

□ *Debra Hall 2021*

♉
♊ ## Tuesday
5

☽♂♅ 12:28 am
☽⚹♆ 6:59 am
☽△♇ 9:46 am v/c
☽→♊ 1:07 pm
☽□♄ 6:50 pm

♊ ## Wednesday
6

☽△♂ 12:44 am
☉♂♅ 4:09 am
☽⚹♀ 12:06 pm
☽□♅ 1:46 pm
☉□☽ 3:21 pm

Waning Half Moon in ♊ Gemini 3:21 pm PDT

♊
♋ ## Thursday
7

☽□♆ 3:21 pm v/c
☽→♋ 10:00 pm

♋ ## Friday
8

☽△♄ 3:43 am
☉△♃ 4:13 am
☽□♂ 1:33 pm
☽⚹♅ 7:57 pm

ALL ASPECTS IN PACIFIC DAYLIGHT TIME; ADD 3 HOURS FOR EDT; ADD 7 HOURS FOR GMT

Of the Sun

Child of the sun, you've been blessed since birth
Your skin is akin to our brown Mother Earth
She kisses your hands and guards every step
Even in dreams, you are carefully kept
For a promise was made to ancestors before you
who brought life to the land with the bounty they grew
    Your people were here since the first rising sun
    Your tie to la tierra cannot be undone
    Mestiza, Hispanic, Latinx, Chicano
    Illegal, Indian, migrant, Mexicano—
    Whatever they call you is merely a name
    Your bloodline, your story remains just the same
Flags will fly, maybe die and leaders will change
But your bond to this land will always remain
From Yámana down south to Inuit in the north
The land's First People will keep pushing forth
To survive and to thrive, despite changing days
holding on to their customs while learning new ways
    If you've planted your roots or traveled quite far
    always remember deep down who you are
    Indigenous. Native. On this land, you may roam
    Wherever life takes you, that means you are home

excerpt © Xelena González 2020

♄♄♄ sábado

♋

Saturday
9

☽⚹♃ 4:38 am
☉⚹☽ 6:48 am
☽⚹♅ 7:34 pm

☉☉☉ domingo

♋
♌

Sunday
10

☽△♆ 2:36 am
☽☍♇ 5:47 am v/c
☽→♌ 9:36 am

The Spiral Way

Walking
    the spiral way,
        circling around,
maybe deeper,
    maybe higher,
        with each revolution.
It is always like this—
    the years circle
        and pile up on each other.
The seasons turn,
    wind around,
        then return.
Once a girl,
    then a mother,
        now a crone,
still walking,
    still turning,
        in the spiral way.
Hair brown,
    hair white,
        hair gone.
Smooth baby skin
    gone coarse,
        now lined and deepened.

Walking the
    endless circuit,
        making the turns,
marking the way
    things change
        and yet remain the same.
Even when the end
    comes for you,
        the earth spirals,
keeps going round,
    keeps turning,
        keeps building,
keeps on.

◻ Maya Spector 2021

Raven *© Colleen Clifford 2017*

Spiral Goddess ◻ *Anne Jewett 2021*

Lunar Fragments

off we fly, souls regenerated,
onward to the next great arc of sky, the
next beautiful unfurling. our eyes are flecked with
nova and starstuff. we are made for this journey.

excerpt ◻ *marna scooter 2020*

September
rujan

Magnolia

♌

Monday
11

)⚹♂ 5:06 am
)♂♀ 12:32 pm
☉⊼♆ 3:40 pm
)□♃ 4:54 pm

♌ ♍

Tuesday
12

)□♅ 8:06 am v/c
)ApG 8:43 am
)→♍ 10:18 pm

♍

Wednesday
13

)☍♄ 3:30 am
)♂♀ 3:04 pm

♍

Thursday
14

)△♃ 5:27 am
☉♂) 6:40 pm
)△♅ 8:37 pm

New Moon in ♍ Virgo 6:40 pm PDT

♍ ♎

Friday
15

)☍♆ 3:30 am
)△♇ 6:49 am v/c
)→♎ 10:44 am
♀D 1:21 pm
☉△♅ 6:24 pm

ALL ASPECTS IN PACIFIC DAYLIGHT TIME; add 3 hours for EDT; add 7 hours for GMT

Hestia, Whispering in the Kitchen

My darling,
the night has shattered its walls for you.
It is as open as a bloom.
Even here, at the sink piled with dishes,
beauty finds itself moving through you
as you make what was soiled
new again beneath the murky stars.
The dark is breathing evenly
throughout the house,
but there is no peace for you
in this untidy room,
lit and warm and overflowing
with what the day has left behind.
I know you are able to nourish yourself
and the ones you carried into this world.
You are the only one who doubts, and so you struggle.
Everything in this world is broken.
Yet, beneath that brokenness, everything remains whole.
Dust and clutter and unwashed laundry cannot make you small
unless you allow them to. And even then,
the smallness you choose to wear is such a poor disguise.
The night will always find you and set you free.

© Megan Welti 2013

Hemp the Wise Woman © *Barb Kobe 2018*

ħħħ subota

Saturday
16

☽ ☌ ♂ 12:52 pm
☽ ⚹ ♀   4:57 pm
♀ ☐ ♃ 11:09 pm

☉☉☉ nedjelja

Sunday
17

☽ ☐ ♇   6:06 pm v/c
☽ → ♏ 9:58 pm

Fall Equinox

There is change in the air. It is traced by the wandering path of silent nighthawks migrating across grey-clouded skies. The seas seethe and ripple with change, the earth heaves and rumbles, the trees bend low offering up their leaves, plants are turning their faces to seed. Our bodies ebb and flow through so much change, ever unfolding. Standing here we can feel the world spin, can feel change whisper, shriek, and howl. There are hurricanes, there are nighthawks, there is a great pulse running through it all. May we listen. May we bear witness. May we change.

As we slip into the liminal space of the Equinox, we may find ourselves wavering between action and stillness. We hear the cries of our sisters, from times long past and times yet to come. They urge us to seize both our joys and courage and set forth, beneath a rising moon beside a ravenous sea, eyes cast upward to catch the silver lining as it breaks forth behind the clouds, feet moving together with resolute purpose, onward and forward.

Molly Remer © Mother Tongue Ink 2022

The Allies *© Lindsay Carron 2016*

Portals

Outlined by light for just an instant, an archway appears. We are invited into the heart of wonder. If we accept the beckoning, we enter a realm just familiar enough to banish fear, leading toward resilient truth.

Sometimes we see a city.

Sometimes wilderness.

Often we take on a new skin of fur or feathers or scales and live for an hour, animal

Once I was a healer with crystals in my palms.

Once a monastic woman whose days were spent in prayer.

Once a mother, daughter, sister, and crone, all in the same dream.

Always changed after these journeys, these indelible lessons, I know to look for the thinnest silver frame, seen best at the edge of the moon.

© Joanne M. Clarkson 2021

Kintsugi Spirit
© *Danielle Helen Ray Dickson 2016*

September

Bhadro

Wisp of Moon
which way does your crescent face
leaning into present grace
the wax and the wane
are one and the same
on either side of a long life
excerpt ¤ Kro 2021

☽☽☽ sombar

Monday
18

☽△♄ 2:18 am
ΨPrH 7:35 am
☽✶☿ 2:52 pm

♂♂♂ mongolbar

Tuesday
19

☽☌♃ 3:15 am
☉☌Ψ 4:17 am
☽□♀ 5:29 am
♂⊼♃ 3:48 pm
☽☌♅ 5:46 pm

☿☿☿ budhbar

Wednesday
20

☽△Ψ 12:06 am
☉✶☽ 1:47 am
☽✶♇ 3:21 am v/c
☽→♐ 7:06 am
☽□♄ 10:58 am
☉△♇ 10:21 pm

♃♃♃ brihospotibar

Thursday
21

☽□☿ 2:13 am
☽✶♂ 1:12 pm
☽△♀ 3:25 pm

♀♀♀ sukrobar

Friday
22

☽□Ψ 6:37 am
☉□☽ 12:32 pm v/c
☽→♑ 1:20 pm
☽✶♄ 4:44 pm
☉→♎ 11:50 pm

Fall Equinox

☉→♎

Waxing Half Moon in ♐ Sagittarius 12:32 pm PDT
Sun in ♎ Libra 11:50 pm PDT

ALL ASPECTS IN PACIFIC DAYLIGHT TIME; ADD 3 HOURS FOR EDT; ADD 7 HOURS FOR GMT

2023 Year at a Glance for ♎ Libra (Sept. 22–Oct. 23)

In continuation from last year, relationships will continue to be a significant focus in 2023. Over the past few years you may have grappled with unmet expectations. Being a cardinal air sign, it is very like you to charge in when those you care about are in need. When your loved ones do not reciprocate, it can be frustrating for you. Try to understand that having expectations is fair, and people will sometimes fall short. Try not to take it too personally—your loved ones are consumed by the various requirements that this life calls for, too. You aren't supposed to over-think your connections; allow them to organically develop. Do not get stuck on how hard it can be to maintain certain friendships; trust that effort will bear fruit. One of the key lessons for you is to learn not to overextend yourself. As significant a role partnerships play, you also have some inner transformation to attend to. It may be difficult for your cardinal energy to relax, but when you cut out the need to overdo yourself, you open up room for personal development. The message here is to focus on yourself and learn how to say "no." This year you will naturally gravitate towards very independent people: Individuals. Firecrackers! Try not to hyper-fixate on romance, even though you may crave the embrace of a lover. Your ability to let go will allow you room to blossom. Take the days slowly and direct your energy towards self-care.

Astrologer Six © Mother Tongue Ink 2022

© *Elizabeth Diamond Gabriel 2017*

ħħħ sonibar

♑

Saturday
23

♀△♇ 1:17 am
☽△♅ 11:24 am
☽△♃ 3:12 pm
☽□♂ 8:17 pm

☉☉☉ robibar

♑
♒

Sunday
24

☽△♅ 4:27 am
☽✶♆ 10:02 am
☽♂♇ 1:05 pm v/c
♂♂♇ 1:06 pm

☽→♒ 4:29 pm
☉△☽ 7:26 pm
☉☍ħ 8:10 pm

September / October
Mí Meán Fomhair / Mí Deireadh Fomhair

Silver Strands
Every year, I find
more silver strands of hair.
Every year, I embody
the magic of the moon
a little bit more.
□ *Astrea Taylor 2019*

─── ꭰꭰꭰ Dé Luain ───

≈

Monday
25

☿△♃ 5:10 am
☽□♃ 4:49 pm

─── ♂♂♂ Dé Máirt ───

≈
♓

Tuesday
26

☽△♂ 12:12 am
☽☍♀   1:47 am
☽□♅   5:38 am v/c
☽→♓   5:18 pm
☽♂♄   8:01 pm

─── ☿☿☿ Dé Céadaoin ───

♓

Wednesday
27

☿⊼♄ 3:30 pm
☽⚹♃ 4:46 pm
☽PrG 5:45 pm
☽☍☿ 11:18 pm

─── ♃♃♃ Dé Ardaoin ───

♓
♈

Thursday
28

☽⚹♅ 5:35 am
☽♂♆ 10:54 am
☽⚹♇ 1:57 pm v/c
☽→♈ 5:17 pm

─── ♀♀♀ Dé Haoine ───

♈

Friday
29

☉☍☽ 2:57 am
♀□♅ 10:52 am

Full Moon in ♈ Aries 2:57 am PDT

All aspects in Pacific Daylight Time; add 3 hours for EDT; add 7 hours for GMT

Thwarting the Arrow of Time

Camping by a river running glacial blue
we drape our backs in blankets,
sit beside a fire,
sipping whiskey out of Mason jars
anticipating the advent of fireflies
who patiently out wait dusk-fleet bats
to light their lamps.

Glasses dry, we chase their glowing wisps
like children, cutting all cords to ordinary life;
breathe in the damp green scent of dewy grasses,
remembering a childhood without magic,
replacing it with this one, newly made,
opening like a sunflower in the blazing glow
of Olympia's imperious disregard
for Time's straight arrow.

◻ *Christine Irving 2020*

Diosa de la Luna © *Kay Kemp 2018*

ㅊㅊㅊ Dé Sathairn

♈
♉

Saturday
30

☾⚹♂ 5:19 am
☾△♀ 7:08 am
☿△♅ 9:55 am
☾□♇ 2:49 pm v/c

☾→♉ 6:18 pm
☾⚹♄ 8:45 pm
♂⚻♅ 9:38 pm

⊙⊙ Dé Domhnaigh

♉

Sunday
1

October

☾♂♃ 6:37 pm

MOON X

139

October
octubre

♉
♊

Monday
2

☿☍Ψ	8:34 am
☽☌♅	8:57 am
☽□♀	1:07 pm
☽⚹Ψ	2:47 pm
☽△♅	3:41 pm
☽△♇	6:19 pm v/c
☽→♊	10:03 pm

♊

Tuesday
3

☽□♄	12:28 am
☿△♇	12:20 pm
☉△☽	5:03 pm
♀⚻Ψ	5:21 pm

♊

Wednesday
4

☿→♎	5:08 pm
☽△♂	8:32 pm
☽□Ψ	9:37 pm
☽⚹♀	11:34 pm v/c

♊
♋

Thursday
5

☽→♋	5:32 am
☽□♅	7:33 am
☽△♄	7:54 am
☿⚻♄	10:03 am
♂⚻Ψ	4:09 pm

♋

Friday
6

♀⚻♇	5:49 am
☉□☽	6:48 am
☽⚹♃	8:29 am

Waning Half Moon in ♋ Cancer 6:48 am PDT

ALL ASPECTS IN PACIFIC DAYLIGHT TIME; ADD 3 HOURS FOR EDT; ADD 7 HOURS FOR GMT

girl, woman, grandmother

I am a mother born a thousand years ago
from tidal currents and seashells.
I am a daughter raised by granite and stone
sap trickling down pines.
I know this, and yet

Most see me as
Girl, waiting.

Only recently, in the in-between,
have some caught the glimpse of a woman
lost deliriously in song

or, in the quiet hours of dawn,
the fresh scent of a woman,
holding fragile blossoms
in her palm.

And even fewer,
perhaps just the owls and moon,
have seen flashes of grandmother,
ancient being reborn,
bones made of bird feather
and sand.

◻ *Geneva Toland 2020*

Mama Moon © *Anna Lindberg 2018*

ㅎㅎㅎ sábado

Saturday
7

☽✶♅ 1:22 am	☽□♂ 10:25 am
☉⊼♃ 2:04 am	☽⚹♇ 12:11 pm v/c
☽△♆ 7:58 am	☽→♌ 4:24 pm

☉☉◎ domingo

Sunday
8

☽✶♉ 4:47 am	
♂□♇ 6:05 pm	
♀→♍ 6:11 pm	
☽□♃ 7:55 pm	

October
listopad

♌

Monday
9

☉⚹☽ 12:07 am
☽□♅ 1:36 pm
☽ApG 8:38 pm
♀☍♄ 11:11 pm

♌
♍

Tuesday
10

☽⚹♂ 2:36 am v/c
☽→♍ 5:02 am
☽☍♄ 7:06 am
☽♂♀ 7:46 am
ED 6:10 pm
♄PrH 11:06 pm
☉☍♅ 11:20 pm

Time to order We'Moon 2024!
Free Shipping within the US October 10–13th!
Promo Code: Lucky13 www.wemoon.ws

♍

Wednesday
11

☽△♃ 8:06 am
♂→♏ 9:04 pm

♍
♎

Thursday
12

☽△♅ 2:01 am
☿⊼♃ 5:32 am
☽☍♆ 8:42 am
☽△♇ 1:10 pm v/c
☽→♎ 5:22 pm

♎

Friday
13

♂△♄ 5:29 am

Girl Friends

innocent of the grown world
we filled our imaginations
to the brim and drank
the strawberry gold of words.
we flew like Amelia Earhart,
young engines chugging ideas
into the great unknown
where "I can do this" hums and
friendship is light as cumulus clouds
in pristine seas of blue.

then adults-only rules invaded
tore the throttle from our hands, broke the compass
believing we couldn't find our way upside down
perform evasive daredevil acrobatics
weave through nimbus rain clouds
cut our engines to dive silently
through hail spinning like cobwebs
and float the descent, skywriting our lives
like jet stream through stratus
waving our vermilion caps at our grown-up selves
to beckon them back home.

¤ Stephanie A. Sellers 2021

───── ᚺᚺᚺ subota ─────

♎

Saturday
14

☽☌☿ 1:58 am
☉☌☽ 10:55 am
☿☌♃ 3:31 pm

New Moon in ♎ Libra 10:55 am PDT
*Annular Solar Eclipse 10:59 am PDT

───── ☉☉☉ nedjelja ─────

♎
♏

Sunday
15

☽□♇ 12:01 am v/c
☽→♏ 4:04 am
☽△♄ 5:41 am

☽☌♂ 8:35 am
☉⚹♅ 12:43 pm
☽⚹♀ 3:51 pm

When Ending Comes

Look into its eyes
until your tears make a Monet's garden of the landscape,
blurring the hard cliff edge
you will step beyond into emptiness.

When ending comes
Be alone with Sorrow
even if she refuses to speak to you,
let the silence become clay on a wound
that draws out your own hidden, essential words.

When ending comes
Greet it like a guest
that will destroy the house
but leave behind a golden cup
you will not know how to drink from right away.

When ending comes
Cradle it in your arms like an egg, warm it with your body
so that someday when your back curves around it with grief
the bared bones of your shoulders
will breathe out wings.

© Sophia Rosenberg 2019

Iniko © *Sandra Stanton 2021*

XI. PASSAGE

Moon XI: October 14–November 13

New Moon in ♎ Libra Oct. 14; Sun in ♏ Scorpio Oct. 23; Full Moon in ♉ Taurus Oct. 28

Condor Corridor © Serena Supplee 2004

October
Ashshin

Dragonfly

© Tamara Phillips 2015

— ☽☽☽ sombar —

Monday
16

☽☌♃ 4:31 am
☽☌♅ 10:01 pm

— ♂♂♂ mongolbar —

Tuesday
17

☽△♆ 4:20 am
☿⊼♅ 7:48 am
☽✶♇ 8:43 am v/c
☽→♐ 12:36 pm
☽□♄ 2:02 pm

— ☿☿☿ budhbar —

Wednesday
18

♂ApH 2:21 am
☽□♀ 4:15 am
☉⊼♆ 8:40 pm

— ♃♃♃ brihospotibar —

Thursday
19

☿⊼♆ 7:11 am
☽□♆ 10:52 am
☽✶☿ 11:25 am
☉✶☽ 12:02 pm v/c
☽→♑ 6:55 pm
☽✶♄ 8:10 pm
☉☌☿ 10:38 pm

— ♀♀♀ sukrobar —

Friday
20

☽✶♂ 4:54 am
☽△♀ 1:59 pm
☽△♃ 4:30 pm
☿□♇ 5:51 pm

ALL ASPECTS IN PACIFIC DAYLIGHT TIME; ADD 3 HOURS FOR EDT; ADD 7 HOURS FOR GMT

Death Altar

Make space for death in your altar
Collect the bodies of bees, and butterflies and beetles
Birds, even
Let your fruits decay
Pick up the bones and feathers you find
Admire them
Take them home
Bury things
And dig them up again
To watch how the Earth has reclaimed them
Take deep breaths and hold them
Burn things
And scatter the ashes on the soil of your plants
Cry
Cry as hard and deep and often as you can
Grieve like it is a community project
Get your family involved
As often as we celebrate life,
we ought to dance and sing for the death that had to come
before, and will inevitably come again.

If you will give it space, death can make something
extraordinarily beautiful on the altar of your life.

© Brittany May Gill 2021

ꓘꓘꓘ sonibar

♑
♒

Saturday
21

☉⊡ᴾ	7:09 am
☽△⛢	9:21 am
☽⚹♆	3:17 pm
☽☌ᴾ	7:33 pm
☉⊡☽	8:29 pm

♀△♃	9:32 pm
☽⊡⛢	11:00 pm v/c
☽→♒	11:06 pm
⛢→♏	11:49 pm

Waxing Half Moon in ♑ Capricorn 8:29 pm PDT

☉☉ robibar

♒

Sunday
22

⛢△♄	9:12 am
☽⊡♂	11:21 am
☽⊡♃	7:27 pm

October
Mí Deireadh Fomhair

Monday
23

☉→♏ 9:21 am
☽□♅ 12:04 pm v/c

☉→♏

Sun in ♏ Scorpio 9:21 am PDT

♒
♓

Tuesday
24

☉△♄ 12:13 am
☽→♓ 1:33 am
☽♂♄ 2:34 am
☉△☽ 2:45 am
☽△♅ 7:57 am
☽△♂ 3:58 pm
☽⚹♃ 8:57 pm

♓

Wednesday
25

☽☌♀ 2:52 am
☽⚹♅ 1:35 pm
☽♂♆ 7:22 pm
☽PrG 7:52 pm
☽⚹♇ 11:39 pm v/c

♓
♈

Thursday
26

☽→♈ 3:01 am
☿ApH 6:05 pm
♀⚻♇ 6:10 pm

♈

Friday
27

No Exact Aspects

ALL ASPECTS IN PACIFIC DAYLIGHT TIME; ADD 3 HOURS FOR EDT; ADD 7 HOURS FOR GMT

2023 Year at a Glance for ♏ Scorpio (Oct. 23–Nov. 22)

Last year you learned the power of choosing to be in the moment, making decisive decisions, and committing yourself to just doing what needs to be done. Congratulations! The ability to lunge at momentary opportunities is a key that will open the door to endless opportunities. There has been a long-standing demand for you to settle down, which can be scary and daunting. It requires a certain degree of conformity, and with all the new knowledge that you're developing, it's likely a struggle to find a home base. The best way to get through the beginning of 2023: acceptance. Accept where you are right now and release the desire to create drastic change, unless you are convinced that a complete change is what you desire. If you spend this year unable to ground yourself, it will be difficult to find your place. Focus on your fitness, develop a structured routine, and pay closer attention to your health. The most difficult part of taking care of yourself is starting, and then it becomes second nature. Towards the end of the year, there will be room for love and romance.

Recognize that not every connection needs to turn into a commitment, and love does come with risks, and those risks should make sense. Remember the responsibility that comes with sustaining an intimate relationship. It's not easy, but it can be meaningful.

Astrologer Six © Mother Tongue Ink 2022

Albedo
© Kimberly Webber 2017

--------- ♄♄♄ Dé Sathairn ---------

♈
♉
Saturday
28

☽□♇ 1:20 am v/c	☉☌☽ 1:24 pm
☽→♉ 4:44 am	☿☌♃ 8:44 pm
☽⚹♄ 5:40 am	☽☌♃ 11:36 pm
♂☌♃ 9:03 am	

--------- ☉☉☉ Dé Domhnaigh ---------

*Partial Lunar Eclipse 1:14 am PDT
Full Moon in ♉ Taurus 1:24 pm PDT

♉
Sunday
29

☽☌♀ 12:00 am	☽△♀ 2:33 pm
☽☌♂ 12:30 am	☽☌♅ 5:36 pm
♀☌♂ 7:22 am	☽⚹♆ 11:50 pm

October / November

octubre / noviembre

☽☽☽ lunes

♉
Ⅱ

Monday
30

☽△♇ 4:36 am v/c
☽→Ⅱ 8:08 am
☽□♄ 9:04 am

♂♂♂ martes

Ⅱ

Tuesday
31

Samhain / Hallowmas

♀△♅ 5:51 am

☿☿☿ miércoles

Ⅱ
♋

Wednesday
1

November

☽□♀ 12:25 am
☽□♆ 5:36 am v/c
☿⊼♂ 8:45 am
♃PrH 2:00 pm
☽→♋ 2:30 pm
☽△♄ 3:28 pm

♃♃♃ jueves

♋

Thursday
2

☉△☽ 9:23 am
☽⚹♃ 10:31 am
☽△♂ 7:01 pm
☉☍♃ 10:02 pm

♀♀♀ viernes

♋

Friday
3

☽△♉ 3:49 am
☽⚹♅ 7:36 am
☽⚹♀ 2:49 pm
☽△♆ 2:50 pm
♀☍♆ 3:05 pm
☽☍♇ 8:28 pm v/c

ALL ASPECTS IN PACIFIC DAYLIGHT TIME; ADD 3 HOURS FOR EDT; ADD 7 HOURS FOR GMT

Samhain

Now we slip between times, the stillpoint where silence descends. It is not too late to remember, sing the stones. We're still here, part of all that survives, to keep carrying the stories, creating the art, making what magic we can. Here in the shadows, with a thin silver moon as company, we persist in brewing together traces of hope. We remember that we have come through famine and fatigue. We have laid our hands on wet earth and shaped it into vessels that can walk through fire. We have crossed continents and nourished countless generations with our bodies, breath, and prayers. We plant our feet on a living earth, lift our arms to an open sky, listen to the night. We honor the nameless, and we persist in mending the web, hands extended, eyes alight, bodies worn but still standing here. Together. It is time to weave new stories from the bones of old and forgotten things, mixing them with the golden seeds of possibility and the flares of inspiration, touching this moment of now.

Molly Remer © Mother Tongue Ink 2022

River in Autumn ◦ *Jeanette M. French 2021*

Season of the Witch

sacred woman
she who plays with fire and night
speaker for the dead
medicine woman, midwife,
healer, mystic, mother, crone
sacred witch
she who casts spells to maintain
order and balance in the spirit realm
an invocation to venerate
sacred witch
crafter of the primordial dark
  she who has been robbed from us
    wisdom stolen and burned
      hundreds of years
        you have been suppressed
        dark goddess
         sacred witch
          reclaiming you I remember
           I carry your teachings and magic
           in my bones and blood
            you are my intuition; ancestor
            I honor you womb walker
             keeper of the autumn deep
             communicator beyond the veil
             thank you for revealing yourself
             weaving yourself into stardust
             in this portal of samhain
             where you and our beloved dead
             dwell closer then ever
             Season of the witch

□ Tasha Zigerelli 2020

Full Moon Magic © Maria Cristina Guerriero 2018

ProtectHer © *Poetically Illustrated 2020*

♋
♌

Saturday
4

♄D   12:03 am
☽→♌   12:21 am
☿♂♅   9:07 am
☽□♃   8:46 pm

———— ☉☉☉ domingo ————

♌

Sunday
5

☉□☽   1:37 am
♂⊼♇   1:44 am
☽□♂   9:00 am
☽□♅   6:11 pm
☽□☿   11:25 pm v/c

Waning Half Moon in ♌ Leo 1:37 am PDT
Daylight Saving Time Ends 2:00 am PDT

November
studeni

♌
♍

Monday
6

♀△♇ 6:38 am
☽→♍ 11:39 am
☽☍♄ 12:42 pm
☽ApG 1:57 pm
☿△♆ 5:36 pm

♍

Tuesday
7

☽△♃ 7:43 am
☉✶☽ 6:54 pm

♍

Wednesday
8

☽✶♂ 1:29 am
♀→♎ 1:30 am
☽△♅ 6:40 am
♀⚻♄ 1:13 pm
☽☍♆ 2:20 pm

☿✶♇ 4:17 pm
☉⚻♅ 7:01 pm
☽△♇ 8:20 pm
☽✶☿ 8:55 pm v/c

♍
♎

Thursday
9

☽→♎ 12:08 am
☽☌♀ 2:23 am
☿→♐ 10:25 pm

♎

Friday
10

☿□♄ 7:07 am

ALL ASPECTS IN PACIFIC STANDARD TIME; ADD 3 HOURS FOR EST; ADD 8 HOURS FOR GMT

Cosmic Laundromat

eventually we all meet here
click clack, in goes our silver
one year at a time.
no need to fret,
go ahead and sit down or
lean over the edge and
watch the sun sleep,
take your time for once
and just think,
start another chapter
tell the kids go ahead
and pick flowers
while the last of what you
have no time for any longer
gets rinsed out for good.
when the spinning halts and
the place goes silent
rest your eyes.
you're made new,
like grandma's linens fresh
with lavender steam.

Gertie with a Poppy in Her Hair
© *Carol Wylie 2010*

when a 3rd-shift waitress
with her pile of aprons
hums a ten spot
into the machine
change spilling out
like Las Vegas
her sparks flying
around your body
jangling bright as gold,
stand into yourself at last
and be on your way.
¤ *Stephanie A. Sellers 2021*

ꑄꑄꑄ subota

Saturday
11

)☐♇   7:05 am v/c
)→♏ 10:39 am
)△♄ 11:43 am
♂☍♅ 1:11 pm

☉☉ nedjelja

♏

Sunday
12

)☍♃   4:09 am

Feed the Fire

Feed the fire dear ones;
listen to the flames.

Inside, there is transformation
Outside it feels like burning.

Almost too much in the moment.
Surrender and alas, the alchemy transpires.

If you're feeling stuck or challenged,
ask yourself:
"When is the last time I sat with a fire?"

"When is the last time I gazed into a flame,
Asking for help,
Asking for clarity,
And at the same,
Feeling its assuring warmth.

Not getting lost is not the goal . . .
The goal, is to allow this lost-ness
To ripen you,
To disorient the rigid ways
That no longer serve.

Those ways,
that only in their decomposition,
Bring new life.

Let the flame of hope
Sing to you, whisper in your dreams,
Promise of this waking
Life, illuminated.

□ *Alexa Iya Soro 2021*

XII. SHE CHANGES

Moon XII: November 13–December 12

New Moon in ♏ Scorpio Nov.13; Sun in ♐ Sagittarius Nov. 22; Full Moon in ♊ Gemini Nov. 27

Sitting with Pele © *Francene Hart Visionary Artist 2018*

November
Kartik

♏︎
♐︎

Monday
13

Lunar Samhain

☉☌☽ 1:27 am
☽☍♅ 2:05 am
♅PrH 3:42 am
☽☌♂ 4:18 am
☽△♆ 9:20 am

☉☍♅ 9:20 am
☽⚹♇ 3:03 pm v/c
☽→♐︎ 6:23 pm
☽□♄ 7:28 pm

New Moon in ♏︎ Scorpio 1:27 am PST

♐︎

Tuesday
14

☽☌♉ 6:04 am
☽⚹♀ 6:44 am

♐︎
♑︎

Wednesday
15

☿⚹♀ 4:48 am
☽□♆ 2:57 pm v/c
☿⊼♃ 7:35 pm
☽→♑︎ 11:41 pm
♀⊼♃ 11:48 pm

♑︎

Thursday
16

☽⚹♄ 12:48 am
☽△♃ 2:48 pm
☽□♀ 4:16 pm

♑︎

Friday
17

♂△♆ 12:36 am
☉△♆ 6:52 am
☽△♅ 11:51 am
☽⚹♆ 6:52 pm
☉⚹☽ 7:49 pm
☽⚹♂ 7:51 pm
☉☌♂ 9:42 pm

ALL ASPECTS IN PACIFIC STANDARD TIME; ADD 3 HOURS FOR EST; ADD 8 HOURS FOR GMT

Liminal Space

In my world we have been pulled taut,
like a yo-yo at apogee,
flung out to rumble trouble
in the raincrushed waters.
We hold out our arms at the radiant moment
of centrifugal possibility.
I'm not sure if I'm ready
for my life to reel me back in
From this sense that
something wonderful might be
about to shift, to change, to happen.

At the same time,
even though I'm partway obliterated,
I'm glad for the inward sweep,
the sense of belonging
Earth's gravity as love,
swinging me back
whole and holy.

excerpt ¤ marna scooter 2020

ᔆᔆᔆ sonibar

♑
♒

Saturday
18

☽☌♇ 12:27 am v/c
☽→♒ 3:27 am
☽□♃ 5:50 pm

☉☉☉ robibar

♒

Sunday
19

☽△♀ 12:12 am
☽⚹☿ 2:39 am
☽□♅ 2:53 pm

November
Mí na Samhna

―――― ꓒꓒꓒ Dé Luain ――――

≈
♓

Monday
20

꒰□♂ 1:38 am
☉□꒰ 2:50 am v/c
꒰→♓ 6:29 am
꒰♂♄ 7:45 am
☉⚹♇ 1:26 pm
☿△♄ 7:08 pm
꒰⚹♃ 8:19 pm

Waxing Half Moon in ≈ Aquarius 2:50 am PST

―――― ♂♂♂ Dé Máirt ――――

♓

Tuesday
21

꒰□♅ 11:16 am
꒰PrG 12:56 pm
♂⚹♇ 5:18 pm
꒰⚹♅ 5:35 pm

―――― ☿☿☿ Dé Céadaoin ――――

♓
♈

Wednesday
22

☉→♐

꒰♂♆ 12:45 am
☉→♐ 6:03 am
꒰⚹♇ 6:29 am
꒰△♂ 7:09 am v/c
♀♂♄ 8:44 am
꒰→♈ 9:19 am
☉△꒰ 9:34 am

Sun in ♐ Sagittarius 6:03 am PST

―――― ♃♃♃ Dé Ardaoin ――――

♈

Thursday
23

☉□♄ 1:47 am
꒰☍♀ 2:57 pm
꒰△☿ 7:52 pm

―――― ♀♀♀ Dé Haoine ――――

♈
♉

Friday
24

☿⚹♅ 1:27 am
♂→♐ 2:15 am
꒰□♇ 9:40 am v/c
꒰→♉ 12:28 pm
꒰⚹♄ 1:59 pm

―――――――――――――――――――――――

2023 Year at a Glance for ♐ Sagittarius (Nov. 22–Dec. 21)

This year is being guided by the spirit of love—how fortunate for you! By the way of love, you can expect new friends, new experiences, and plenty of reasons to keep a travel bag ready. If you're ready to learn and keep an open mind, the Universe has plenty to offer you. After a few years that have forced you to strip down and recognize yourself without frills, this year is granting you the ability to reinvent your style. You will be challenged to be creative, think outside of the box. Be bold and style yourself with fabulously breathtaking fashion inventions, or bring bold new ideas about uplifting your community or supporting habitats, local or abroad. Try not to be scattered at the beginning of this year; taking on too many romantic pursuits can steer you off your path. As the year progresses, you'll be able to find your focus through caring for yourself. If you aren't part of a wellness community, the summer of 2023 is a great time to take part in one. You'll develop a lot of little pearls of wisdom that will prove to aid you in your personal growth. This year you are supposed to focus on setting a solid foundation. Cultivating the home of your dreams, connecting with your soul society, and understanding how best to care for yourself will transform your life for the better. There is no rush when it comes to personal growth; thankfully the stars are on your side.

Astrologer Six © Mother Tongue Ink 2022

You have to go through the fire to come out gold
◻ *Emma Abel 2021*

ℏℏℏ Dé Sathairn

♉ ◖

Saturday
25

☽♂♃   1:42 am
♂□♄   8:57 am

☉☉☉ Dé Domhnaigh

♉ ◗
♊

Sunday
26

☽♂⛢   12:03 am
☽⚹♆   7:42 am
♀⚻⛢   7:49 am
☽△♇   1:52 pm v/c

☽→♊   4:40 pm
☽□♄   6:22 pm
☽☍♂   8:08 pm

November / December
noviembre / diciembre

Mushroom Studies
▢ *Zoe Zum 2020*

☽☽☽ lunes

♊

Monday
27

☉☍☽ 1:16 am
☿☐♆ 5:27 am

Full Moon in ♊ Gemini 1:16 am PST

♂♂♂ martes

♊
♋

Tuesday
28

☽△♀ 9:54 am
☽☐♆ 1:30 pm
☽☍♅ 5:03 pm v/c
☽→♋ 10:54 pm

☿☿☿ miércoles

♋

Wednesday
29

☽△♄ 12:51 am
☉⚻♃ 9:38 am
☽✶♃ 12:21 pm

♃♃♃ jueves

♋

Thursday
30

♀⚻♆ 2:13 am
☽✶♅ 1:20 pm
☽△♆ 10:04 pm

♀♀♀ viernes

♋
♌

Friday
1

December

☽☐♀ 12:09 am
☽☍♇ 5:07 am v/c
♅→♈ 6:31 am
☽→♌ 8:00 am
☽△♂ 6:48 pm
☽☐♃ 9:44 pm

ALL ASPECTS IN PACIFIC STANDARD TIME; ADD 3 HOURS FOR EST; ADD 8 HOURS FOR GMT

Dark Harbingers of Light

They bind earth together   push through mud:
morels, shaggy manes, chanterelles—
slimy harbingers of light in darkness
whispering foreign tongues
They keep forests breathing,
such odd brilliant creatures
often invisible to human eyes
Diligent creamy fungi transform
poisons to potions   or bloom scarlet
with white dots, exotic children
from distant planets peeking
through rubble and twigs

No need to fear them   mostly
but examine them closely
Sort dangerous from edible ones
and gentle hallucinogens
Forage   then mindfully devour
but allow these geniuses
to spin their power

© Claire Blotter 2018
previously published in Fungi Magazine

Fungi Love © *Kristen Roderick 2020*

ℏℏℏ sábado

♌

Saturday
2

⊙△☽ 3:45 am
☿⚹♄ 7:27 am

☊☊☊ domingo

♌
♍

Sunday
3

☽□♅ 12:13 am
♀□♇ 5:29 am
♂⚻♃ 3:20 pm

☽⚹♀ 6:11 pm v/c
☽→♍ 7:50 pm
☽☍♄ 10:26 pm

December
prosinac

 ♍

Monday
4

☽△♅ 2:12 am
☽△♃ 9:32 am
☽ApG 10:48 am
♀→♏ 10:51 am
☽□♂ 10:52 am
☉□☽ 9:49 pm

──── ♂♂♂ utorak ──────────── Waning Half Moon in ♍ Virgo 9:49 pm PST

 ♍

Tuesday
5

☽△♅ 12:45 pm
♀△♄ 2:51 pm
☽☍♆ 10:17 pm

──────── ☿☿☿ srijeda ────────

 ♍
♎

Wednesday
6

♆D 5:22 am
☽△♇ 5:50 am v/c
☽→♎ 8:34 am
☽□♅ 8:00 pm

──────── ♃♃♃ četvrtak ────────

 ♎

Thursday
7

☽⚹♂ 3:16 am
☉⚹☽ 3:37 pm
☉△♅ 4:12 pm
☿△♃ 8:08 pm

──────── ♀♀♀ petak ────────

 ♎
♏

Friday
8

☽□♇ 5:05 pm v/c
☽→♏ 7:35 pm
☽△♄ 10:33 pm

ALL ASPECTS IN PACIFIC STANDARD TIME; ADD 3 HOURS FOR EST; ADD 8 HOURS FOR GMT

Gobsmacked

Listen, I intend to be gobsmacked
By the beauty of blossom
In every spring I live for
Bewildered by the majesty of the sky
Transformed by the light in my friends' faces
Let me tell you
I am not going to be serious when playing is allowed
I have come through too many dark places
To waste any time censoring what is permitted
To bring me joy
I got here on knees and on wings
With a heart
Surprised daily
At its elastic greatness
Somehow, I made
Straw into gold
Coal into diamonds
Pain into fuel
Because I pledged to
Keep loving
This crazy world
© *Nell Aurelia 2021*

Rebirth © *Raven Borgilt 2021*

ᚻᚻᚻ subota

♏ Saturday
9

☽☌♀ 6:23 am
☽☍♃ 7:41 am
☽⚹♅ 9:46 am
♀☍♃ 7:35 pm

☉☉☉ nedjelja

♏ Sunday
10

☽☍♅ 9:03 am
☽△♆ 5:58 pm

The Nature of Me

My skin, easily created from mud, the earth and rain
that pools in low places and hides from sun to make
life, tadpoles and minnows, possible. My bones, a
calcium totem pole that says, Here I stand, There I
run, Over by that place I fell, and yet through it all
I am here. My face, the moon of day and night, what
watches, what refuses to look away, what knows her
home as self among the stars. My blood, the river
that sustains hills and valleys, how it runs freely and
feeds every inch of me. There is no Lewis or Clark
who can discover my mystery. My hands, these tools
of transformation, how they do what I tell them,
their soldier fingers in formation, always at the ready.
My breath, the smooth and ragged winds of what
goes in and out of me, taking what I need, giving back
endlessly, the miraculous moments of abundant being.
My toes, the tiny balancing dancers who are the last
to kiss the land as I leap up, right or wrong, however
I come down, they stay with me and welcome the
earth back to my body. Earth, rain, mud, calcium,
moon, river, hills, valleys, mystery, winds and
dancing, jumping and returning; these are the elements
and magical motions that are the nature of me.

¤ *Cassie Premo Steele 2021*

XIII. GIFTS & PROMISES

Moon XIII: December 12–January 11

New Moon in ♐ Sagittarius Dec. 12; Sun in ♑ Capricorn Dec. 21; Full Moon in ♋ Cancer Dec. 26

Into the Light © Catherine Molland 2020

When Darkness Rolls Over You

Step out into your sacred circle
Gather up the accolades the Universe
Has stockpiled for you like stars in the sky
In anticipation of your arrival
Knowing you are beloved of the Goddess
Fling your heart into life and dance

excerpt ¤ Deborah K. Tash / White Wolf Woman 2013

December
Ogrohaeon

♏
♐

Monday
11

D✶♇ 12:57 am v/c
D→♐ 3:11 am
D□♄ 6:13 am
☿✶♀ 11:18 am
☉⊼♅ 10:21 pm

Knitting Together a Life © *Melissa Harris 2014*

♐

Tuesday
12

D♂♂ 2:05 am
☉♂D 3:32 pm
D□♆ 10:48 pm v/c
☿R 11:09 pm

New Moon in ♐ Sagittarius 3:32 pm PST

♐
♑

Wednesday
13

D→♑ 7:31 am
D✶♄ 10:39 am
D△♃ 5:51 pm
D♂♅ 9:47 pm

♑

Thursday
14

D✶♀ 2:55 am
D△♅ 5:00 pm

♑
♒

Friday
15

D✶♆ 1:27 am
D♂♇ 8:03 am v/c
D→♒ 9:56 am
♂△♃ 2:55 pm
D□♃ 7:52 pm

This Joy in Nothing

Sometimes you wake up with this Inexplicable Joy
with your gut curled up into a Cheshire smile
and your left shoulder pulls back into a wink
that no one else can see.

and you look around
for the source of this smug delight

but can't, at a glance, find its origin
in any particular thing
not in the whisper of a morning
that gently beckoned you awake just in time

Before anyone else would even think of rising
at this Mad Hatter coffee-over-tea hour
Before the light of the sun has even risen
so, you know that even Beauty is not to blame

Not for this.

This is the best joy.
This is the first joy.
This is the last joy.

This joy in nothing.

© Nhien Vuong 2019

ᚻᚻᚻ sonibar

 ### Saturday
16

☽□♀ 9:33 am
☽PrG 10:58 am
☽⚹♂ 12:52 pm
☽□♅ 6:53 pm
☉□♆ 7:43 pm

◉◉◉ robibar

 ### Sunday
17

☉⚹☽ 4:04 am v/c
♀⚹♫ 11:49 am
☽→♓ 11:58 am

☽♂♄ 3:32 pm
☽⚹♃ 9:49 pm
☽⚹♀ 10:20 pm

Wish © *Brianna Capra 2015*

Winter Solstice

Rejoice! For the Light is birthed once more, and we discover anew that the body and divinity are made of the same things. There is the breath of the holy across every lip, the kiss of renewal on every brow, the new-birthed cry of awareness in every throat, the fresh taste of wonder on every tongue, the touch of joy beneath each fingertip, rebirthed this day.

In the depths of cave time, when the silver glow of moonshadow and the leaping heartfires of home comfort us, we gather fibers to knit our communities whole. There may be stripes of uncertainty and patches of pain, long gray stretches and bursts of color, but each of us contributes to the pattern of the World Soul.

Let's give up our notions of too late, never, and not enough time, and let our fingers trail through our lives, gathering experiences of last year and holding them tenderly, both the sweet and the spiky. Breathe easy. Keep your eyes on those irrepressible silver linings, and keep your hands open. There is much work yet to be done.

Molly Remer © Mother Tongue Ink 2022

Healing Water Wounds

Pray for the waters. Heal the waters in yourself and in your communities, allow yourself to be supported, while [continuing] to offer relentless support and pour your gifts into stopping the pipelines, undamming the rivers, healing the forests, singing to the wilds. Be more loving and daring than ever in your actions thus far in the name of the earth and the water, cross more barriers than you could imagine.

Hold healing ceremonies for the water and for all of our bodies and sing out our names. Heal yourself and the earth more and more and more. Sing to the earth and sing to each other and sing to each other's thriving and life-filled bodies. Sing to your beauty, your lives, your dreams, your pain, your grief, your terror and traumas and wounds. Sing to all beings in all their ways. Teach each other to cry. Invoke the undamming of the waters in your body, in all our bodies in all the rivers. May the waters rage. May the waters ravage. May the waters regenerate, renew, and heal.

excerpt ¤ amara hollow bones 2021

Emissary ¤ *Melissa Winter 2017*

December
Mí na Nollag

—— ꒰꒰꒰ Dé Luain ——

Monday
18

☿△♃ 6:28 am
☽△♀ 4:30 pm
☽□♂ 5:58 pm
☽✶♅ 9:14 pm

—— ♂♂♂ Dé Máirt ——

Tuesday
19

☽♂♆ 6:07 am
☉□☽ 10:39 am
☽✶♇ 1:03 pm v/c
☽→♈ 2:47 pm
☽□♅ 9:42 pm

—— ☿☿☿ Dé Céadaoin ——

Waxing Half Moon in ♓ Pisces 10:39 am PST

Wednesday
20

♀☍♅ 11:04 pm

—— ♃♃♃ Dé Ardaoin ——

Thursday
21

☽△♂ 12:23 am
☿✶♄ 4:33 am
♂⚼♅ 6:44 am
☽□♇ 5:11 pm
☉△☽ 6:47 pm v/c

☽→♉ 6:50 pm
☉→♑ 7:27 pm
☽△☿ 9:21 pm
☽✶♄ 11:08 pm

Winter Solstice

Sun in ♑ Capricorn 7:27 pm PST

—— ♀♀♀ Dé Haoine ——

Friday
22

☽♂♃ 4:53 am
☉♂☿ 10:54 am
☿PrH 6:20 pm
☿→♐ 10:17 pm

2023 Year at a Glance for ♑ Capricorn (Dec. 21–Jan. 20)

Capricorn, the world is your playground. Regardless of where you live there is inspiration to be found. If your domain is in a concrete jungle, take note of how the wildlife around you interacts with the pavement. For those of you who live around lush greenery, pay careful attention to the detailing of nature. Every plant, stream of water, and cloud has a story to tell you if you're willing to be patient and pay attention. There is plenty of wisdom to attain when you look at your environment through new eyes. Become reacquainted with your surroundings; approach life as if you are a visitor with fresh eyes and the willingness to explore. Allowing yourself the space to be imaginative and creative will bring life to even the most mundane aspects of your day. Practice documenting your everyday observations. What seems meaningless and normal one day can prove to have been the foreshadowing of your next creative venture. Take time to find out what brings you joy and puts a smile on your face. Financially, you will have to watch your wallet during 2023. Try not to overspend— make use of what you already have. As the year begins to approach its end, you'll find that your creative energy is flowing freely and with ease. You may struggle to express all the thoughts and ideas that are bubbling in your brain; try not to worry about rushing your process. When you are ready to speak the words will flow.

Astrologer Six © Mother Tongue Ink 2022

──────── ♄♄♄ Dé Sathairn ────────

♉ ☾ **Saturday**
23

☽♂♉ 5:33 am
☽☍♀ 11:04 am
☽⚹♆ 3:12 pm
☽△♇ 10:40 pm v/c

──────── ☉☉☉ Dé Domhnaigh ────────

♉ ☾
♊ **Sunday**
24

☽→♊ 12:15 am
☽□♄ 4:58 am
☉⚹♄ 9:28 am

Sitting Pretty
© Poetically Illustrated 2018

December
diciembre

♊

Monday
25

♀△♆ 9:15 am
☽⚹♂ 6:08 pm
☽□♆ 9:57 pm
☽⚹♅ 11:55 pm v/c

♊
♋

Tuesday
26

☽→♋ 7:15 am
☽△♄ 12:29 pm
☉⚹☽ 4:33 pm
☽⚹♃ 5:45 pm
♃D 5:50 pm
☿□♆ 11:42 pm

Full Moon in ♋ Cancer 4:33 pm PST

♋

Wednesday
27

☉△♃ 7:28 am
☿♂♂ 4:31 pm
☽⚹♅ 8:04 pm

♋
♌

Thursday
28

☽△♆ 6:45 am
☽△♀ 2:12 pm
♂□♆ 2:15 pm
☽⚹♇ 2:57 pm v/c
☽→♌ 4:23 pm
♀⚹♇ 10:01 pm

♌

Friday
29

☽□♃ 3:17 am
♀→♐ 12:23 pm

Offerings

I carried a bucket of sunshine
into the kitchen this morning

how could I have missed
such pleasure
such magic
all these years?

what's free is generous
like the daily feathers
I've been receiving

I could say finding
but they are not lost
they are the shed offerings
that lift
into heaven from earth

with a lightness of being
I want to remember
excerpt © Valerie A Szarek 2021

Yelapa Woman *© Margriet Seinen 2014*

♄♄♄ sábado

♌

Saturday
30

☽□♅ 6:39 am
☽△☿ 1:00 pm
♃D 6:40 pm
☽△♂ 9:18 pm v/c

☉☉☉ domingo

♌
♍

Sunday
31

☽→♍ 3:53 am
☽□♀ 8:23 am
☽☍♄ 10:24 am
☽△♃ 3:10 pm

January 2024
siječanj

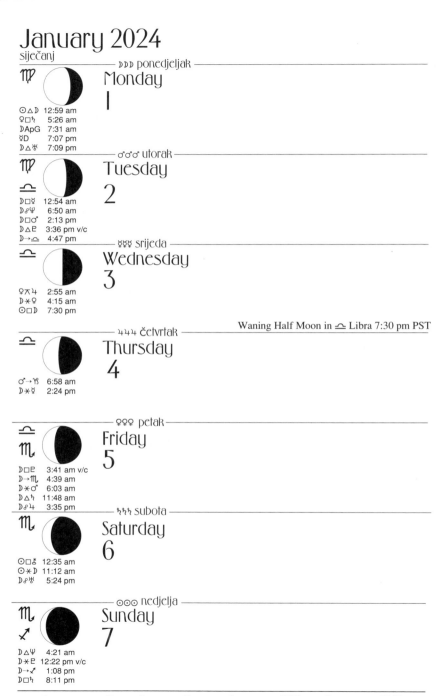

— ☽☽☽ ponedjeljak —

Monday
1

☉△☽	12:59 am
♀□♄	5:26 am
☽ApG	7:31 am
☿D	7:07 pm
☽△♅	7:09 pm

— ♂♂♂ utorak —

Tuesday
2

☽□♉	12:54 am
☽☍♆	6:50 am
☽□♂	2:13 pm
☽△♇	3:36 pm v/c
☽→♎	4:47 pm

— ☿☿☿ srijeda —

Wednesday
3

♀⚼♃	2:55 am
☽✶♀	4:15 am
☉□☽	7:30 pm

Waning Half Moon in ♎ Libra 7:30 pm PST

— ♃♃♃ četvrtak —

Thursday
4

| ♂→♑ | 6:58 am |
| ☽✶♉ | 2:24 pm |

— ♀♀♀ petak —

Friday
5

☽□♇	3:41 am v/c
☽→♏	4:39 am
☽✶♂	6:03 am
☽△♄	11:48 am
☽☍♃	3:35 pm

— ♄♄♄ subota —

Saturday
6

☉□⚷	12:35 am
☉✶☽	11:12 am
☽☍♅	5:24 pm

— ☉☉☉ nedjelja —

Sunday
7

☽△♆	4:21 am
☽✶♇	12:22 pm v/c
☽→♐	1:08 pm
☽□♄	8:11 pm

All aspects in Pacific Standard Time; add 3 hours for EST; add 8 hours for GMT

First Light

A weathered hand, rough and gnarled,
reaches down to stroke your cheek,
as you lay curled in the darkness. Waiting.
Grandmother Moon.
"Reach in your apron pocket, child,
and see what seeds there are to be sown.
We have much to do."
With a barely audible creak,
like the opening door of an ancient farmhouse,
a sliver of light is revealed in the night sky.
Now, here is the Moon in her maiden form.
Can you feel the energy rising?
"What path shall you choose?" she asks.
"Come, it is time to get started. I'll light the way."

And so we begin again . . .

◻ *Heather Esterline 2018*

Wolf
© *Sigita Mockute (Psigidelia) 2021*

We'Moon Evolution: A Community Endeavor

We'Moon is rooted in womyn's community. The datebook was originally planted as a seed in Europe where it sprouted on women's lands in the early 1980s. Transplanted to Oregon in the late '80s, it flourished as a cottage industry on We'Moon Land near Portland in the '90s and early 2000s, and now thrives in rural Southern Oregon.

The first We'Moon was a handwritten, pocket-size women's diary and handbook in Gaia Rhythms, translated in five languages! It was self-published under the name of Mother Tongue Ink, by me and my partner Nada in 1981, in France—in collaboration with friends from Kvindelandet ("women's land") in Denmark. We'Moon was inspired by our experience of living there together in a lively international community of 20–40 lesbian feminists in the late 1970s.

The first five editions of We'Moon were created by friends in different countries in Europe, voluntarily, as a "labor of love"—publicized mostly by word-of-mouth and distributed by backpack over national borders. When I returned to America with We'Moon, it changed to a larger, more user-friendly format as we entered the computer age. We grew into the business of publishing by the seat of our pants, as a community-run cottage industry on We'Moon Land, from 1988–2008. Starting with a little seed money, we recycled the proceeds into printing the next We'Moon, each year. By the early '90s, we finally sold enough copies to be able to pay for our labor. We'Moon Company was incorporated (dba) Mother Tongue Ink, and it has grown abundantly with colorful new fruits ever since! For a full listing of current We'Moon publications: (see pp 231–233).

Whew! It was always exciting, and a lot more work than we ever imagined! We learned how to do what was needed. We met and overcame major hurdles that brought us to a new level each time. The publishing industry has transformed: independent distributors, women's bookstores and print-based publications have declined. Nonetheless, We'Moon's loyal and growing customer base continues to support our unique womyn-created products. This home-grown publishing company is staffed by a resilient and highly skilled multi-generational team—embedded in women's community—who inspire, create, produce and distribute We'Moon year in and year out.

Every year, We'Moon is created by a vast web of womyn. Our Call for Contributions goes out to thousands of women, inviting art and writing on that year's theme (see p. 234). Women are invited to attend

Selection Circles to review submissions and give feedback. In 2020, the pandemic and social distancing requirements turned those circles into virtual Zoom meetings . . . which had the beneficial effect of extending our outreach world-wide! The We'Moon Creatrix then collectively selects, designs, edits, and weaves the material together in the warp and woof of natural cycles through the thirteen Moons of the year. All the activity that goes into creating We'Moon is the inbreath; everything else we do to get it out into the world to you is the outbreath in our annual cycle. To learn more about the herstory of We'Moon, the art and writing that have graced its pages, and the Spirit that has breathed through it for 42 years now, check out the Anthology: *In the Spirit of We'Moon* (see page 231).

WE'MOON LAND

We'Moon Land (former publication home base for We'Moon products) is a residential womyn's land community—a nature sanctuary for womyn (wemoon by nature) that has been held by and for womyn, since 1973—one of the longest surviving womyn's lands communities in the world. Generations of wemoon (mostly lesbians) have made home here over the years in a community committed to living together in harmony with one another and all our relations. We live in wemoon-built houses, grow organic food, on 52 beautiful acres of forests and fields, an hour from Portland. We host individual and group events, retreats, visitors, camping, workshops, land workdays, seasonal holy days, circles, celebrations and gatherings of, by and for wemoon.

Founded on feminist values, ecological practices and earth-based women's spirituality, we are calling for a more diverse, generationally interwoven community of wemoon who love wemoon, and share our vision of creative spirit-centered life on the land, to come join us! We are at a crucial point of generational succession now, and are looking for new potential residents who are committed to live and work on the land (preferably, with experience and skills in healthy community, communication, conflict-resolution, organic gardening, building, permaculture . . .). Join us in carrying on this womyn's land community for years to come—in the Spirit of We'Moon. We will be celebrating our 50th Anniversary Gathering in 2023! FFI about We'Moon Land and our non-profit organizations (We'Moon Homestead and We'Moonivrsity), contact: wemoonland@gmail.com, wemoonland.org, wemoon.ws

Musawa ¤ Mother Tongue Ink 2022

DIVINING THE TIMING OF THE WE'MOON TAROT

It has been tricky trying to announce the much-anticipated release of the We'Moon Tarot accurately—two years ahead of time— especially during the last two unpredictable years. Much to our chagrin, and the disappointment of all who have been eagerly awaiting it, we prematurely announced its arrival in the last two editions of We'Moon—as if it was a done deal—when it turned out not to be true. So sorry! No more promises. Let's open the deck, pick some cards, and see what clues they might reveal about the mystery of the unveiling of the We'Moon Tarot.

XVIII. The Moon/Lunar Power: *Lunar consciousness is the Moon's special magic, the right-brained intuitive link between worlds.* Tarot is first and foremost a divinatory art, based on tapping into your own intuition, or lunar consciousness for navigating the past, present and future mysteries in life.

XVI. Tower/Collapse: Quantum Leap: *The collapse of this "House of Cards" represents a wemoon's version of the Tower card: what countless people have to deal with in everyday life, from the fall-out of systemic collapse.* The main cause of delays in completing the We'Moon Tarot was due to unexpected personal losses I experienced in 2020–2021 (my sister's sudden death; shingles; a broken ankle, and fractured vertebrae) that incapacitated me for months at a time, derailing my creative process in the final stretch.

XII. The Hanged One/Chrysalis: *Metamorphosis. You are knocked off your feet, can't proceed as planned, are completely immobilized by the immediate situation. You may feel like you are falling apart, but maybe you just have to turn back in on yourself . . . and let go!* The delays were compounded by the tight annual production schedule the We'Moon team has to keep, so trying to fit the We'Moon Tarot in—while it was still in the process of creation— couldn't work as hoped.

VII. The Charioteer: Holding Course: *You may face crosswinds and have to tack back and forth to get to your destination right now, but hold on and stay the course.* And so we shall. We look forward to sharing with you the full array of We'Moon Tarot wisdom in its own magical time. Stay tuned by signing up for our newsletter at wemoon.ws

© *Musawa 2022*

Staff Appreciation

It is said that the We'Moon cohort lives into the theme that we are creating, and that was true for the *2022 Magical Dark* theme, and most recently, for our 2023 theme of *Silver Lining*. We begin creating each edition almost two full years before you will begin using this book. And so, we edge-walk out to the boundaries of Now in order to feel the foreshadowing of the future world.

During the creation of this edition, in 2021, we each ventured out from physical isolation, taking careful precautions to keep ourselves and each other healthy. It was a "modified-normal," as I imagine so many of you are familiar with, complete with testing, masking, keeping safer distances, learning to use our words more explicitly rather than leaning on facial expressions to speak for us. We carried over some of the skills and virtual technology that worked well for us during the previous year, allowing more of us to participate from home.

Silver Linings are only made moonifest by the clouds: We relished being in each other's company after so long apart, even if masked. Decisions were able to be made more swiftly, compared with the previous year's moratorium on in-person collaboration. People clamored and rejoiced to get their hands on the new edition that was two months delayed, between the shipping, porting, and trucking backlogs of 2021. We were beyond antsy! Thank you all for your patience.

I am truly blessed to get to work with each of these amazing women. As a team, we navigated these precarious times and collaborated to make another gorgeous edition of We'Moon. Thank you. And Dana, your constant company in the office will be missed, but your quick humor and camaraderie will remain. Thank you for your many years of service in the shipping department. Erin, welcome aboard! We look forward to working with you!

Blessings to all of you who make We'Moon possible. We hope that your Silver Linings shine brightly this year, and in every year to come.

Barbara Dickinson © Mother Tongue Ink 2022

WE'MOON ANCESTORS

We honor wemoon who have gone between the worlds of life and death recently, beloved contributors to wemoon culture who continue to bless us from the other side. We appreciate receiving notice of their passing.

Alix Dobkin (1940–2021) was a folk singer-songwriter, memoirist, and lesbian feminist activist. Coming from progressive Jewish and communist roots, Alix was a legend in the women's music scene, performing at women's music festivals across the country and the world for decades. Before turning to a life of music, she studied painting at Temple University. She was briefly married and had a daughter. A photo of her in 1975 wearing a t-shirt sporting "The Future is Female" (originally the slogan of New York City's first women's bookstore) went viral 40 years later, inspiring a whole new generation of feminists.

bell hooks (1952–2021) was a beloved author, professor, feminist, and social activist. Her name, bell hooks, borrowed from her maternal great grandmother, and lower case intentionally, was meant to focus on the "substance of books, not who I am." Anchoring all activism in love, bell's work as a Black Feminist scholar and professor at Stanford University, Yale University, and The City College of New York sought to end sexism, racism, and all forms of oppression and injustice. In later life, she returned to her hometown Kentucky community and created the bell hooks Institute at Berea College.

She made accessible the intersectionality of class, race, and sex for white women. Her core beliefs were that community, education, and love are the seeds of liberation, and that feminism is for everyone.

Carol Christ (1945–2021) was a foremother of the Goddess movement. Author, theologian, feminist historian, she offered spiritual and intellectual leadership with her 1978 essay "Why Women Need the Goddess." She understood clearly that religious centrality of male gods is critically associated with the oppression of women, and that to affirm Goddess is to uplift female power. Celebrating Goddess iconography honors the female body. Carol

authored six influential books on women's spirituality and co-edited two collections of rituals and feminist theology. As Director of the Ariadne Institute, she led pilgrimages to sacred Goddess sites in Greece, studying artifacts of matriarchal religions. She lived for many years on Lesbos.

Ivy Bottini (1926–2021) was one of the She-roes of lesbian feminist activism, beginning in 1966 when she helped found the NYC chapter of NOW, and then introduced feminist consciousness-raising to their work. In 1970, she was among lesbians expelled from NOW. A colorful, magnetic woman, Ivy was a performing

Thoughtful Pelican *© Marianne Moskowitz 2010*

artist, a visual artist, and a consummate innovator for women's rights, gay and lesbian equality. Her activism was prominent for decades in California, fighting against homophobia, initiating support for LGBT communities (e.g. AIDS care, Elder Housing). Often the first out lesbian or gay appointee to official boards and commissions, Ivy broke ground as a woman/feminist/lesbian in governance.

Joan Didion (1934–2021) was a celebrated writer, essayist, memoirist, and novelist. Joan's early published works were a window into 1960s counterculture. Her highly observant prose made meaning of her life, and her essays normalized being open about mental health struggles. She worked with her husband on screenplays, and together they adopted a daughter. Her memoirs on their deaths gave us a template for grief. She received the National Humanities Medal in 2013.

Marianne Moskowitz (1936–2021) was a painter, writer, gifted school psychologist and devoted mom. She came out as a lesbian in the heyday of feminist activism, and participated in the groundbreaking Los Angeles Women's Community Chorus. In 1997, she moved to Oregon with her partner Renée Côté to be part of lesbian land culture. Her gardens and her artistry flourished. Sharing mutual inspiration with other lesbian artists, Marianne painted exquisite reflections of her environment. She wrote poems and memoir, including poignant accounts of growing up as a German child during World War II. The importance of these stories, told by a European woman of her generation, is immeasurable.

Sally Miller Gearhart (1931–2021) was a charismatic mover-and-shaker in the lesbian feminist movement. Her presence was majestic, and her brilliance legendary. Activist, educator, author, environmental champion, she was revered for her forthright wisdom, undaunted humor, and compassion for all earth-life. She helped found the field of Women's Studies, and was the first out lesbian to become a tenured professor. Sally worked mightily against anti-gay bias, including proposed legislation to ban LGBT teachers from public schools. Her 1978 visionary novel *The Wanderground* inspired scores of women creating lesbian lands, and foreshadowed Sally's own "retirement" in California hill country where she continued her lesbian feminist revolution as a land dyke.

Tangren Alexander (1940–2021) was a beloved and imaginative teacher, writer, artist, and mainstay of Southern Oregon's vibrant lesbian feminist community. The first woman granted a PhD in Philosophy from the University of Oregon (1975), she taught and wrote about feminism and philosophy, women and ethics, death, history, and reverence for the universe. She created art and story with dolls: dozens of Barbie-esque dolls, re-costumed, staged often in intricately furnished doll houses—filmed and photographed enacting feminist history, lesbian family, social justice movements. (See tangrenalexander.com)

Tangren's creative brilliance and sense of wonder shimmered with magic and wit, and will continue to inspire us.

© Copyrights and Contacting Contributors

Copyrights for most of the work published in We'Moon belong to each individual contributor. Please honor the copyrights: ©: do not reproduce without the express permission of the artist, author, publisher or Mother Tongue Ink, depending on whose name follows the copyright sign. Some wemoon prefer to free the copyright on their work: ✺: this work may be passed on among women who wish to reprint it "in the spirit of We'Moon." In all cases, give credit to the author/artist and to We'Moon, and send each a copy. If the artist has given permission, We'Moon may release contact information. Contact mothertongue@wemoon.ws or contact contributors directly.

Contributor Bylines and Index
See page 236 for info about how YOU can become a We'Moon contributor!

A. Levemark (Tranas, Sweden) I'm a gardener and an illustrator, who is passionate about permaculture. My roots are in Scandinavia and Britain, and I'm drawn to the folklore of both places. levemark@protonmail.com avalanasart.co.uk **p. 97**

Alexa Iya Soro (Wakefield, RI) is a therapist in a long line of generations playing a humble role of helping the new world usher itself in more deeply towards harmony. Alexa guides people back to greater self-love, an enriched quality of life, and service of Heartsong through counseling, retreats, plant ally-ship and ritual. alexaiyasoros@gmail.com livinglovingbeing.life **p. 156**

Alexa Sunshine Rose (Port Townsend, WA) is a mother, musician, artist and visionary. Find her music and learn more at alexasunshinerose.com **p. 18**

amara hollow bones (Somes Bar, CA) amara's drawings emerge out of lived experiences in wild places; singing songs of reverence, grief, and awe for the earth. They are prayers for the return of magic, the resilience of wildness, for remembering our ancestors and home. amarahollowbones.com **p. 171**

Amy Haderer-Swagman (Thornton, CO) is an artist, muralist, circus aerialist, doula, and mama of six living in Denver, CO. Her mandala work (mandalajourney.com) concentrates on birth, motherhood, and the divine feminine, while her most recent work (willowaerial.com) depicts circus artists, aerialists, and dancers. **p. 49**

Angela Bigler (Lancaster, PA) is playing with words and spirit among the trees and cornfields. Visit her at dreambigwords.com or email at angelabigler42@gmail.com **p. 94**

Anna Lindberg (Stockholm, Sweden) I am a professional artist working from my home studio. I often use the Divine Feminine as my source of inspiration, depicting Goddesses from many different cultures, using different techniques, in my artwork. I wish to inspire and empower women all over the world through my art. annalindbergart.com IG: @anna.lindberg.art **p. 141**

Anna McKay (Christchurch, New Zealand) specializes in digital art with a focus on portraiture and a love for the mystical. She is a Virgo sun, Scorpio ascendant and Aquarius moon. To see more work: IG:@annamckayartist **p. 95**

Anne Jewett (Crawfordville, FL) is a clay sculptor, painter and Priestess of the Goddess. I put blessings and prayers for Healing, Joy and Love. IG: @purple_full_moon_studio, purplefullmoonstudio.com **p. 67, 131**

Annika Gemlau aSombrasDelSur (Essen, Germany) Astist, Illustrator and Expert for Anti-Discrimination, Vulnerability and Empowerment. asombrasdelsur.com IG: @asombrasdelsur, annikagemlau@gmail.com **p. 120**

Astrea Taylor (Kettering, OH) is the author of *Air Magic and Intuitive Witchcraft: How to Use Intuition to Elevate your Craft* (Llewellyn Worldwide). She presents workshops and rituals online and at festivals across the country. astreataylor.com **p. 138**

Astrologer Six, MSW (Lehigh Acres, FL) Six is the creator of BlackWomenBeing, a lifestyle blog that focuses on the astrology of love and beauty. Six graduated from Columbia University where she earned a Master of Social Work degree. Six can be reached at blackwomenbeing.com or on Twitter/instagram @ blackwomenbeing **p. 15, 39, 51, 63, 75, 87, 99, 111, 125, 137, 149, 161, 173**

Barb Kobe (Minneapolis, MN) Artist, Author, Teaching Artist, Mentor, Creativity Coach; Barb guides, mentors, teaches and supports women who want to reconnect with their intuition, bodies, emotions and wisdom using art-doll making and other creative processes. barbkobe.com, healingdollways.com and barbkobe@healingdollways.com **p. 133**

Barbara Dickinson (Sunny Valley, OR) is trundling happily along on this adventure of life, ever curious, always learning, constantly course-correcting. May we all harvest every last drop of joy from each moment. **p. 181**

Barbara Landis (San Francisco, CA) is a fine art photographer creating images locally and abroad. Practicing Nichiren Shoshu Buddhism since 1968, she belongs to Myoshinji Temple. Also a member of San Francisco Women Artists. IG:@ barbara_landis_photography **p. 132**

Beate Metz (Berlin, Germany) was an astrologer, feminist, translator & mainstay of We'Moon's German edition & the European astrological community. **p. 205**

Bethroot Gwynn (Myrtle Creek, OR) 27 years as We'Moon's Special Editor & 47 at Fly Away Home women's land, growing food, theater & ritual. For info about spiritual gatherings, summertime visits send SASE to POB 593, Myrtle Creek, OR 97457. For info about her book of poetry and plays, *Preacher Woman for the Goddess,* see p. 231. **p. 23, 25**

Betty LaDuke (Ashland, OR) "Your creations are filled with joy, delight, and hope, all of which we desperately need right now."—Gov Kate Brown, 2020. bettyladuke.com **p. 98**

Brianna Capra (Menomonie, WI) is an illustrator, artist, environmental activist, gardener and mom from rural Wisconsin. See her portfolio at bcaprastudioarts. com, follow on social media @briannacapra_studioarts, or purchase prints and wearables through Etsy and Redbubble. **p. 170**

Brighdelynne Stewart (East Sussex, England) Echoes to the past—The Venuses of Willendorf & Laussel, the Sleeping Maltese Goddess & many more, inspire me to create, & to celebrate. I try to interpret these ancient images in a way that hopefully has resonance today, creating sculptures that are reflections of the real wimmin we are, expressing joy and confidence in the beauty of the voluptuous female form. **p. 56**

Brigidina (Elgin, IL) I am a TreeSister, and my Sacred Earth Art is created using natural pigments, sacred cedar & rose oils, peace fire coals, honey, and waters from 54 sacred sites. brigidina.com, treesisters.org **p. 71**

Brittany May Gill (Kamloops, BC) is an artist, water protector, earth activist and mother. She aspires to lead a life outside of the current system to empower others to live on their own terms. **p. 147, 160**

Carol Wylie (Saskatoon, SK) is a portrait artist living on the Canadian prairies, Treaty 6 Territory and the traditional homeland of the Metis. She specializes in portraiture, loving people and faces of all kinds! carolwylie.ca, IG: @carol.wylie.71 **p. 155**

Casey Sayre Boukus (Nantucket, MA) is a witch, masseuse, fabric artist, mother of teenagers and cats, and wild pagan soul whose sacred work involves the art of make-believe. She loves books, wine, dancing, costume, ritual and gathering with family and friends. bycasendra.massagetherapy.com **p. 172**

Cassie Premo Steele (Columbia, SC) is a lesbian, ecofeminist, mother, poet, novelist, and essayist whose writing focuses on the themes of trauma, healing, creativity, mindfulness and the environment. She lives in South Carolina with her wife. cassiepremosteele.com **p. 80, 166**

Catherine Molland (Santa Fe, NM) My life is reflected in my Art. My new series SeedPod is about homesteading. On my lovely 5 acres, I grow my organic food, raise chickens for eggs and make compost. Here's to Makers everywhere! catherinemolland.com **p. 167**

Cathy McClelland (Kings Beach, CA) paints from her heart and imagination. Her love for nature, cross-cultural mythical subjects, magical, sacred places and symbols fuel her creative spirit. cathymcclelland.com **Front Cover**

Christine Irving (Denton, TX) Priestess and poet, Christine draws meaningful connections between the past and present, ordinary and numinous while revealing their relevance to contemporary women's lives: christineirving.com contains samples, information and links to buy her books. **p. 119, 139**

Christine Lowther (Tofino, BC) served as Tofino Poet Laureate 2020–22. She is compiling two anthologies of tree poems: one for kids & youth, one for adults. She lives for ancient temperate rainforests, west coast of Cascadia. FB: christinelowtherauthor, christinelowther.blogspot.com **p. 59**

Claire Blotter (San Rafael, CA) writes and performs poems with movement and body percussion. She teaches writing and performance to elementary and high school students. Her award-winning video doc, *Wake-up Call: Saving the Songbirds* is distributed by Video Project. She loves darkness. claireblotter.com **p. 163**

Colleen Clifford (Humboldt, CA) is a stained glass artist who enlightens with light, line, color, and texture. colleencliffordart.com **p. 130**

Corinne "Bee Bop" Trujillo (Denver, CO) is one-half of the collaboration duo Koco Collab. In her work, she explores the odyssey of womxn. corinnebeebop.com **p. 38, 86**

Cosmic Gazer Art (Keaau, HI) was birthed by a creatress that was activated on the Big Island of Hawaii and took up painting in 2015. She feels a deep connection to space, star beings, sacred geometry and combining these elements. "I love sharing my work because I feel the energy that comes through raises your vibration." cosmicgazerart.com **p. 28**

D. Woodring – Portrait Priestess (Milwaukee, WI) I am Damara Woodring, The Portrait Priestess. I create works of art that are centered around ancestral connection, spiritual education, Self-love and empowerment, reconnecting us back to spirit, to nature, to the wisdoms of our mothers before us. IG: @dwoodring_portraitpriestess, portraitpriestess.com **p. 69, 99**

Dana Wheeles (Charlottesville, VA) is an artist, a wayfinder, and a mandala maker living in Central Virginia. Learn more at deerhawkhealing.com **p. 48**

Danielle Helen Ray Dickson (Nanaimo, BC) considers her art to have the power to heal people, change lives and shed light on the world in a new way. She infuses this into her work with each intentional brush stroke. danielledickson.com **p. 135**

Deborah K. Tash/White Wolf Woman (San Francisco, CA) calls on Spirit Guides, Animal Allies, Angels and archetypes to create, as a spiritual practice in honor of the Divine Feminine and as means of self-expression as both visual artist and poet. Her art is available at inherimagestudio.com **p. 167**

Debra Hall (Dumfriesshire, Scotland) I am a meditation teacher, rite of passage guide, champion of nature and women, soulmaker, poet, artist and natural healer. herwholenature.com, IG: @her_whole_nature **p. 65, 128**

Diana Denslow (Poulsbo, WA) is a mother, artist, crone, and cat lady now emerging from 5 years of sabbatical. Diana can be reached at dianaherself66@ gmail.com and her artwork can now be seen on Etsy at etsy.com/shop/ MysticVisionsGallery **p. 33, 101**

Diane Norrie (Coquitlam, BC) Visual artist and teacup reader. I live in the Fraser River Valley in Small Red Salmon, BC. I am strongly influenced by spiritual connection. It makes my work constantly changing and evolving. **p. 22**

Dorrie Joy (Somerset, UK) is a prolific intuitive artist working in many mediums. Grandmother, builder, Moon lodge dweller, she is committed to active decolonization and teaches traditional craft and ancestral skills. Books, prints, wildcraft, original art: dorriejoy.co.uk **p. 123**

Eefje Jansen (Flevoland, The Netherlands) is a Dutch intuitive artist and lightworker whose paintings and drawings unfold from her inner world. She creates earthly, magical pieces filled with light, love, strength and healing. eefje-jansen.com **p. 55, 75**

Elizabeth Diamond Gabriel (St. Paul, MN) is a professional artist, illustrator, writer and teacher-in-practice since 1975. She loves animals, nature, a good veggie burrito and long listening walks among her beloved Minnesota woods and lake waters. **p. 46, 137**

Elspeth McLean (Pender Island, BC) creates vivid, vibrant paintings completely out of dots. Each dot is like a star in the universe. Elspeth hopes her art connects the viewer with their inner child. elspethmclean.com **p. 80**

Emily Kedar (Toronto, ON) is a poet, writer and psychotherapist working and living on Salt Spring Island. You can contact her about poetry or her therapy work at emilykedar.com **p. 36, 103**

Emily Kell (Boulder, CO) witchy fem visions, IG:@emilythefunkypriestess, on the web at: emilykell.com **p. 150**

Emma Abel (West Sussex, UK) is a yogic practitioner, teacher and artist who creates from a space of stillness and connection to the Divine, that lives and moves within all. @emma.abel.art, emmabeldrawings.com **p. 121, 161**

Erin Guntis (Asheville, NC) Erin's favorite pastime is staying up late and taking walks under the quiet moon. When not teaching yoga and doing massage for friends and family, she is busy loving her four boys and writing a poem or two. You can reach her at hometreeyogamassagetherapy.com **p. 29**

Francene Hart Visionary Artist (Honaunau, HI) is an internationally recognized visionary artist whose work utilizes the wisdom and symbolic imagery of sacred geometry, reverence for the Natural Environment and interconnectedness between all things. francenehart.com **p. 157**

Geneva Toland (Middletown, RI) is a writer, singer, farmer and teacher currently residing on occupied Munsee Lenape territory along the Hudson River. She spends her time creating reciprocal relationships with seeds, birds, water, trees, and people in her community. IG: @evtoland **p. 52, 141**

Gloria Campuzano (Cottage Grove, OR) Native of Colombia. Yoga teacher. Retired Nutritionist. Loves painting for peace and hand stitching dolls and whimsical creatures for healing and forgiveness. Volunteers in rural Oregon. Loves nature, husband, pets, kindred spirits . . . Visionary. goyayoga@icloud.com **p. 1**

Gretchen Butler (Cazadero, CA) Life and art are nestled between forest and meadows. Visit her website chock full of art and stories from an off-the-grid remote area of Northern California. gretchenbutlerwildart.com **p. 103**

Gretchen Lawlor (Mexico and Whidbey Island, WA) We'Moon oracle, now mentor to new oracles & astrologers. Astrology is my great passion—the stars my friends, my loves, my allies. Let me help connect you to these wise guides. Readings in person, skype or zoom. 206-698-3741 (call or text) light@whidbey.com; gretchenlawlor.com **p. 11, 12**

Haley Neddermann (Torrington, CT) I am an educator, poet, and herbalist with a passion for exploring nature's magic and the kinship of all beings. May my words be medicine for your heart and for the earth. sweetfernbotanicals.com **p. 67**

Heather Esterline (Walloon Lake, MI) is an old kitchen witch living in Northern Michigan. I have a love affair with the beautiful woods all around me, and am a long-time user and gatherer of herbal medicinals. I make my own formulas, tinctures and salves. **p. 177**

Heather Roan Robbins (Ronan, MT) ceremonialist, counselor, and astrologer for over 40 years, creator of the *Starcodes Astro-Oracle* deck, author of *Moon Wisdom, Everyday Palmistry,* and several children's books, writes the weekly Starcodes column for We'Moon and the Santa Fe New Mexican and works with people in person in MT and by phone or Zoom. roanrobbins.com **p. 8, 202, 203**

Heidi Van Impe (Salt Spring Island, BC) is an artist and art therapist who enjoys bringing vitality and regeneration through the arts to elders in care homes. Birds and nature are a large influence in her work as well as part of her internal symbolism. heidivanimpe.com **p. 57**

Helen Smith (Herefordshire, UK) is a druid, therapist, poet and artist from the Welsh Marshes. Her work is inspired by mythology, the relationship between people and nature, and the landscape of the human body. FB: earthbodyartstudio IG: @earth.body.art **p. 90**

Jana Parkes (Grants Pass, OR) Art created through my heart. I never know beforehand what I will paint. I simply ask with an open heart for the highest good. My hope is that others find art as healing and inspiring as I do. janaparkesart.com **p. 126**

Jakki Moore (Co. Leitrim, Ireland) Life circumstances led Jakki to a magical cottage in the west of Ireland. Surrounded by nature, she paints, writes and leads the occasional tour to Goddess Sites. jakkiart.com **p. 34, 72**

Janet Newton (Peoria, IL) is a retired graphic design professor who finally has time to pursue her love of drawing and painting. **p. 109**

Janey Brims (Somerset, UK) I am an artist and lover of light, squirreled away, happily living my best life. Contact: thewillowballerina@gmail.com or through Naomi at Inanna's Festival, 2 St. Andrews Hill, Norwich, UK **p. 76**

Janis Dyck (Golden, BC) I am an artist and art therapist and am humbled and in awe of women's creativity and its capacity to transform lives. I am honored to work in a lineage of creative women; their strength and the beauty of our planet give me inspiration and guidance. janisdyck.com **p. 101**

Jeannette M. French (Gresham, OR) My purpose is to inspire relationship with Spirit through portals of light, love, beauty, joy, hope and gratitude. See more at jeanette-french.pixels.com **p. 151, Back Cover**

Jennifer Highland (Plymouth, NH) practices Osteopathy in a solar-powered office in central New Hampshire. She also spends her time growing vegetables and poems, hiking, and practicing Tai Chi. **p. 89**

Jiling Lin L.Ac. (Venture, CA) is an Earth-centered acupuncturist, herbalist, and yoga teacher. She nourishes resilience through clinics, classes, and retreats integrating wilderness, creativity, and Spirit. Visit Jiling at jilinglin.com **p. 58**

Joan Zehnder (Louisville, KY) Check out my facebook artist page @ joanzehnderstudio and Saatchi page saatchiart.com/joanzehnder. **p. 16**

Joanne M. Clarkson (Port Townsend, WA) Joanne's lifelong spiritual and artistic practice has been writing poetry. Her most recent book is *The Fates* from Bright Hill Press. She is also a palm and Tarot reader taught by her grandmother. See more at joanneclarkson.com **p. 55, 93, 123, 135**

Johanna Elise (Salt Spring Island, BC) lives close to nature teaching children to love the earth and all beings. She sings, writes, dances, and brews chai to express her creative spirit. **p. 35**

Joy Brady (San Francisco, CA) an elder, uses art, poetry as expressions of her second half of life experiences. She has a practice in symbolic consultation in San Francisco. sacredintention@gmail.com **p. 116**

Julia Jenkins Art (Haiku, HI) is a painter deeply inspired by femininity, dreams and our connection to Mother Earth. She creates with her soul on the island of Maui. juliajenkinsart.com, IG: @juliajenkins_ **p. 127**

Karen L. Culpepper (DC, Maryland, Virginia tri state area) is a momma, creative, dreamer, herbalist and practitioner. She loves depth in her relationships, sunshine, being in saltwater, and laughter. Let's connect: karenculpepper.com, IG: @rhythmicbotanicals, rhythmicbotanicals@gmail.com **p. 18**

Karen Russo (Elmira, OR) Working with clay and paint, my sculptures are a tapestry of form, texture and color. My artwork embodies the maternal archetype; highlighting her emotion and spirit, as well as her vulnerability and resiliency. karenrusso.studio **p. 89**

Katheryn M. Trenshaw (Devon, UK) is the founder of *Passionate Presence Center for Creative Expression*. She revels in the spaces in between and becomes comfortable with discomfort. Her life, art & teaching uncover what is already there waiting to be revealed as love and as already whole. She lives and makes art on an organic smallholding in the remarkably funky rural town of Totnes in Devon UK overlooking Dartmoor. katheryntrenshaw.com **p. 25**

Katie Ree (Durham, NC) is fascinated by the subtle energies that connect us to all, and she expresses them through lines and colors. Her hope is that we can all come back to ourselves—our best selves—in nature. katieree.com **p. 31**

Katya Sabaroff Taylor (Tallahassee, FL) is a poet/writer/author whose great joy is inciting others to find their authentic voices through "the wisdom of the pen." She is the author of *My Haiku Life*, and *Prison Wisdom: Writing With Inmates*. katyata@earthlink.net, creativeartsandhealing.com **p. 92**

Kay Kemp (Bastrop, TX) delights in creating heart-centered art that honors & inspires the power of the spirit. She is the founder of *Spirit Works 4 U*, where she seeks to amplify a message of love and respect around the world. Spiritworks4u.com **p. 64, 139**

Kimberly Webber (Taos, NM) is a contemporary symbolist painter who works with pure powdered earth pigments, pine pitch, beeswax, the archetypes, medicine animals and birds to create visual alchemy. The paintings are offerings of inspiration, healing and hope. kimberlywebber.com **p. 149**

Koco Collab (Denver, CO) is the coalescence of Aiko Szymczak and Corinne Trujillo. In our practice, we unravel our lineages ad explore our pasts. As women and people of color, it has become essential in our practice to disentangle and weave new stories. IG: @kococollab **p. 45**

Kristen Roderick (Toronto, ON) is a ceremonialist, writer, mama and rites of passage guide. When she's not designing courses, she's foraging through the woods looking for mushrooms or apprenticing herself to the ancient ways of weaving and fibre art. spiritmoving.org **p. 163**

Kro (Chicago, IL) is a spoken word artist, on-demand typewriter poet, queer/nonbinary Druid, small business owner, and lifelong Chicago local. Follow their poetry on IG and TikTok: @kroetry and contact them at knkroger@gmail.com linktr.ee/Kroetry **p. 136**

KT InfiniteArt (Freeport, NY) Creatrix, artist, writer inspired by sensuality & spirit. IG: @KTInfiniteArt. Visit infiniteartworld.com to check out more artwork & prints **p. 12, 63, 200**

L. Sixfingers (Sacramento, CA) (she/they) is an intersectional herbalist and witch who helps folks to come home to their magick. She hosts online courses for starry-hearted healers as well as teaching and offering in-person services grounded in inclusivity and justice. wortsandcunning.com **p. 104, 120**

Lani Kai Weis (Flagstaff, AZ) is a visionary artist, inspired by the beautiful technologies and patterns that the natural world presents. She hopes to provide nourishment for the eyes of hungry souls and inspiration for creative hearts. Follow on social media: @lanikai_art **p. 105**

Leah Marie Dorian (Prince Albert, SK) An interdisciplinary Métis artist, Leah's paintings honor the spiritual strength of Aboriginal women, the Sacred Feminine. She believes women play a key role in passing on vital knowledge for all humanity, which is deeply reflected in her artistic practice. Visit her at leahdorion.ca **p. 79**

Leah Markman (Eugene, OR) A Tarot enthusiast, astrology lover and leather craftswoman. She spends her time in the sunshine with her dog, horse and VW Bus. Visit her etsy for more writings and leatherwork! etsy.com/shop/DreamtenderLeather IG: @DreamtenderLeather **p. 4, 22**

Lindsay Carron (Los Angeles, CA) Lindsay's drawings and murals are a vibrant ode to the spirit of this planet and tell a story brimming with hope. Her work is dedicated to social and environmental justice and resilience. lindsaycarron.com **p. 134**

Lindy Kehoe (Gold Hill, OR) I am in ever-flowing gratitude to be part of this wonderful weaving of creating womyn! Living in the awesomely inspiring Rogue Valley of Southern Oregon, and painting from a place of wonder. lindykehoe.com **p. 20**

lisa kemmerer (Ocean Shores, WA) Retired in order to work for the earth, anymals, and all who are marginalized and disempowered. lisa is an artist, scholar, and founder of *Tapestry*. For more information, please visit lisakemmerer.com **p. 84**

LorrieArt (Cleveland, OH) I am in my crone phase of life. I love animals, and you can see them often in my artwork. I am healing from trauma and fight my own mental illness battles with chronic depression, social anxiety and agoraphobia. These aspects of my life contribute to my unique tapestry and unite me with so many other women, maybe even you. IG: @lattesmith05, email: lattesmith@yahoo.com **p. 65**

Lyla June (Albuquerque, NM) is an Indigenous musician, scholar & community organizer of Diné (Navajo), Tsétsêhéstâhese (Cheyenne) & European lineages. Her dynamic, multi-genre presentation style has engaged audiences across the globe towards personal, collective and ecological healing. She blends studies in Human Ecology at Stanford, graduate work in Indigenous Pedagogy, & the traditional worldview she grew up with to inform her music, perspectives & solutions. She is currently pursuing her doctoral degree, focusing on Indigenous food systems revitalization. lylajune@dreamwarriors.co **p. 41**

Mandalamy Arts (Tokepa, KS) Amy Allen is an artist, psychologist, life learner/homeschooling mom. She finds inspiration from nature, wildlife, stargazing, hiking, travel, yoga, art, and music. She can be found on FB and IG as Mandalamy Arts. **p. 3, 14**

Margriet Seinen (Redway, CA) discovered silk painting in the early 80s. She painted scarves, pillow covers and then moved into fine art, including images of mermaids, nature devas, scenery and mandalas. She also teaches mandala classes where students learn silk painting. seinensilk.com **p. 175**

Maria Cristina Guerriero (Punalu'u, HI) is a nurse educator and artist. Her images focus on the Divine Feminine and nature. Email: marieange2001@hotmail.com, IG: @mariacristinaguerriero **p. 152**

Marianne Moskowitz (Sunny Valley, OR) was a visual artist, writer, gifted school psychologist, and devoted mom to three daughters. Read more about her life on page 183. **p. 182**

marna scooter (Portland, OR) catalyzes earth creativity in regenerative Goddess gardens and tends stars and dreams for priestesses of earthly flourishing (deeperharmony.com), as a visitor guest on the traditional lands of Chinookan Nations. **p. 26, 116, 131, 159**

Marnie Recker (Tofino, BC) Photographer and painter. My photographs are time capsules of people, places, light and love. I create paintings to honour the spirit of creativity and to celebrate the beauty and cycles of life. marnierecker.com **p. 100**

Maya Spector (Oakland, CA) is a poet, ritualist, SoulCollage® Facilitator and retired children's librarian. She authored a book of poetry, *The Persephone Cycle*, has been published in several poetry anthologies, and has performed at many Rumi's Caravan spoken word events. Blog: hangingoutwithhecate.blogspot.com **p. 130**

Megan Welti (Clarksburg, MA) is an artist, poet and energy worker living in Western Massachusetts with her husband, four children, and many fur babies. You can find prints of her original watercolors at redrootrising.squarespace.com **p. 33, 117, 133**

Melissa Harris (West Hurley, NY) Artist, author, and intuitive. Join me for one of my Art and Spirit retreats in magical locations. Author of *100 Keys to a Creative Life* (Amazon), *Anything is Possible* activation cards and *Goddess on the Go* affirmation cards. melissaharris.com **p. 168**

Melissa Kae Mason, "MoonCat!" (EARTH) Traveling Astrologer, Artist, Radio DJ, Photographer, Jewelry Creator, PostCard Sender, Goddess Card Inventor, Seer of Patterns, Adventurer and Home Seeker. See LifeMapAstrology.com Contact: LifeMapAstrology@gmail.com **p. 204**

Melissa Winter (San Antonio, TX) Prints and original paintings may be found at Melissa's website: honeybart.com. For commissions, please contact Melissa at mwinter1103@gmail.com **p. 171**

Meridian Azura (New Boston, NH) is a mixed media artist and witch working with the Divine Feminine. You can find her work on IG:@meridian.azura or on her website: meridianazura.com **p. 106**

Mindi Meltz (Hendersonville, NC) is the author of themed *Animal Wisdom Cards* and several mythical novels exploring the divine feminine and nature as dream-mirror for the soul. She lives off-grid in the Blue Ridge Mountains. To read more: mindimeltz.com **p. 48, 107**

Mojgan Abolhassani (Vancouver, BC) is an artist and Expressive Art Therapist. She also obtained solid training in a wide variety of intuitive art programs: Cyclic Meditation, Theta Healing and many other healing modalities. mojgana66@gmail.com **p. 40**

Molly Remer, MSW, D.Min (Rolla, MO) is a priestess facilitating women's circles, seasonal rituals, & family ceremonies. Molly & her husband, Mark, co-create original Story Goddesses at Brigid's Grove (brigidsgrove.etsy.com). Molly is the author of nine books, including *Walking with Persephone, Whole and Holy, Womanrunes, & The Goddess Devotional.* She is the creator of the devotional experience #30DaysofGoddess & she loves savoring small magic & everyday enchantment. **p. 20, 43, 60, 64, 79, 100, 108, 115, 124, 134, 151, 170**

Monika Denise (Rockingham, VA) I follow the red unraveling thread, leaving the monoliths of the old paradigm towards freedom. May my own liberation aid in the restoration of interconnection, aliveness, wholeness, beauty, and love between peoples and nature. mburkholder12@gmail.com **p. 83**

Morgen Maier (Arcata, CA) Artist mama dwelling in the mountain, Redwood, ocean energy of N. Cali. Earthen Furrow Studio is where I transmute the everyday magic of the natural world as I see it. We are surrounded by ecstatic beauty & my art just strives to honor that! IG: @earthen_furrow, earthenfurrowstudio.org **p. 53**

Moss Wildwing (Arcata, CA) (they/them) is a queer artist & songwriter working towards becoming a licensed therapist specializing in using the expressive arts in healing trauma. Youtube: Moss Wildwing & mindfulnetdesigns.com **p. 119**

Musawa (Estacada, OR and Tesuque, NM) We are celebrating the 50th anniversary of We'Moon Land this Summer—one of the first intentional women's land communities in this country! Having started it in 1973, when I was in my 20s, I am now in my

70s, and am looking for new generations of wemoon who wish to support carrying on this inter-generational land dyke community in the spirit of We'Moon—for the next 50 years! FFI: wemoonland@gmail.com **p. 6, 178, 180, 196**

Natasza Zurek (Naramata, BC) In the spirit of play, I use the visual language of shadow and light to create dimensions of possibility where colourful dreams and visions can be shared to learn about the world and explore the limitlessness of human potential. nataszazurekart.com, IG: @natka01 **p. 91**

Nell Aurelia (Devon, UK) is a writer, performer, mother and counselor. Writing of trauma; transformation; grief, grace and grit; radical self-love; smashing the patriarchy; love affairs with nature. IG: @nellaureliapoetry **p. 82, 165**

Nhein Vuong, J.D., M.Div. (Kansas City, MO) Founder of *Evolving Enneagram* and ordained interspiritual Unity minister, Rev. Nhien Vuong is an internationally recognized counselor, consultant, and community builder focused on transformation using the Enneagram as a map for our conscious, collective evolution. evolvingenneagram.com **p. 169**

Oak Chezar (Jamestown, CO) is a radical dyke in the Rocky Mountains of Colorado and a frequent contributor to We'Moon. oakchezar.com **p. 77**

PamTaylorPhotography (Sedona, AZ) Her website, pamtaylormultimedia. com demonstrates a full 4-decade career. Beginning with photojournalism, Pam progressed to performance photography and more lyrical images. Her recent work explores psychological, spiritual storytelling. **p. 115**

Patricia Soper (Patchogue, NY) Exploring and deepening in the wisdom of crone, nature, Spirit, Sacred Feminine and ancient ways. **p. 44**

Patricia Wyatt (Santa Fe, NM) a graphic painter, using collage, watercolor paper, canvas and printed papers, and texture and embossed papers to create a sense of a spiritual connection to the land, the sky, the animals, the birds and the plants. patriciawyatt.com **p. 113**

Poetically Illustrated (Murfreesboro, TN) Destiney Powell is a visual artist specializing in visual storytelling of black culture through colorful paintings. Learn more at poeticallyillustrated.net **p. 153, 173**

Rachel Creager Ireland (Austin, TX) is good at building campfires and remembering dreams. She self-published *Flight of Unknown Birds: Poems About the Wildness and the Weirdness Within*, and she blogs at veronicasgarden.wordpress.com. **p. 32**

Raven Borgilt (Ashland, OR) studied art throughout her childhood. She has always taken inspiration from nature, and the animals around her. She is now a practicing massage therapist and artist in Southern Oregon. thrivemassageashland.com **p. 165**

Robin Lea Quinlivan (Thomas, WV) is an oil painter who lives in the wilds of the Appalachian Mountains where she co-owns an art gallery. She is inspired by her love for the natural world, as well as the mutable nature and interconnectedness of all things. robinquinlivan.etsy.com **p. 19**

Sabina Jones (Taos, NM) has been writing since she knew how. She is 23 and on a pilgrimage of heart. She writes poetry for people on the streets with her vintage Corona-Smith. You can pick the topic and she writes the poem. Find her and her musings at eartothelight.tumblr.com **p. 122**

Sandra Pastorius (Ashland, OR) has been a practicing Astrologer since 1979, and a Featured Writer for We'Moon since 1990. Look for her collected We'Moon essays, "Galactic Musings" under Resources at wemoon.ws. With Sun in Gemini, she delights in blending the playful and the profound. Sandra offers individual and couples charts, readings and transit updates in person or by phone. Email her about astrology classes at: sandrapastorius@gmail.com. Read more articles here: wemoon. ws/blogs/sandras-cosmic-trip. Peace Be! **p. 10, 16, 206**

Sandra Stanton (Farmington, ME) Continuing to explore empathic connections between people, other species and Mother Earth. World Goddesses & tree lore combine in *The Green World Oracle*, with Kathleen Jenks, published by Schiffer. goddessmyths.com, sandrastantonart.com **p. 144**

Sandy Bot-Miller (St. Cloud, MN) loves playing with words, fibers and oil pastels. She creates to nurture her own well-being and to connect with others in making the world a better place for all. sandybotmiller@gmail.com **p. 85**

Serena Supplee (Moab, UT) Forty years of living and loving the Colorado Plateau serve as the current of inspiration for her joyous artwork. She paints with watercolors and oils, working from her drawings rather than photos, trusting her creative process. serenasupplee.com **p. 44, 145**

Shauna Crandall (Driggs, ID) lives in the beautiful Teton Valley and is inspired by the feminine found in myth, nature and the cosmos. shaunacrandall.com & skcrandall@yahoo.com **p. 50**

Sierra Lonepine Briano (Gaston, OR) Celebrating my Cronedom, I am coming into myself as an artist, painter, Witch, lover of Earth Mother and the Ocean. I want, now, to paint my friends, my "Cronies" and how we are connected to the Earth, both in this life and the next. FB: Sierra Briano TripOut **p. 110**

Sigita Mockute (Psigidelia) (Lithuania) Inspired by nature and everyday living experiences, these drawings come from Inner World, beyond personal identity, vibrating through the deepest layers of my own being and expressing onto paper. I use colour pencils as a medium to download them onto paper. For more please visit psigidelia.com **p. 43, 177**

Sophia Faria (Salt Spring Island, BC) is a Sex & Relationship Coach working with individuals, couples, and groups. As a Creative Consultant, she offers embodied leaders practical support to soundboard, design, refine, and birth their content & online businesses. Connect: sophiafaria.com **p. 95**

Sophia Rosenberg (Lasqueti Island, BC) Thank you, We'Moon creatrixes, for helping us keep track of the days and moons of our lives, as well as inspiring and supporting women's creativity for decades. sophiarosenberg.com, Blue Beetle Studio on Etsy **p. 144**

Stephanie A. Sellers (Fayetteville, PA) So grateful to be part of the We'Moon community again this year and add my voice to this beautiful collective of womyn. I founded an international network of support for women (and anyone) who has been shunned by their family of origin: sednasdaughters.com **p. 69, 96, 113, 143, 155**

Susa Silvermarie (Ajijic, Mexico) I channel Spirit into poetry. At 76 I turn myself over to my largest art, the creation of harmony in my life and the world. Please visit me at susasilvermarie.com or email me ssilvermarie@gmail.com **p. 31, 72, 127**

Susan Baylies (Durham, NC) sells her lunar phases as cards, larger print charts and posters at snakeandsnake.com Email her at sbaylies@gmail.com **p. 226**

Susan Levitt (San Francisco, CA) is an astrologer, tarot card reader, and feng shui consultant since 1986. Her publications include *Taoist Astrology* and *The Complete Tarot Kit*. Follow Susan's lunar astrology newsletter for new Moon and full Moon updates. susanlevitt.com **p. 19, 197**

Suzanne Grace Michell (Sacramento, CA) I am passionate about and delighted by the interplay between spirit, humanity, the natural world and creativity. These connections inspire my life and art. It is my joy to share it with you. rockmama.com **p. 73, 230**

Tamara Phillips (Vancouver, BC) is a Canadian watercolour artist inspired by the raw beauty of the natural world and our connection to it. She explores the depth between myth, dream, intuition, and reality. See more of her work at tamaraphillips.ca **p. 37, 61, 146**

Tara deForest Hansen (Camas, WA) is a self-taught artist, specializing in oil painting. She hopes to bring, as well as express, beauty and change in this world. IG: @tara_de_forest_hansen Website: janesinspiration.com **p. 81**

Tasha Zigerelli (Santa Cruz, CA) is a grief guide & educator, writer, singer, death/birth worker. She uses her writing & creativity to curate ceremonies, poetry & music from her deepest wounds, held & inspired by her beloved dead. IG: @tendingtogrief **p. 47, 152**

Terri Watrous Berry (Erie, MI) Terri's work has appeared over the past four decades in several anthologies, journals, magazines, and newspapers. A septuagenarian since last September, she resides in Michigan and can be reached via email at tgwberry@yahoo.com **p. 57**

Tessa Mythos (Hornby Island, BC)is a visual artist from Hornby Island B.C. She is deeply inspired by the wild beauty and magic of nature and the divine. She may be found on her website www.artbymythos.com, fb: Art by Mythos and IG: tessa_mythos **p. 27**

Tonya J. Cunningham (Lake Forest Park, WA) As a preschool teacher, and mother, I'm privileged to see the wonder in the world around me, every day. As a poet, I hope to share that wonder and create a spark of hope and empathy with my writing. **p. 70**

Valerie A Szarek (Louisville, CO) is a Performance Poet, Native American Flute player, and Shamanic Practitioner/Healer. She teaches Soul-centered writing workshops online and in Louisville, Colorado. poetval.com to hear her poems and music. **p. 175**

Van Lefan (Mission, BC) For blog, music, social media links visit my website: vanessalyuen.com **p. 4**

Verlena Lisa Johnson (Tarzana, CA) Work by the artist can be seen on her website: verlenajohnson.com **p. 87**

Viandara (Hillsboro, OR) I am an emissary of love, dreaming into being a new cosmology. Painting mystic metarealism: pictorial poetry where image converges with myth. I create heART offerings from our collective evolution. viandarasheart.com **p. 125**

Xelena González (San Antonio, TX) practices the healing arts through writing and movement. She is the author of the acclaimed picture books *All Around Us* and *Where Wonder Grows* and the divination guide *Loteria Remedios*. Connect at xelena. space or xelenag@gmail.com **p. 129**

Zoe Zum (Victoria, BC) is a visionary artist based out of Vancouver Island Canada. Her work is inspired by an ongoing study of magic, dreams, visions, animals and folklore. Her work can be viewed on FB & IG:@zoezum as well as on etsy: ZoeZumArt **p. 162**

Errors/Corrections

We misspelled two words in *We'Moon 2022*: "courageous" in the chart on page 21, and "Katharyn" on page 26. Apologies, Katharyn, your "a" went "couraageous."

We appreciate all the feedback we get, so please let us know if you find anything amiss. Please visit our "Errata and Corrigenda" web page near the beginning of the year to see any corrections published for this issue of We'Moon.

WE'MOON SKY TALK

Gaia Rhythms: We show the natural cycles of the Moon, Sun, planets and stars as they relate to Earth. By recording our own activities side by side with those of other heavenly bodies, we may notice what connection, if any, there is for us. The Earth revolves around her axis in one day; the Moon orbits around the Earth in one month ($29^1/_2$ days); the Earth orbits around the Sun in one year. We experience each of these cycles in the alternating rhythms of day and night, waxing and waning, summer and winter. The Earth/Moon/Sun are our inner circle of kin in the universe. We know where we are in relation to them at all times by the dance of light and shadow as they circle around one another.

The Eyes of Heaven: As seen from Earth, the Moon and the Sun are equal in size: "the left and right eye of heaven," according to Hindu (Eastern) astrology. Unlike the solar-dominated calendars of Christian (Western) patriarchy, We'Moon looks at our experience through both eyes at once. The **lunar eye of heaven** is seen each day in the phases of the Moon, as she is both reflector and shadow, traveling her $29^1/_2$-day path around the Earth in a "Moon" Month (from each new moon to the next, 13 times in a lunar year). Because Earth is orbiting the Sun at the same time, it takes the Moon $27^1/_3$ days to go through all the signs of the Zodiac—a sidereal month. The **solar eye of heaven** is apparent at the turning points in the Sun's cycle. The year begins with Winter Solstice (in the Northern Hemisphere), the dark renewal time, and journeys through the full cycle of seasons and balance points (solstices, equinoxes and the cross-quarter days in between). The **third eye** of heaven may be seen in the stars. Astrology measures the cycles by relating the Sun, Moon and all other planets in our universe through the backdrop of star signs (the zodiac), helping us to tell time in the larger cycles of the universe.

Measuring Time and Space: Imagine a clock with many hands. The Earth is the center from which we view our universe. The Sun, Moon and planets are like the hands of the clock. Each one has its own rate of movement through the cycle. The ecliptic, a 17° band of sky around the Earth within which all planets have their orbits, is the outer band of the clock where the numbers are. Stars along the ecliptic are grouped into constellations forming the signs of the zodiac—the twelve star signs are like the twelve numbers of the clock. They mark the movements of the planets through the 360° circle of the sky, the clock of time and space.

Whole Earth Perspective: It is important to note that all natural cycles have a mirror image from a whole Earth perspective—seasons occur at opposite times in the Northern and Southern Hemispheres, and day and night are at opposite times on opposite sides of the Earth as well. Even the Moon plays this game—a waxing crescent moon

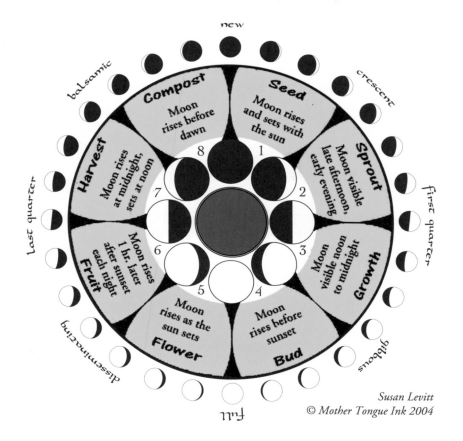

new

balsamic

crescent

Compost
Moon rises before dawn

Seed
Moon rises and sets with the sun

Harvest
Moon rises at midnight, sets at noon

Sprout
Moon visible late afternoon, early evening

Last quarter

first quarter

Fruit
Moon rises 1 hr. later after sunset each night

Growth
Moon visible noon to midnight

8

1

7

2

6

3

5

4

Flower
Moon rises as the sun sets

Bud
Moon rises before sunset

disseminating

gibbous

full

Susan Levitt
© *Mother Tongue Ink 2004*

in Australia faces right (☽), while in North America, it faces left (☽). We'Moon uses a Northern Hemisphere perspective regarding times, holy days, seasons and lunar phases. Wemoon who live in the Southern Hemisphere may want to transpose descriptions of the holy days to match seasons in their area. We honor a whole Earth cultural perspective by including four rotating languages for the days of the week, from different parts of the globe.

Whole Sky Perspective: It is also important to note that all over the Earth, in varied cultures and times, the dome of the sky has been interacted with in countless ways. The zodiac we speak of is just one of many ways that hu-moons have pictured and related to the stars. In this calendar we use the Tropical zodiac, which keeps constant the Vernal Equinox point at 0° Aries. Western astrology primarily uses this system. Vedic or Eastern astrology uses the Sidereal zodiac, which bases the positions of signs relative to fixed stars, and over time the Vernal Equinox point has moved about 24° behind 0° Aries.

Musawa © *Mother Tongue Ink 2008*

ASTROLOGY BASICS

Planets: Like chakras in our solar system, planets allow for different frequencies or types of energies to be expressed. See Mooncat's article (p.204) for more detailed planetary attributes.

Signs: The twelve signs of the zodiac are a mandala in the sky, marking off 30° segments of a circle around the earth. Signs show major shifts in planetary energy through the cycles.

Glyphs are the symbols used to represent planets and signs.

Sun Sign: The Sun enters a new sign once a month (on or around the 21st), completing the whole cycle of the zodiac in one year. The sun sign reflects qualities of your outward shining self.

Moon Sign: The Moon changes signs approximately every 2 to $2^{1}/_{2}$ days, going through all twelve signs of the zodiac every $27^{1}/_{3}$ days (the sidereal month). The Moon sign reflects qualities of your core inner self.

Moon Phase: Each calendar day is marked with a graphic representing the phase of the Moon.

Lunar Quarter Phase: At the four quarter-points of the lunar cycle (new, waxing half, full and waning half moons), we indicate the phase, sign and exact time for each. These points mark off the "lunar week."

Day of the Week: Each day is associated with a planet whose symbol appears in the line above it (e.g., ☽☽☽ for Moon: Moonday)

Eclipse: The time of greatest eclipse is given, which is near to, but not at the exact time of the conjunction (☉☌☽) or opposition (☉☍☽). See "Eclipses" (p. 10).

Aspects (□ △ ☍ ☌ ✶ ⊼) are listed in fine print under the Moon sign each day, and show the angle of relationship between different planets as they move. Daily aspects provide something like an astrological weather forecast, indicating which energies are working together easily and which combinations are more challenging.

Transits are the motion of the planets and the moon as they move among the zodiacal constellations and in relationship to one another.

Ingresses (→): When the Sun, Moon and planets move into new signs.

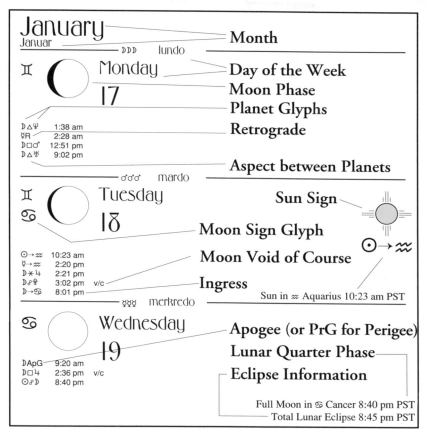

January
Januar ⠀⠀⠀ ⠀ ⠀ ⠀DDD ⠀⠀ lundo ⠀⠀⠀⠀ **Month**

♊ ⠀ **Monday** ⠀⠀⠀ **Day of the Week**
⠀⠀⠀⠀⠀⠀ 17 ⠀⠀⠀⠀ **Moon Phase**
⠀⠀⠀⠀⠀⠀⠀⠀⠀⠀⠀⠀⠀ **Planet Glyphs**

D△Ψ ⠀ 1:38 am ⠀⠀⠀ **Retrograde**
☿R ⠀⠀ 2:28 am
D□♂ ⠀ 12:51 pm
D△♅ ⠀ 9:02 pm

⠀⠀⠀⠀⠀⠀⠀⠀⠀⠀⠀⠀ **Aspect between Planets**

⠀⠀⠀⠀⠀⠀ ♂♂♂ ⠀ mardo

♊ ⠀ **Tuesday** ⠀⠀⠀ **Sun Sign**
♋ ⠀⠀⠀ 18 ⠀⠀⠀ **Moon Sign Glyph**

⊙→♒ ⠀ 10:23 am ⠀⠀⠀ **Moon Void of Course**
☿→♒ ⠀ 2:20 pm
D✳4 ⠀ 2:21 pm ⠀⠀⠀ **Ingress**
D♂♀ ⠀ 3:02 pm ⠀ v/c
D→♋ ⠀ 8:01 pm ⠀⠀⠀⠀ Sun in ♒ Aquarius 10:23 am PST

⠀⠀⠀⠀⠀⠀ ☿☿☿ ⠀ merkredo

♋ ⠀ **Wednesday** ⠀⠀⠀ **Apogee (or PrG for Perigee)**
⠀⠀⠀⠀⠀⠀ 19 ⠀⠀⠀ **Lunar Quarter Phase**
⠀⠀⠀⠀⠀⠀⠀⠀⠀⠀⠀⠀ **Eclipse Information**

DApG ⠀ 9:20 am
D□4 ⠀ 2:36 pm ⠀ v/c
⊙♂D ⠀ 8:40 pm

⠀⠀⠀⠀⠀⠀⠀⠀⠀ Full Moon in ♋ Cancer 8:40 pm PST
⠀⠀⠀⠀⠀⠀⠀⠀⠀ Total Lunar Eclipse 8:45 pm PST

Sample calendar page for reference only

Moon "Void of Course" (D v/c): The Moon is said to be "void of course" from the last significant lunar aspect in each sign until the Moon enters a new sign. This is a good time to ground and center yourself.

Super Moon is a New or Full Moon that occurs when the Moon is at or within 90% of perigee, its closest approach to Earth. On average, there are four to six Super Moons each year. Full Super Moons could appear visually closer and brighter, and promote stronger tides. Personally, we may use the greater proximity of Super Moons to illuminate our inner horizons and deepen our self-reflections and meditations.

Apogee (ApG): The point in the Moon's orbit that is *farthest* from Earth. At this time, the effects of transits may be less noticeable immediately, but may appear later. Also, **Black Moon Lilith**, a hypothetical center point of the Moon's elliptical orbit around the Earth, will be conjunct the Moon.

Perigee (PrG): The point in the Moon's orbit that is *nearest* to Earth. Transits with the Moon, when at perigee, will be more intense.

Aphelion (ApH): The point in a planet's orbit that is *farthest* from the Sun. At this time, the effects of transits (when planets pass across the path of another planet) may be less noticeable immediately, but may appear later.

Perihelion (PrH): The point in a planet's orbit that is *nearest* to the Sun. Transits with planets, when they are at perihelion, will be more intense.

Lunar Nodes: The most Northern and Southern points in the Moon's monthly cycle when it crosses the Sun's ecliptic or annual path, offering to integrate the past (South) and future (North) directions in life.

Direct or Retrograde (D or R): These are times when a planet moves forward (D) or backward (R) through the signs of the zodiac (an optical illusion, as when a moving train passes a slower train that appears to be going backward). When a planet is in direct motion, planetary energies are more straightforward; in retrograde, planetary

energies turn back in on themselves and are more involuted. See "Mercury Retrograde" (p. 10).
© *Mother Tongue Ink*
2000

The Regal Moon and Her Phases
© *KT InfiniteArt 2020*

SIGNS AND SYMBOLS AT A GLANCE

PLANETS

Personal Planets are closest to Earth.

☉ **Sun**: self radiating outward, character, ego
☽ **Moon**: inward sense of self, emotions, psyche
☿ **Mercury**: communication, travel, thought
♀ **Venus**: relationship, love, sense of beauty, empathy
♂ **Mars**: will to act, initiative, ambition

Asteroids are between Mars and Jupiter and reflect the awakening of feminine-defined energy centers in human consciousness.

Social Planets are between personal and outer planets.

♃ **Jupiter**: expansion, opportunities, leadership
♄ **Saturn**: limits, structure, discipline

Note: The days of the week are named in various languages after the above seven heavenly bodies.

⚷ **Chiron**: is a small planetary body between Saturn and Uranus representing the wounded healer.

Transpersonal Planets are the outer planets.

♅ **Uranus**: cosmic consciousness, revolutionary change
♆ **Neptune**: spiritual awakening, cosmic love, all one
♇ **Pluto**: death and rebirth, deep, total change

ZODIAC SIGNS

♈ Aries
♉ Taurus
♊ Gemini
♋ Cancer
♌ Leo
♍ Virgo
♎ Libra
♏ Scorpio
♐ Sagittarius
♑ Capricorn
♒ Aquarius
♓ Pisces

ASPECTS

Aspects show the angle between planets; this informs how the planets influence each other and us. We'Moon lists only significant aspects:

☌ CONJUNCTION (planets are 0–5° apart)
Linked together, energy of aspected planets is mutually enhancing.
☍ OPPOSITION (planets are 180° apart)
Polarizing or complementing, energies are diametrically opposite.
△ TRINE (planets are 120° apart)
Harmonizing, energies of this aspect are in the same element.
□ SQUARE (planets are 90° apart)
Challenging, energies of this aspect are different from each other.
✶ SEXTILE (planets are 60° apart)
Cooperative, energies of this aspect blend well.
⚻ QUINCUNX (planets are 150° apart)
Variable, energies of this aspect combine contrary elements.

OTHER SYMBOLS

☽ v/c–Moon is "void of course" from last lunar aspect until it enters new sign.
ApG–Apogee: Point in the orbit of the Moon that's farthest from Earth.
PrG–Perigee: Point in the orbit of the Moon that's nearest to Earth.
ApH–Aphelion: Point in the orbit of a planet that's farthest from the Sun.
PrH–Perihelion: Point in the orbit of a planet that's nearest to the Sun.
D or R–Direct or Retrograde: Describes when a planet moves forward (D) through the zodiac or appears to move backward (R).

Constellations of the Zodiac

These stations of the zodiac were named thousands of years ago for the constellations that were behind them at the time. The signs of the zodiac act like a light filter, coloring the qualities of life force. As the Sun, Moon and other planets move through the zodiac, the following influences are energized:

♒ **Aquarius** (Air): Community, ingenuity, collaboration, idealism. It's time to honor the philosophy of love and the power of community.

♓ **Pisces** (Water): Introspection, imagination, sensitivity and intuition. We process and gestate our dreams

♈ **Aries** (Fire): Brave, direct, rebellious, energized. Our inner teenager comes alive; our adult self needs to direct the energy wisely.

♉ **Taurus** (Earth): Sensual, rooted, nurturing, material manifestation. We slow down, get earthy, awaken our senses, begin to build form, roots, and stubborn strength.

♊ **Gemini** (Air): Communication, networking, curiosity, quick witted. We connect with like minds and build a network of understanding.

♋ **Cancer** (Water): Family, home, emotional awareness, nourishment. We need time in our shell and with our familiars.

♌ **Leo** (Fire): Creativity, charisma, warmth, and enthusiasm. Gather with others to celebrate and share bounty.

♍ **Virgo** (Earth): Mercurial, curious, critical, and engaged. The mood sharpens our minds and nerves, and sends us back to work.

♎ **Libra** (Air): Beauty, equality, egalitarianism, cooperation. We grow more friendly, relationship oriented, and incensed by injustice.

♏ **Scorpio** (Water): Sharp focus, perceptive, empowered, mysterious. The mood is smoky, primal, occult, and curious; still waters run deep.

♐ **Sagittarius** (Fire): Curiosity, honesty, exploration, playfulness. We grow more curious about what's unfamiliar.

♑ **Capricorn** (Earth): family, history, dreams, traditions. We need mountains to climb and problems to solve.

adapted from Heather Roan Robbins' Sun Signs and Sun Transits
© *Mother Tongue Ink 2016*

Moon Transits

The Moon changes signs every 2½ days. The sign that the Moon is in sets the emotional tone of the day.

♒ Moon in Aquarius calls us to the circle and away from private concerns; it reminds us of the sacredness of collaboration and collectivity. It's time to search for new allies, to network, and to live our philosophy.

♓ Moon in Pisces makes us aware, sometimes painfully, of our emotions. It heightens compassion, intuition. We may have to strengthen boundaries. Explore the temple of imagination.

♈ Moon in Aries accesses our fire; temper, impatience and passion. We feel an urgency to focus, but we can lose our empathy. It's time to do what truly makes us feel alive, to initiate projects and set boundaries.

♉ Moon in Taurus slows us down; roots grow deep in this stubborn, creative, sensual time. It's time to cultivate our earthly resources: garden, home, and body. Plant seeds in fertile loam, listen to the Earth's magic.

♊ Moon in Gemini speeds our thoughts and nerves. It's time to weave words: talk, listen, laugh, sing and write. Network, negotiate, rearrange; juggle possibilities; just don't get spread too thin.

♋ Moon in Cancer reconnects us with our emotions. We may get overwhelmed and defensive, or we can nourish ourselves and reconnect with our true feelings. Water is healing; bathe, hydrate, make soup.

♌ Moon in Leo gets us into the heart of the action. It's time to let our light shine, express ourselves and appreciate other's unique stories. Celebrate, ritualize, dramatize. Share with true Leonine generosity.

♍ Moon in Virgo sharpens our minds and nerves. It helps us digest information and assess the situation. Invoke Virgoan compassion and brilliant problem-solving. Clean, organize, edit, weed and heal.

♎ Moon in Libra warms our hearts and heightens our aesthetics. Beauty, fairness and balance feed us. We want everyone to get along, and we become allergic to discord in the culture and with our beloveds.

♏ Moon in Scorpio turns us inward, deepens our curiosity and focus, but gives us attitude. We need privacy, as moods may be prickly. Clear the deadwood of soul or garden. Seek deep, refreshing contemplation.

♐ Moon in Sagittarius gets us moving around the globe, or into our minds. It loans us fresh (often tactless) honesty, an adventurous spark, philosophical perspective and easy rapport with the natural world.

♑ Moon in Capricorn whets our ambition and tests our sense of humor. It's time to put sweat-equity into our dreams; organize, build, manifest. Set clear short-term goals and feel the joy of accomplishment.

adapted from Heather Roan Robbins' Moon Signs and Moon Transits

Know Yourself—Map of Planetary Influences

Most people, when considering astrology's benefits, are familiar with their Sun Sign; however, each of the planets within our solar system has a specific part to play in the complete knowledge of "The Self." Here is a quick run-down of our planets' astrological effects:

☉ **The Sun** represents our soul purpose—what we are here on Earth to do or accomplish, and it informs how we go about that task. It answers the age-old question "Why am I here?"

☽ **The Moon** represents our capacity to feel or empathize with those around us and within our own soul as well. It awakens our intuitive and emotional body.

☿ **Mercury** is "The Thinker," and involves our communication skills: what we say, our words, our voice, and our thoughts, including the Teacher/Student, Master/Apprentice mode. Mercury affects how we connect with all the media tools of the day—our computers, phones, and even the postal, publishing and recording systems!

♀ **Venus** is our recognition of love, art and beauty. Venus is harmony in its expressed form, as well as compassion, bliss and acceptance.

♂ **Mars** is our sense of "Get Up and GO!" It represents being in motion and the capacity to take action and do. Mars can also affect our temperament.

♃ **Jupiter** is our quest for truth, living the belief systems that we hold and walking the path of what those beliefs say about us. It involves an ever-expanding desire to educate the Self through knowledge toward higher law, the adventure and opportunity of being on that road—sometimes literally entailing travel and foreign or international culture, language and/or customs.

♄ **Saturn** is the task master: active when we set a goal or plan then work strongly and steadily toward achieving what we have set out to do. Saturn takes life seriously along the way and can be rather stern, putting on an extra load of responsibility and effort.

⚷ **Chiron** is the "Wounded Healer," relating to what we have brought into this lifetime in order to learn how to fix it, to perfect it, make it the best that it can possibly be! This is where we compete with ourselves to better our own previous score. In addition, it connects to our health-body—physiological and nutritional.

♅ **Uranus** is our capacity to experience "The Revolution," freedom to do things our own way, exhibiting our individual expression or even "Going Rogue" as we blast towards a future collective vision. Uranus inspires individual inclination to "Let me be ME" and connect to an ocean of humanity doing the same.

♆ **Neptune** is the spiritual veil, our connection to our inner psychology and consciousness, leading to the experience of our soul. Psychic presence and mediumship are influenced here too.

E Pluto is transformation, death/rebirth energy—to the extreme. In order for the butterfly to emerge, the caterpillar that it once was must completely give up its life! No going back; burn the bridge down; the volcano of one's own power explodes. Stand upon the mountaintop and catch the lightning bolt in your hand!

Ascendant or Rising Sign: In addition, you must consider the sign of the zodiac that was on the horizon at the moment of your birth. Your Rising sign describes how we relate to the external world and how it relates back to us—what we look like, how others see us and how we see ourselves.

It is the combination of all of these elements that makes us unique among all other persons alive! We are like snowflakes in that way! Sharing a Sun sign is not enough to put you in a singular category. Here's to our greater understanding! Know Yourself!

Melissa Kae Mason, MoonCat! © Mother Tongue Ink 2011

GODDESS PLANETS: CERES, PALLAS, JUNO AND VESTA

"Asteroids" are small planets, located between the inner, personal planets (Sun to Mars) that move more swiftly through the zodiac, and the outer, social and collective planets (Jupiter to Pluto) whose slower movements mark generational shifts. Ceres, Pallas, Juno and Vesta are faces of the Great Goddess who is reawakening in our consciousness now, quickening abilities so urgently needed to solve our many personal, social, ecological and political problems.

♀ Ceres (Goddess of corn and harvest) symbolizes our ability to nourish ourselves and others in a substantial and metaphoric way. As in the Greek myth of Demeter and Persephone, she helps us to let go and die, to understand mother-daughter dynamics, to re-parent ourselves and to educate by our senses.

✳ Juno (Queen of the Gods and of relationships) shows us what kind of committed partnership we long for, our own individual way to find fulfillment in personal and professional partnering. She wants partners to be team-workers, with equal rights and responsibilities.

♀ Pallas (Athena) is a symbol for our creative intelligence and often hints at the sacrifice of women's own creativity or the lack of respect for it. She brings to the fore father-daughter issues, and points to difficulties in linking head, heart and womb.

⚶ Vesta (Vestal Virgin/Fire Priestess) reminds us first and foremost that we belong to ourselves and are allowed to do so! She shows us how to regenerate, to activate our passion, and how to carefully watch over our inner fire in the storms of everyday life.

excerpt Beate Metz © Mother Tongue Ink 2009
See p. 213 for Asteroid Ephemeris

EPHEMERIS 101

A Planetary Ephemeris provides astronomical data showing the daily positions of celestial bodies in our solar system.

The planets have individual and predictable orbits around the sun and pathways through the constellations that correlate with the astrological signs of the Zodiac. This regularity is useful for sky viewing and creating astro charts for a particular date.

The earliest astrologers used these ephemeris tables to calculate individual birth and event charts. These circular maps plot planetary positions and the aspects—angles of relationships—in a "state of the solar system" as a permanent representation of a moment in time. The ephemeris can then be consulted to find when real-time or "transiting" planets will be in the same sign and degree as planets in the birth or event chart. For instance, use the ephemerides to follow the Sun through the houses of your own birth chart, and journal on each day the Sun conjuncts a planet. The sun reveals or sheds light on a sign or house, allowing those qualities to shine and thrive. Ephemerides can also be used to look up dates of past events in your life to learn what planets were highlighted in your chart at that time. In addition, looking up dates for future plans can illuminate beneficial timing of available planetary energies.

Read across from a particular date, ephemerides provide the sign and degree of all the Planets, the Sun and Moon and nodes of the Moon on that day. The lower box on the page offers a quick look at Astro data such as, when a planet changes sign (an ingress occurs), aspects of the outer planets, their retrograde periods and much more. The larger boxes represent two different months as labeled. Signs and Symbols at a Glance (p. 201) is a handy key to the planet, sign and aspects glyphs.

Sandra Pastorius © Mother Tongue Ink 2018

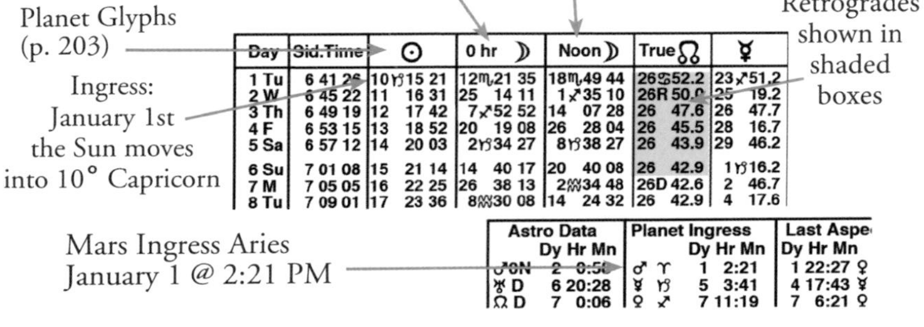

Moon: O hr=Midnight and Noon=12PM

R=Planet Retrogrades shown in shaded boxes

Planet Glyphs (p. 203)

Ingress: January 1st the Sun moves into 10° Capricorn

Day	Sid.Time	☉	0 hr ☽	Noon ☽	True ☊	☿
1 Tu	6 41 25	10♑15 21	12♏21 35	18♏49 44	26♋52.2	23♐51.2
2 W	6 45 22	11 16 31	25 14 11	1♐35 10	26R 50.0	25 19.2
3 Th	6 49 19	12 17 42	7♐52 52	14 07 28	26 47.6	26 47.7
4 F	6 53 15	13 18 52	20 19 08	26 28 04	26 45.5	28 16.7
5 Sa	6 57 12	14 20 03	2♑34 27	8♑38 27	26 43.9	29 46.2
6 Su	7 01 08	15 21 14	14 40 17	20 40 08	26 42.9	1♑16.2
7 M	7 05 05	16 22 25	26 38 13	2♒34 48	26D 42.6	2 46.7
8 Tu	7 09 01	17 23 36	8♒30 08	14 24 32	26 42.9	4 17.6

Mars Ingress Aries January 1 @ 2:21 PM

Astro Data			Planet Ingress		Last Aspe
	Dy Hr Mn			Dy Hr Mn	Dy Hr Mn
♂ON	2 0:50		♂ ♈	1 2:21	1 22:27 ♀
⚷ D	6 20:28		♀ ♐	5 3:41	4 17:43 ⚷
☊ D	7 0:06		♀ ♐	7 11:19	7 6:21 ♀

2023 Planetary Ephemeris

LONGITUDE — January 2023

Day	Sid.Time	☉	0 hr ☽	Noon☽	True☊	☿	♀	♂	⚳	♃	♄	♅	♆	♇
1 Su	6 41 33	10♑16 59	3♉38 16	9♉57 50	11♉45.0	23♑42.1	27♑22.9	9♊04.0	3♎09.3	1♈11.6	22♒25.1	15♉08.9	22♓52.2	27♑39.5
2 M	6 45 30	11 18 08	16 13 36	22 26 01	11R45.1	23R05.8	28 38.0	8R54.8	3 21.9	1 18.9	22 31.1	15R07.8	22 53.2	27 41.4
3 Tu	6 49 26	12 19 16	28 35 33	4♊42 33	11 43.6	22 18.1	29 53.2	8 46.4	3 34.2	1 26.4	22 37.2	15 06.7	22 54.2	27 43.3
4 W	6 53 23	13 20 24	10♊47 26	16 50 28	11 39.5	21 20.0	1♒08.3	8 38.9	3 46.1	1 34.0	22 43.3	15 05.7	22 55.2	27 45.2
5 Th	6 57 19	14 21 32	22 51 58	28 52 09	11 32.6	20 13.0	2 23.4	8 32.2	3 57.8	1 41.8	22 49.5	15 04.8	22 56.3	27 47.1
6 F	7 01 16	15 22 40	4♋51 15	10♋49 27	11 23.0	18 59.0	3 38.5	8 26.3	4 09.1	1 49.7	22 55.7	15 03.9	22 57.4	27 49.0
7 Sa	7 05 13	16 23 48	16 46 55	22 43 47	11 11.1	17 40.3	4 53.6	8 21.3	4 20.2	1 57.8	23 02.0	15 03.1	22 58.5	27 51.0
8 Su	7 09 09	17 24 56	28 40 15	4♌36 26	10 57.9	16 19.7	6 08.7	8 17.0	4 30.9	2 06.0	23 08.3	15 02.3	22 59.7	27 52.9
9 M	7 13 06	18 26 04	10♌32 33	16 28 45	10 44.5	14 59.6	7 23.7	8 13.6	4 41.2	2 14.4	23 14.7	15 01.5	23 00.9	27 54.9
10 Tu	7 17 02	19 27 11	22 25 18	28 22 27	10 31.9	13 42.5	8 38.8	8 11.0	4 51.3	2 22.9	23 21.1	15 00.8	23 02.1	27 56.8
11 W	7 20 59	20 28 18	4♍20 30	10♍19 48	10 21.2	12 30.7	9 53.8	8 09.1	5 00.9	2 31.6	23 27.5	15 00.2	23 03.4	27 58.8
12 Th	7 24 55	21 29 26	16 20 44	22 23 46	10 13.1	11 26.0	11 08.8	8D08.0	5 10.3	2 40.4	23 34.0	14 59.6	23 04.6	28 00.7
13 F	7 28 52	22 30 33	28 29 21	4♎38 01	10 07.8	10 29.5	12 23.8	8 07.8	5 19.3	2 49.4	23 40.5	14 59.0	23 05.9	28 02.7
14 Sa	7 32 48	23 31 40	10♎50 19	17 06 51	10 05.1	9 42.3	13 38.8	8 08.2	5 27.9	2 58.4	23 47.1	14 58.5	23 07.3	28 04.6
15 Su	7 36 45	24 32 47	23 28 10	29 54 52	10D04.4	9 04.7	14 53.7	8 09.5	5 36.2	3 07.7	23 53.7	14 58.1	23 08.6	28 06.6
16 M	7 40 42	25 33 54	6♏27 31	13♏06 37	10R04.6	8 36.9	16 08.7	8 11.5	5 44.1	3 17.0	24 00.4	14 57.7	23 10.0	28 08.6
17 Tu	7 44 38	26 35 01	19 52 35	26 45 46	10 04.3	8 18.6	17 23.6	8 14.2	5 51.6	3 26.5	24 07.1	14 57.4	23 11.5	28 10.5
18 W	7 48 35	27 36 07	3♐46 20	10♐54 18	10 02.4	8D09.4	18 38.6	8 17.7	5 58.7	3 36.1	24 13.8	14 57.1	23 12.9	28 12.5
19 Th	7 52 31	28 37 14	18 09 29	25 31 27	9 58.1	8 09.0	19 53.5	8 21.8	6 05.5	3 45.8	24 20.5	14 56.8	23 14.4	28 14.5
20 F	7 56 28	29 38 20	2♑59 32	10♑32 49	9 50.8	8 16.6	21 08.4	8 26.7	6 11.9	3 55.7	24 27.3	14 56.7	23 15.9	28 16.4
21 Sa	8 00 24	0♒39 26	18 10 10	25 50 15	9 41.0	8 31.7	22 23.2	8 32.3	6 17.9	4 05.7	24 34.2	14 56.5	23 17.4	28 18.4
22 Su	8 04 21	1 40 31	3♒31 36	11♒12 42	9 29.6	8 53.7	23 38.1	8 38.6	6 23.5	4 15.8	24 41.0	14D56.5	23 19.0	28 20.4
23 M	8 08 17	2 41 35	18 52 00	26 28 05	9 17.9	9 21.9	24 52.9	8 45.6	6 28.6	4 26.1	24 47.9	14 56.4	23 20.6	28 22.3
24 Tu	8 12 14	3 42 39	3♓59 39	11♓25 37	9 07.4	9 55.9	26 07.7	8 53.2	6 33.4	4 36.4	24 54.8	14 56.5	23 22.2	28 24.3
25 W	8 16 11	4 43 41	18 45 09	25 57 36	8 59.0	10 34.9	27 22.5	9 01.5	6 37.8	4 46.9	25 01.8	14 56.5	23 23.8	28 26.3
26 Th	8 20 07	5 44 43	3♈02 39	10♈00 10	8 53.5	11 18.7	28 37.3	9 10.4	6 41.7	4 57.5	25 08.8	14 56.7	23 25.5	28 28.2
27 F	8 24 04	6 45 43	16 50 12	23 33 01	8 50.6	12 06.6	29 52.0	9 20.0	6 45.3	5 08.2	25 15.8	14 56.9	23 27.1	28 30.2
28 Sa	8 28 00	7 46 43	0♉08 58	6♉38 33	8 49.7	12 58.4	1♓06.7	9 30.2	6 48.4	5 19.0	25 22.8	14 57.1	23 28.8	28 32.1
29 Su	8 31 57	8 47 41	13 02 17	19 20 47	8 49.7	13 53.6	2 21.4	9 40.9	6 51.1	5 29.9	25 29.8	14 57.4	23 30.6	28 34.1
30 M	8 35 53	9 48 38	25 34 38	1♊44 28	8 49.1	14 52.0	3 36.0	9 52.3	6 53.4	5 40.9	25 36.9	14 57.7	23 32.3	28 36.0
31 Tu	8 39 50	10 49 34	7♊50 53	13 54 25	8 47.0	15 53.3	4 50.7	10 04.2	6 55.2	5 52.0	25 44.0	14 58.1	23 34.1	28 37.9

LONGITUDE — February 2023

Day	Sid.Time	☉	0 hr ☽	Noon☽	True☊	☿	♀	♂	⚳	♃	♄	♅	♆	♇
1 W	8 43 46	11♒50 28	19♊55 38	25♊55 00	8♉42.3	16♑57.2	6♓05.2	10♊16.7	6♎56.6	6♈03.3	25♒51.1	14♉58.6	23♓35.9	28♑39.9
2 Th	8 47 43	12 51 22	1♋52 59	7♋49 58	8R34.6	18 03.4	7 19.8	10 29.7	6 57.6	6 14.6	25 58.2	14 59.1	23 37.7	28 41.8
3 F	8 51 40	13 52 14	13 46 17	19 42 16	8 23.9	19 11.8	8 34.3	10 43.3	6R58.2	6 26.0	26 05.3	14 59.6	23 39.5	28 43.7
4 Sa	8 55 36	14 53 05	25 38 10	1♌34 12	8 10.9	20 22.3	9 48.8	10 57.3	6 58.3	6 37.5	26 12.5	15 00.3	23 41.4	28 45.6
5 Su	8 59 33	15 53 55	7♌30 33	13 27 23	7 56.3	21 34.6	11 03.2	11 11.9	6 58.0	6 49.2	26 19.7	15 00.9	23 43.3	28 47.5
6 M	9 03 29	16 54 43	19 24 51	25 23 06	7 41.3	22 48.6	12 17.6	11 27.0	6 57.3	7 00.9	26 26.9	15 01.6	23 45.2	28 49.4
7 Tu	9 07 26	17 55 31	1♍22 15	7♍22 30	7 27.3	24 04.3	13 32.0	11 42.5	6 56.1	7 12.7	26 34.1	15 02.4	23 47.1	28 51.3
8 W	9 11 22	18 56 17	13 23 59	19 26 55	7 15.2	25 21.4	14 46.4	11 58.6	6 54.5	7 24.6	26 41.3	15 03.2	23 49.0	28 53.2
9 Th	9 15 19	19 57 02	25 31 32	1♎38 06	7 05.8	26 40.0	16 00.7	12 15.0	6 52.4	7 36.5	26 48.5	15 04.1	23 51.0	28 55.0
10 F	9 19 15	20 57 46	7♎46 56	13 58 23	6 59.6	27 59.9	17 14.9	12 32.0	6 49.9	7 48.6	26 55.7	15 05.0	23 52.9	28 56.9
11 Sa	9 23 12	21 58 29	20 12 50	26 30 43	6 56.2	29 21.0	18 29.2	12 49.3	6 47.0	8 00.7	27 02.9	15 06.0	23 54.9	28 58.7
12 Su	9 27 09	22 59 11	2♏52 30	9♏18 40	6D55.0	0♒43.4	19 43.4	13 07.1	6 43.6	8 13.0	27 10.2	15 07.0	23 56.9	29 00.6
13 M	9 31 05	23 59 52	15 49 40	22 25 58	6R55.1	2 07.0	20 57.5	13 25.3	6 39.8	8 25.3	27 17.4	15 08.0	23 59.0	29 02.4
14 Tu	9 35 02	25 00 31	29 08 01	5♐56 11	6 55.2	3 31.6	22 11.6	13 43.9	6 35.6	8 37.7	27 24.7	15 09.2	24 01.0	29 04.2
15 W	9 38 58	26 01 10	12♐50 43	19 51 48	6 54.0	4 57.4	23 25.7	14 02.9	6 30.9	8 50.2	27 31.9	15 10.3	24 03.0	29 06.0
16 Th	9 42 55	27 01 48	26 59 26	4♑13 27	6 50.8	6 24.2	24 39.8	14 22.3	6 25.8	9 02.7	27 39.2	15 11.6	24 05.1	29 07.8
17 F	9 46 51	28 02 24	11♑33 27	18 58 51	6 44.9	7 52.0	25 53.8	14 42.1	6 20.2	9 15.3	27 46.5	15 12.8	24 07.2	29 09.6
18 Sa	9 50 48	29 02 59	26 28 50	4♒02 24	6 36.7	9 20.9	27 07.7	15 02.3	6 14.3	9 28.0	27 53.7	15 14.1	24 09.3	29 11.3
19 Su	9 54 45	0♓03 33	11♒38 20	19 15 19	6 26.8	10 50.7	28 21.7	15 22.8	6 07.9	9 40.8	28 01.0	15 15.5	24 11.4	29 13.1
20 M	9 58 41	1 04 06	26 51 58	4♓26 52	6 16.4	12 21.5	29 35.6	15 43.7	6 01.1	9 53.7	28 08.2	15 16.9	24 13.5	29 14.8
21 Tu	10 02 38	2 04 37	11♓58 42	19 26 14	6 06.9	13 53.3	0♈49.4	16 05.0	5 53.8	10 06.6	28 15.5	15 18.4	24 15.7	29 16.5
22 W	10 06 34	3 05 06	26 48 26	4♈04 29	5 59.3	15 26.0	2 03.2	16 26.6	5 46.2	10 19.6	28 22.7	15 19.9	24 17.8	29 18.2
23 Th	10 10 31	4 05 33	11♈13 44	18 15 49	5 54.2	16 59.8	3 16.9	16 48.5	5 38.2	10 32.6	28 30.0	15 21.5	24 20.0	29 19.9
24 F	10 14 27	5 05 58	25 10 33	1♉57 58	5D51.7	18 34.4	4 30.6	17 10.7	5 29.8	10 45.7	28 37.2	15 23.1	24 22.1	29 21.6
25 Sa	10 18 24	6 06 22	8♉38 14	15 11 42	5 51.2	20 10.1	5 44.2	17 33.3	5 21.1	10 58.9	28 44.4	15 24.7	24 24.3	29 23.2
26 Su	10 22 20	7 06 44	21 38 47	28 00 00	5 51.9	21 46.7	6 57.8	17 56.2	5 11.9	11 12.1	28 51.7	15 26.4	24 26.5	29 24.9
27 M	10 26 17	8 07 04	4♊15 57	10♊27 15	5R52.6	23 24.3	8 11.3	18 19.3	5 02.5	11 25.4	28 58.9	15 28.2	24 28.7	29 26.5
28 Tu	10 30 13	9 07 22	16 34 30	22 38 21	5 52.3	25 02.9	9 24.8	18 42.8	4 52.6	11 38.7	29 06.1	15 29.9	24 30.9	29 28.1

Astro Data

	Dy Hr Mn
☊R	1 15:26
♄⚺♆	6 7:57
♂D	12 20:58
♃0N	13 5:57
☽0S	13 15:34
☊D	15 2:21
☊R	16 6:34
☿D	18 13:13
♅D	22 23:00
☽0N	26 5:33
⚳R	3 19:14
☽0S	9 20:32
☊D	12 7:35
☊R	13 16:10
♀0N	22 2:56

Planet Ingress

		Dy Hr Mn
♀	♒	3 2:11
☉	♒	20 8:31
♀	♓	27 2:34
☿	♒	11 11:23
☉	♓	18 22:35
♀	♈	20 7:57

☽0N22 15:01
☊ D24 18:59
☊ R27 7:58

Last Aspect / ☽ Ingress

Last Aspect Dy Hr Mn		☽ Ingress Dy Hr Mn
2 22:18 ♇ △	♊	3 2:45
5 0:09 ♆ □	♋	5 14:16
7 22:24 ♇ ☍	♌	8 2:41
10 1:54 ♄ ☍	♍	10 15:16
12 23:08 ♇ △	♎	13 2:58
15 8:41 ♇ □	♏	15 12:09
17 14:28 ♇ ⚹	♐	17 17:34
19 10:10 ♄ ⚹	♑	19 19:13
21 15:53 ♇ ☌	♒	21 18:30
23 10:20 ♀ ☌	♓	23 17:37
25 16:13 ♇ ⚹	♈	25 18:49
27 21:02 ♇ □	♉	27 23:44
30 5:53 ♇ △	♊	30 8:36

Last Aspect / ☽ Ingress

Last Aspect Dy Hr Mn		☽ Ingress Dy Hr Mn
1 11:59 ♄ △	♋	1 20:13
4 6:20 ♇ ☍	♌	4 8:50
6 14:17 ♄ ☍	♍	6 21:15
9 6:41 ♇ △	♎	9 8:48
11 16:42 ♇ □	♏	11 18:36
13 23:53 ♇ ⚹	♐	14 1:32
16 1:07 ♄ ⚹	♑	16 5:01
18 4:19 ♇ ☌	♒	18 5:36
20 2:01 ♄ ☌	♓	20 4:57
22 4:07 ♇ ⚹	♈	22 5:15
24 7:23 ♇ □	♉	24 8:30
26 14:44 ♇ △	♊	26 15:49

☽ Phases & Eclipses

Dy Hr Mn	
6 23:09	○ 16♋22
15 2:11	☾ 24♎38
21 20:54	● 1♒33
28 15:20	☽ 8♉26
5 18:30	○ 16♌41
13 16:02	☾ 24♏40
20 7:07	● 1♓22
27 8:07	☽ 8♊27

Astro Data

1 January 2023
Julian Day # 44926
SVP 4♓56'29"
GC 27♐09.6 ⚴ 20♋49.4R
Eris 23♈55.8R ⚵ 24♓34.1
⚷ 11♈58.1 ⚶ 14♓01.2
☽ Mean ☊ 10♉12.1

1 February 2023
Julian Day # 44957
SVP 4♓56'23"
GC 27♐09.7 ⚴ 11♋47.2R
Eris 23♈57.5 ⚵ 9♈05.9
⚷ 12♈38.2 ⚶ 26♓51.8
☽ Mean ☊ 8♉33.7

*Giving the positions of planets daily at midnight, Greenwich Mean Time (0:00 UT)
Each planet's retrograde period is shaded gray.

2023 Planetary Ephemeris

March 2023

LONGITUDE

Day	Sid.Time	☉	0 hr ☽	Noon ☽	True ☊	☿	♀	♂	⚳	♃	♄	♅	♆	♇
1 W	10 34 10	10♓07 38	28♊39 25	4♋38 19	5♉50.3	26♒42.5	10♈38.2	19♊06.6	4♎42.5	11♈52.1	29♒13.2	15♉31.8	24♓33.1	29♑29.7
2 Th	10 38 07	11 07 52	10♋35 35	16 31 46	5R46.0	28 23.1	11 51.6	19 30.6	4R32.0	12 05.6	29 20.4	15 33.7	24 35.4	29 31.3
3 F	10 42 03	12 08 04	22 27 21	28 22 47	5 39.4	0♓04.7	13 04.9	19 54.9	4 21.2	12 19.1	29 27.6	15 35.6	24 37.6	29 32.8
4 Sa	10 46 00	13 08 13	4♌18 27	10♌14 44	5 30.8	1 47.4	14 18.1	20 19.4	4 10.1	12 32.7	29 34.7	15 37.5	24 39.8	29 34.3
5 Su	10 49 56	14 08 21	16 11 54	22 10 14	5 21.1	3 31.2	15 31.3	20 44.3	3 58.7	12 46.3	29 41.8	15 39.6	24 42.1	29 35.9
6 M	10 53 53	15 08 27	28 09 57	4♍11 15	5 10.9	5 16.0	16 44.4	21 09.3	3 47.1	12 59.9	29 48.9	15 41.6	24 44.3	29 37.3
7 Tu	10 57 49	16 08 31	10♍14 16	16 19 10	5 01.3	7 01.9	17 57.4	21 34.6	3 35.1	13 13.6	29 56.0	15 43.7	24 46.6	29 38.8
8 W	11 01 46	17 08 33	22 26 04	28 35 05	4 53.2	8 48.9	19 10.4	22 00.2	3 23.0	13 27.4	0♓03.1	15 45.8	24 48.8	29 40.3
9 Th	11 05 42	18 08 34	4♎46 19	10♎59 55	4 47.0	10 37.0	20 23.3	22 25.9	3 10.6	13 41.1	0 10.1	15 48.0	24 51.1	29 41.7
10 F	11 09 39	19 08 32	17 16 01	23 34 46	4 43.2	12 26.2	21 36.2	22 51.9	2 58.0	13 55.0	0 17.1	15 50.2	24 53.3	29 43.1
11 Sa	11 13 36	20 08 29	29 56 21	6♏20 59	4D41.6	14 16.6	22 49.0	23 18.1	2 45.2	14 08.8	0 24.1	15 52.4	24 55.6	29 44.5
12 Su	11 17 32	21 08 24	12♏48 53	19 20 18	4 41.8	16 08.0	24 01.7	23 44.5	2 32.2	14 22.7	0 31.1	15 54.7	24 57.9	29 45.9
13 M	11 21 29	22 08 17	25 55 29	2♐34 41	4 43.0	18 00.6	25 14.3	24 11.2	2 19.1	14 36.7	0 38.0	15 57.1	25 00.2	29 47.2
14 Tu	11 25 25	23 08 09	9♐18 09	16 06 06	4 44.4	19 54.3	26 26.9	24 38.0	2 05.7	14 50.7	0 44.9	15 59.4	25 02.4	29 48.5
15 W	11 29 22	24 07 59	22 58 41	29 56 01	4R45.1	21 49.0	27 39.4	25 05.1	1 52.3	15 04.7	0 51.8	16 01.8	25 04.7	29 49.9
16 Th	11 33 18	25 07 47	6♑58 06	14♑04 50	4 44.5	23 44.9	28 51.9	25 32.3	1 38.8	15 18.8	0 58.7	16 04.3	25 07.0	29 51.1
17 F	11 37 15	26 07 34	21 15 59	28 31 13	4 42.2	25 41.7	0♉04.3	25 59.7	1 25.1	15 32.8	1 05.5	16 06.8	25 09.3	29 52.4
18 Sa	11 41 11	27 07 19	5♒50 01	13♒11 42	4 38.2	27 39.4	1 16.6	26 27.4	1 11.4	15 47.0	1 12.3	16 09.3	25 11.6	29 53.6
19 Su	11 45 08	28 07 03	20 35 31	28 00 33	4 33.2	29 38.1	2 28.8	26 55.2	0 57.6	16 01.1	1 19.1	16 11.8	25 13.8	29 54.8
20 M	11 49 05	29 06 44	5♓25 48	12♓50 16	4 27.6	1♈37.5	3 41.0	27 23.2	0 43.7	16 15.3	1 25.8	16 14.4	25 16.1	29 56.0
21 Tu	11 53 01	0♈06 24	20 12 54	27 32 43	4 22.5	3 37.5	4 53.0	27 51.4	0 29.8	16 29.5	1 32.5	16 17.0	25 18.4	29 57.2
22 W	11 56 58	1 06 01	4♈48 47	12♈00 19	4 18.5	5 38.1	6 05.0	28 19.7	0 16.0	16 43.8	1 39.2	16 19.7	25 20.6	29 58.3
23 Th	12 00 54	2 05 37	19 06 37	26 07 12	4 16.0	7 38.9	7 17.0	28 48.2	0 02.1	16 58.0	1 45.8	16 22.3	25 22.9	29 59.4
24 F	12 04 51	3 05 10	3♉01 41	9♉49 54	4D15.1	9 39.9	8 28.8	29 16.9	29♍48.3	17 12.3	1 52.4	16 25.1	25 25.2	0♒00.5
25 Sa	12 08 47	4 04 42	16 31 47	23 07 26	4 15.6	11 40.8	9 40.6	29 45.8	29 34.5	17 26.6	1 58.9	16 27.8	25 27.4	0 01.6
26 Su	12 12 44	5 04 11	29 37 05	6♊01 02	4 17.0	13 41.4	10 52.3	0♋14.8	29 20.8	17 40.9	2 05.4	16 30.6	25 29.7	0 02.6
27 M	12 16 40	6 03 38	12♊19 42	18 33 34	4 18.7	15 41.2	12 03.9	0 44.0	29 07.2	17 55.3	2 11.9	16 33.4	25 31.9	0 03.6
28 Tu	12 20 37	7 03 03	24 43 09	0♋49 01	4 20.1	17 40.0	13 15.4	1 13.3	28 53.7	18 09.6	2 18.3	16 36.2	25 34.2	0 04.6
29 W	12 24 34	8 02 25	6♋51 45	12 51 57	4R20.7	19 37.5	14 26.8	1 42.8	28 40.3	18 24.0	2 24.7	16 39.1	25 36.4	0 05.6
30 Th	12 28 30	9 01 45	18 50 14	24 47 10	4 20.3	21 33.2	15 38.1	2 12.4	28 27.1	18 38.4	2 31.0	16 42.0	25 38.7	0 06.5
31 F	12 32 27	10 01 03	0♌43 20	6♌39 17	4 18.7	23 26.8	16 49.3	2 42.1	28 14.1	18 52.8	2 37.3	16 44.9	25 40.9	0 07.4

April 2023

LONGITUDE

Day	Sid.Time	☉	0 hr ☽	Noon ☽	True ☊	☿	♀	♂	⚳	♃	♄	♅	♆	♇
1 Sa	12 36 23	11♈00 18	12♌35 33	18♌32 36	4♉16.1	25♈17.8	18♉00.5	3♋12.0	28♍01.2	19♈07.3	2♓43.5	16♉47.9	25♓43.1	0♒08.3
2 Su	12 40 20	11 59 31	24 30 53	0♍30 49	4R12.8	27 05.9	19 11.5	3 42.0	27R48.5	19 21.7	2 49.7	16 50.8	25 45.3	0 09.2
3 M	12 44 16	12 58 42	6♍32 47	12 37 04	4 09.2	28 50.6	20 22.4	4 12.2	27 36.0	19 36.1	2 55.9	16 53.8	25 47.5	0 10.0
4 Tu	12 48 13	13 57 51	18 43 57	24 53 39	4 05.8	0♉31.6	21 33.2	4 42.5	27 23.7	19 50.6	3 02.0	16 56.9	25 49.7	0 10.8
5 W	12 52 09	14 56 57	1♎06 22	7♎22 13	4 03.0	2 08.5	22 44.0	5 12.9	27 11.7	20 05.0	3 08.0	16 59.9	25 51.9	0 11.6
6 Th	12 56 06	15 56 02	13 41 19	20 03 42	4 01.1	3 41.0	23 54.6	5 43.4	26 59.9	20 19.5	3 14.0	17 03.0	25 54.1	0 12.3
7 F	13 00 02	16 55 04	26 29 26	2♏58 30	4D00.1	5 08.8	25 05.1	6 14.0	26 48.4	20 34.0	3 20.0	17 06.1	25 56.2	0 13.0
8 Sa	13 03 59	17 54 04	9♏30 53	16 06 34	4 00.0	6 31.6	26 15.5	6 44.7	26 37.2	20 48.4	3 25.8	17 09.2	25 58.4	0 13.7
9 Su	13 07 56	18 53 03	22 45 30	29 27 37	4 00.7	7 49.1	27 25.7	7 15.6	26 26.2	21 02.9	3 31.7	17 12.3	26 00.5	0 14.4
10 M	13 11 52	19 52 00	6♐12 52	13♐01 12	4 01.7	9 01.1	28 35.9	7 46.6	26 15.6	21 17.4	3 37.5	17 15.5	26 02.6	0 15.0
11 Tu	13 15 49	20 50 55	19 52 31	26 46 44	4 02.9	10 07.5	29 46.0	8 17.7	26 05.2	21 31.9	3 43.2	17 18.7	26 04.8	0 15.7
12 W	13 19 45	21 49 48	3♑43 45	10♑43 27	4 03.8	11 08.1	0♊55.9	8 48.9	25 55.2	21 46.4	3 48.8	17 21.9	26 06.9	0 16.2
13 Th	13 23 42	22 48 39	17 45 39	24 50 09	4R04.2	12 02.7	2 05.8	9 20.2	25 45.5	22 00.8	3 54.5	17 25.1	26 09.0	0 16.8
14 F	13 27 38	23 47 29	1♒56 44	9♒05 07	4 04.2	12 51.3	3 15.5	9 51.6	25 36.1	22 15.3	4 00.0	17 28.3	26 11.0	0 17.3
15 Sa	13 31 35	24 46 17	16 14 55	23 25 46	4 03.7	13 33.6	4 25.1	10 23.1	25 27.1	22 29.8	4 05.5	17 31.6	26 13.1	0 17.8
16 Su	13 35 32	25 45 04	0♓37 12	7♓48 43	4 02.9	14 09.8	5 34.6	10 54.7	25 18.5	22 44.3	4 10.9	17 34.9	26 15.1	0 18.3
17 M	13 39 28	26 43 48	14 59 47	22 09 48	4 02.0	14 39.7	6 43.9	11 26.4	25 10.2	22 58.7	4 16.3	17 38.2	26 17.2	0 18.7
18 Tu	13 43 25	27 42 31	29 18 13	6♈24 26	4 01.2	15 03.3	7 53.2	11 58.2	25 02.2	23 13.2	4 21.6	17 41.5	26 19.2	0 19.1
19 W	13 47 21	28 41 12	13♈27 53	20 28 03	4 00.6	15 20.6	9 02.3	12 30.1	24 54.7	23 27.6	4 26.8	17 44.8	26 21.2	0 19.5
20 Th	13 51 18	29 39 51	27 24 27	4♉16 40	4D00.4	15 31.8	10 11.3	13 02.1	24 47.6	23 42.1	4 32.0	17 48.1	26 23.2	0 19.9
21 F	13 55 14	0♉38 29	11♉04 24	17 47 23	4 00.4	15R36.9	11 20.1	13 34.2	24 40.8	23 56.5	4 37.1	17 51.5	26 25.2	0 20.2
22 Sa	13 59 11	1 37 04	24 25 28	0♊58 36	4 00.5	15 36.1	12 28.8	14 06.4	24 34.5	24 10.9	4 42.1	17 54.8	26 27.1	0 20.5
23 Su	14 03 07	2 35 37	7♊26 49	13 50 15	4 00.7	15 29.6	13 37.4	14 38.6	24 28.5	24 25.3	4 47.1	17 58.2	26 29.0	0 20.7
24 M	14 07 04	3 34 09	20 09 04	26 23 35	4R00.8	15 17.6	14 45.8	15 11.0	24 23.0	24 39.7	4 52.0	18 01.6	26 31.0	0 21.0
25 Tu	14 11 00	4 32 38	2♋34 09	8♋41 09	4 00.8	15 00.5	15 54.1	15 43.4	24 17.9	24 54.1	4 56.8	18 05.0	26 32.9	0 21.2
26 W	14 14 57	5 31 05	14 45 03	20 46 22	4 00.7	14 38.7	17 02.2	16 16.0	24 13.2	25 08.4	5 01.6	18 08.4	26 34.7	0 21.4
27 Th	14 18 54	6 29 30	26 45 37	2♌43 21	4D00.6	14 12.7	18 10.2	16 48.6	24 08.9	25 22.8	5 06.3	18 11.8	26 36.6	0 21.5
28 F	14 22 50	7 27 53	8♌40 09	14 36 35	4 00.6	13 42.9	19 18.0	17 21.3	24 05.0	25 37.1	5 10.9	18 15.2	26 38.4	0 21.7
29 Sa	14 26 47	8 26 14	20 33 15	26 30 43	4 00.7	13 10.0	20 25.6	17 54.1	24 01.5	25 51.4	5 15.4	18 18.7	26 40.3	0 21.7
30 Su	14 30 43	9 24 33	2♍29 33	8♍30 16	4 01.0	12 34.6	21 33.1	18 26.9	23 58.5	26 05.7	5 19.9	18 22.1	26 42.1	0 21.8

Astro Data Dy Hr Mn	Planet Ingress Dy Hr Mn	Last Aspect Dy Hr Mn	☽ Ingress Dy Hr Mn	Last Aspect Dy Hr Mn	☽ Ingress Dy Hr Mn	☽ Phases & Eclipses Dy Hr Mn	Astro Data
♄⚺♇ 3 22:27	☿ ♓ 2 22:53	1 1:08 ♄ △	♋ 1 2:41	2 6:04 ☿ △	♍ 2 10:58	7 12:42 ○ 16♍40	1 March 2023
☽0S 9 1:55	♄ ♓ 7 13:36	3 14:24 ♇ ☍	♌ 3 15:17	4 13:51 ♆ ☍	♎ 4 21:52	15 2:09 ☾ 24♐13	Julian Day # 44985
☊D 11 8:56	♀ ♉ 16 22:35	6 3:20 ♄ ☍	♍ 6 3:40	6 12:44 ♃ ☍	♏ 7 6:30	21 17:24 ● 0♈50	SVP 4♓56'20"
☊R 15 2:21	☿ ♈ 19 4:25	8 14:08 ♇ △	♎ 8 14:45	9 9:10 ♀ ☍	♐ 9 12:58	29 2:34 ☽ 8♋09	GC 27♐09.8 ⚳ 11♋12.9
♃⚺♅ 19 22:07	☉ ♈ 20 21:26	10 23:38 ♇ □	♏ 11 0:07	11 10:49 ♆ □	♑ 11 17:34		Eris 24♈07.5 ⚵ 24♈01.1
☿0N 20 10:54	⚳ ♍R 23 3:39	13 7:00 ♇ ⚹	♐ 13 7:22	13 14:15 ♆ ⚹	♒ 13 20:43	6 4:36 ○ 16♎07	⚷ 13♈50.8 ⚶ 9♈15.2
☉0N 20 21:26	♇ ♒ 23 12:14	15 8:51 ♀ △	♑ 15 12:07	15 15:17 ☉ ⚹	♓ 15 22:58	13 9:13 ☾ 23♑11	☽ Mean ☊ 7♉04.7
♃∠♄ 21 9:27	♂ ♋ 25 11:46	17 14:15 ♇ ☌	♒ 17 14:26	17 18:58 ♆ ☌	♈ 18 1:10	20 4:14 ● 29♈50	
☽0N 22 1:33		19 10:34 ♂ △	♓ 19 15:13	20 4:14 ☉ ☌	♉ 20 4:31	20 4:17:56 ◐ AT01'16"	1 April 2023
☊D 24 2:10	☿ ♉ 3 16:23	21 15:59 ♇ ⚹	♈ 21 16:02	22 3:42 ♆ ⚹	♊ 22 10:12	27 21:21 ☽ 7♌21	Julian Day # 45016
☊R 29 2:29	♀ ♊ 11 4:48	23 17:14 ♂ ⚹	♉ 23 18:43	24 12:16 ♆ □	♋ 24 19:00		SVP 4♓56'16"
☽0S 5 8:55	☉ ♉ 20 8:15	25 16:20 ♆ ⚹	♊ 26 0:43	26 23:42 ♆ △	♌ 27 6:31		GC 27♐09.8 ⚳ 18♋23.3
☊D 7 13:56		28 1:40 ♆ □	♋ 28 10:23	29 10:54 ♃ △	♍ 29 19:00		Eris 24♈25.3 ⚵ 11♉40.5
☊R 13 9:37		30 13:47 ♆ △	♌ 30 22:32				⚷ 15♈34.5 ⚶ 23♈18.9
☽0N 18 10:57							☽ Mean ☊ 5♉26.2

*Giving the positions of planets daily at midnight, Greenwich Mean Time (0:00 UT)
Each planet's retrograde period is shaded gray.

2023 Planetary Ephemeris

LONGITUDE — May 2023

Day	Sid.Time	☉	0 hr ☽	Noon ☽	True ☊	☿	♀	♂	⚳	♃	♄	♅	♆	♇
1 M	14 34 40	10♉22 49	14♍33 23	20♍39 24	4♉01.6	11♉57.3	22♊40.4	18♋59.8	23♍55.9	26♈19.9	5♓24.3	18♉25.6	26♓43.8	0♒21.8
2 Tu	14 38 36	11 21 04	26 48 44	3♎01 45	4 02.3	11R 19.0	23 47.5	19 32.8	23R 53.7	26 34.1	5 28.6	18 29.0	26 45.6	0R 21.9
3 W	14 42 33	12 19 17	9♎18 47	15 40 05	4 03.0	10 40.1	24 54.5	20 05.9	23 51.9	26 48.3	5 32.8	18 32.5	26 47.3	0 21.8
4 Th	14 46 29	13 17 27	22 05 52	28 36 12	4R 03.6	10 01.6	26 01.2	20 39.0	23 50.5	27 02.5	5 37.0	18 35.9	26 49.0	0 21.8
5 F	14 50 26	14 15 36	5♏11 10	11♏50 40	4 03.8	9 23.9	27 07.8	21 12.2	23 49.6	27 16.6	5 41.1	18 39.4	26 50.7	0 21.7
6 Sa	14 54 23	15 13 44	18 34 37	25 22 48	4 03.5	8 47.9	28 14.1	21 45.4	23D 49.0	27 30.7	5 45.1	18 42.9	26 52.4	0 21.6
7 Su	14 58 19	16 11 49	2♐14 55	9♐10 39	4 02.6	8 14.0	29 20.3	22 18.8	23 48.9	27 44.8	5 49.0	18 46.3	26 54.0	0 21.5
8 M	15 02 16	17 09 53	16 09 35	23 11 18	4 01.2	7 42.8	0♋26.3	22 52.2	23 49.2	27 58.9	5 52.8	18 49.8	26 55.7	0 21.3
9 Tu	15 06 12	18 07 56	0♑15 18	7♑21 08	3 59.4	7 14.8	1 32.0	23 25.6	23 49.9	28 12.9	5 56.6	18 53.3	26 57.3	0 21.1
10 W	15 10 09	19 05 57	14 28 17	21 36 18	3 57.7	6 50.4	2 37.6	23 59.2	23 51.0	28 26.9	6 00.3	18 56.7	26 58.8	0 20.9
11 Th	15 14 05	20 03 57	28 44 43	5♒53 07	3 56.2	6 29.9	3 42.9	24 32.8	23 52.5	28 40.9	6 03.9	19 00.2	27 00.4	0 20.7
12 F	15 18 02	21 01 55	13♒01 07	20 08 22	3D 55.4	6 13.5	4 48.1	25 06.4	23 54.3	28 54.8	6 07.4	19 03.7	27 01.9	0 20.4
13 Sa	15 21 59	21 59 53	27 14 32	4♓19 22	3 55.3	6 01.5	5 53.0	25 40.1	23 56.6	29 08.7	6 10.8	19 07.2	27 03.4	0 20.1
14 Su	15 25 55	22 57 49	11♓22 36	18 24 02	3 56.0	5 54.0	6 57.6	26 13.9	23 59.3	29 22.5	6 14.1	19 10.7	27 04.9	0 19.8
15 M	15 29 52	23 55 43	25 23 27	2♈20 39	3 57.1	5D 51.0	8 02.1	26 47.7	24 02.4	29 36.3	6 17.4	19 14.1	27 06.3	0 19.4
16 Tu	15 33 48	24 53 37	9♈15 28	16 07 43	3 58.5	5 52.7	9 06.3	27 21.6	24 05.8	29 50.1	6 20.6	19 17.6	27 07.8	0 19.0
17 W	15 37 45	25 51 29	22 57 14	29 43 51	3R 59.6	5 59.0	10 10.2	27 55.6	24 09.7	0♉03.8	6 23.6	19 21.0	27 09.2	0 18.6
18 Th	15 41 41	26 49 20	6♉27 23	13♉07 42	3 59.9	6 09.9	11 13.9	28 29.6	24 13.9	0 17.5	6 26.6	19 24.5	27 10.5	0 18.2
19 F	15 45 38	27 47 09	19 44 39	26 18 07	3 59.1	6 25.2	12 17.4	29 03.7	24 18.5	0 31.1	6 29.5	19 28.0	27 11.9	0 17.7
20 Sa	15 49 34	28 44 57	2♊48 01	9♊14 17	3 57.0	6 45.1	13 20.6	29 37.9	24 23.5	0 44.7	6 32.3	19 31.4	27 13.2	0 17.2
21 Su	15 53 31	29 42 44	15 36 53	21 55 53	3 53.8	7 09.2	14 23.5	0♌12.1	24 28.9	0 58.3	6 35.1	19 34.9	27 14.5	0 16.7
22 M	15 57 28	0♊40 30	28 11 20	4♋23 22	3 49.7	7 37.6	15 26.1	0 46.3	24 34.6	1 11.8	6 37.7	19 38.3	27 15.8	0 16.2
23 Tu	16 01 24	1 38 14	10♋32 12	16 38 03	3 45.2	8 10.1	16 28.4	1 20.6	24 40.7	1 25.2	6 40.2	19 41.7	27 17.0	0 15.6
24 W	16 05 21	2 35 56	22 41 15	28 42 09	3 40.7	8 46.6	17 30.5	1 55.0	24 47.1	1 38.6	6 42.7	19 45.1	27 18.2	0 15.0
25 Th	16 09 17	3 33 37	4♌41 08	10♌38 40	3 36.8	9 27.0	18 32.2	2 29.4	24 53.9	1 51.9	6 45.0	19 48.5	27 19.4	0 14.4
26 F	16 13 14	4 31 17	16 35 16	22 31 26	3 34.0	10 11.1	19 33.6	3 03.9	25 01.0	2 05.2	6 47.3	19 51.9	27 20.5	0 13.8
27 Sa	16 17 10	5 28 55	28 27 44	4♍24 46	3D 32.5	10 58.9	20 34.6	3 38.4	25 08.5	2 18.5	6 49.4	19 55.3	27 21.6	0 13.1
28 Su	16 21 07	6 26 31	10♍23 07	16 23 23	3 32.3	11 50.2	21 35.3	4 13.0	25 16.3	2 31.6	6 51.5	19 58.7	27 22.7	0 12.4
29 M	16 25 03	7 24 06	22 26 12	28 32 09	3 33.2	12 45.0	22 35.7	4 47.6	25 24.5	2 44.8	6 53.5	20 02.0	27 23.8	0 11.7
30 Tu	16 29 00	8 21 40	4♎41 48	10♎55 42	3 34.8	13 43.2	23 35.7	5 22.3	25 33.0	2 57.8	6 55.4	20 05.4	27 24.8	0 11.0
31 W	16 32 57	9 19 12	17 14 21	23 38 10	3 36.3	14 44.6	24 35.3	5 57.0	25 41.8	3 10.8	6 57.1	20 08.7	27 25.8	0 10.2

LONGITUDE — June 2023

Day	Sid.Time	☉	0 hr ☽	Noon ☽	True ☊	☿	♀	♂	⚳	♃	♄	♅	♆	♇
1 Th	16 36 53	10♊16 43	0♏07 30	6♏42 38	3♉37.2	15♉49.2	25♋34.5	6♌31.8	25♍50.9	3♉23.7	6♓58.8	20♉12.0	27♓26.8	0♒09.4
2 F	16 40 50	11 14 12	13 23 42	20 10 44	3R 36.9	16 56.9	26 33.3	7 06.6	26 00.3	3 36.6	7 00.4	20 15.4	27 27.7	0R 08.6
3 Sa	16 44 46	12 11 41	27 03 38	4♐02 09	3 34.9	18 07.7	27 31.7	7 41.5	26 10.1	3 49.4	7 01.9	20 18.6	27 28.6	0 07.8
4 Su	16 48 43	13 09 08	11♐05 53	18 14 18	3 31.1	19 21.4	28 29.6	8 16.4	26 20.1	4 02.2	7 03.3	20 21.9	27 29.5	0 06.9
5 M	16 52 39	14 06 35	25 26 45	2♑42 28	3 25.9	20 38.1	29 27.1	8 51.3	26 30.5	4 14.9	7 04.6	20 25.2	27 30.4	0 06.1
6 Tu	16 56 36	15 04 00	10♑00 35	17 20 14	3 19.8	21 57.7	0♌24.2	9 26.3	26 41.1	4 27.5	7 05.8	20 28.4	27 31.2	0 05.2
7 W	17 00 32	16 01 25	24 40 30	2♒00 29	3 13.6	23 20.2	1 20.8	10 01.4	26 52.0	4 40.0	7 06.9	20 31.7	27 32.0	0 04.3
8 Th	17 04 29	16 58 49	9♒19 22	16 36 26	3 08.1	24 45.5	2 16.9	10 36.5	27 03.2	4 52.5	7 08.0	20 34.9	27 32.7	0 03.3
9 F	17 08 26	17 56 13	23 51 01	1♓02 37	3 04.1	26 13.7	3 12.5	11 11.6	27 14.7	5 04.9	7 08.9	20 38.1	27 33.5	0 02.4
10 Sa	17 12 22	18 53 36	8♓10 50	15 15 24	3D 01.9	27 44.6	4 07.6	11 46.8	27 26.5	5 17.3	7 09.7	20 41.2	27 34.1	0 01.4
11 Su	17 16 19	19 50 58	22 16 09	29 13 01	3 01.5	29 18.3	5 02.2	12 22.0	27 38.5	5 29.5	7 10.4	20 44.4	27 34.8	0 00.4
12 M	17 20 15	20 48 20	6♈05 59	12♈55 09	3 02.2	0♊54.7	5 56.2	12 57.3	27 50.8	5 41.7	7 11.0	20 47.5	27 35.4	29♑59.4
13 Tu	17 24 12	21 45 41	19 40 35	26 22 28	3 03.3	2 33.9	6 49.6	13 32.6	28 03.4	5 53.8	7 11.5	20 50.6	27 36.0	29 58.4
14 W	17 28 08	22 43 02	3♉00 54	9♉36 03	3R 03.9	4 15.8	7 42.5	14 07.9	28 16.2	6 05.9	7 12.0	20 53.7	27 36.6	29 57.3
15 Th	17 32 05	23 40 22	16 08 02	22 37 00	3 03.0	6 00.4	8 34.7	14 43.4	28 29.3	6 17.8	7 12.3	20 56.7	27 37.1	29 56.2
16 F	17 36 01	24 37 42	29 03 01	5♊26 11	3 00.2	7 47.7	9 26.4	15 18.8	28 42.6	6 29.7	7 12.5	20 59.8	27 37.6	29 55.1
17 Sa	17 39 58	25 35 02	11♊46 34	18 04 13	2 54.9	9 37.6	10 17.3	15 54.3	28 56.2	6 41.5	7R 12.6	21 02.8	27 38.1	29 54.0
18 Su	17 43 55	26 32 21	24 19 11	0♋31 33	2 47.4	11 30.0	11 07.6	16 29.9	29 10.0	6 53.2	7 12.6	21 05.8	27 38.5	29 52.9
19 M	17 47 51	27 29 39	6♋41 21	12 48 43	2 38.2	13 24.9	11 57.2	17 05.5	29 24.1	7 04.8	7 12.6	21 08.8	27 38.9	29 51.8
20 Tu	17 51 48	28 26 57	18 53 43	24 56 32	2 27.9	15 22.2	12 46.1	17 41.1	29 38.4	7 16.3	7 12.4	21 11.7	27 39.3	29 50.6
21 W	17 55 44	29 24 15	0♌57 21	6♌56 24	2 17.6	17 21.8	13 34.2	18 16.8	29 52.9	7 27.8	7 12.1	21 14.6	27 39.7	29 49.4
22 Th	17 59 41	0♋21 31	12 53 58	18 50 23	2 08.3	19 23.5	14 21.6	18 52.5	0♎07.7	7 39.1	7 11.7	21 17.5	27 40.0	29 48.3
23 F	18 03 37	1 18 47	24 46 02	0♍41 21	2 00.6	21 27.3	15 08.1	19 28.3	0 22.7	7 50.4	7 11.3	21 20.4	27 40.2	29 47.1
24 Sa	18 07 34	2 16 02	6♍36 48	12 32 56	1 55.1	23 32.8	15 53.7	20 04.1	0 37.9	8 01.6	7 10.7	21 23.2	27 40.5	29 45.8
25 Su	18 11 30	3 13 17	18 30 17	24 29 28	1 51.9	25 39.9	16 38.5	20 39.9	0 53.3	8 12.6	7 10.0	21 26.0	27 40.7	29 44.6
26 M	18 15 27	4 10 31	0♎31 06	6♎35 49	1D 50.7	27 48.3	17 22.4	21 15.8	1 09.0	8 23.6	7 09.2	21 28.8	27 40.8	29 43.4
27 Tu	18 19 24	5 07 45	12 44 15	18 57 03	1 50.8	29 57.8	18 05.3	21 51.7	1 24.8	8 34.5	7 08.4	21 31.5	27 41.0	29 42.1
28 W	18 23 20	6 04 57	25 14 50	1♏38 11	1R 51.4	2♋08.0	18 47.2	22 27.7	1 40.9	8 45.2	7 07.4	21 34.2	27 41.1	29 40.8
29 Th	18 27 17	7 02 10	8♏07 36	14 43 32	1 51.4	4 18.8	19 28.1	23 03.7	1 57.1	8 55.9	7 06.4	21 36.9	27 41.2	29 39.5
30 F	18 31 13	7 59 22	21 26 18	28 16 05	1 49.8	6 29.9	20 07.9	23 39.7	2 13.6	9 06.5	7 05.2	21 39.6	27R 41.2	29 38.2

Astro Data

	Dy Hr Mn
♇ R	1 17:10
☽ 0S	2 17:17
♃⚺♆	2 22:05
☊ R	4 21:56
⚳ D	6 19:25
☊ D	12 14:36
☿ D	15 3:18
☽ 0N	15 17:55
☊ R	17 19:36
♃□♇	18 1:12
☊ D	27 15:15
☽ 0S	30 1:50
☊ R	1 6:24
☊ D	10 19:43
☽ 0N	11 22:58

Planet Ingress

		Dy Hr Mn
♀	♋	7 14:26
♃	♉	16 17:21
♂	♌	20 15:33
☉	♊	21 7:10
♀	♌	5 13:48
♇	♑R	11 9:48
☿	♊	11 10:28
⚳	♎	21 11:31
☉	♋	21 14:59
☿	♋	27 0:25

Last Aspect / ☽ Ingress (May)

Last Aspect Dy Hr Mn			☽ Ingress	Dy Hr Mn
1 23:54	♆	☍	♎	2 6:10
4 9:18	♃	☍	♏	4 14:33
6 14:39	♆	△	♐	6 20:05
8 20:29	♃	△	♑	8 23:34
10 23:53	♃	□	♒	11 2:07
13 3:16	♃	⚹	♓	13 4:40
15 2:58	♆	☌	♈	15 7:57
17 9:11	♂	□	♉	17 12:29
19 17:52	♂	⚹	♊	19 18:49
21 22:13	♆	□	♋	22 3:30
24 9:13	♆	△	♌	24 14:36
26 6:39	♅	□	♍	27 3:06
29 9:47	♆	☍	♎	29 14:52
31 14:55	♀	□	♏	31 23:46

Last Aspect / ☽ Ingress (June)

Last Aspect Dy Hr Mn			☽ Ingress	Dy Hr Mn
3 0:52	♀	△	♐	3 5:05
5 3:25	♆	□	♑	5 7:32
7 4:41	♆	⚹	♒	7 8:43
9 4:25	☿	□	♓	9 10:15
11 13:21	♇	⚹	♈	11 13:22
13 18:28	♇	□	♉	13 18:32
16 1:38	♇	△	♊	16 1:47
18 6:25	♆	□	♋	18 10:59
20 21:44	♇	☍	♌	20 22:05
22 17:02	♅	□	♍	23 10:36
25 22:25	♇	△	♎	25 22:58
28 8:20	♇	□	♏	28 8:57
30 14:21	♇	⚹	♐	30 15:01

☽ Phases & Eclipses

Dy Hr Mn	
5 17:35	○ 14♏58
5 17:24	• A 0.963
12 14:29	☾ 21♒37
19 15:54	● 28♉25
27 15:23	☽ 6♍06
4 3:43	○ 13♐18
10 19:33	☾ 19♓40
18 4:38	● 26♊43
26 7:51	☽ 4♎29

Astro Data

1 May 2023
Julian Day # 45046
SVP 4♓56'13"
GC 27♐09.9 ⚴ 29♋18.7
Eris 24♈44.9 ⚵ 29♉17.4
⚷ 17♈18.6 ⚶ 6♉54.7
☽ Mean ☊ 3♉50.9

1 June 2023
Julian Day # 45077
SVP 4♓56'08"
GC 27♐10.0 ⚴ 12♌23.4
Eris 25♈02.5 ⚵ 17♊32.3
⚷ 18♈49.4 ⚶ 20♉39.7
☽ Mean ☊ 2♉12.4

*Giving the positions of planets daily at midnight, Greenwich Mean Time (0:00 UT)
Each planet's retrograde period is shaded gray.

2023 Planetary Ephemeris

July 2023

LONGITUDE

Day	Sid.Time	☉	0 hr ☽	Noon☽	True☊	☿	♀	♂	⚳	♃	♄	♅	♆	♇
1 Sa	18 35 10	8♋56 34	5♐12 57	12♐16 44	1♉46.0	8♋40.9	20♌46.6	24♌15.8	2♎30.2	9♉16.9	7♓04.0	21♉42.2	27♓41.2	29♑36.9
2 Su	18 39 06	9 53 45	19 27 06	26 43 30	1R 39.8	10 51.5	21 24.1	24 51.9	2 47.0	9 27.3	7R 02.6	21 44.8	27R 41.2	29R 35.6
3 M	18 43 03	10 50 56	4♑05 12	11♑31 16	1 31.4	13 01.6	22 00.4	25 28.1	3 04.0	9 37.6	7 01.2	21 47.3	27 41.1	29 34.3
4 Tu	18 47 00	11 48 07	19 00 36	26 32 02	1 21.7	15 10.9	22 35.5	26 04.3	3 21.2	9 47.7	6 59.7	21 49.8	27 41.1	29 33.0
5 W	18 50 56	12 45 18	4♒04 18	11♒36 08	1 11.7	17 19.2	23 09.3	26 40.5	3 38.6	9 57.8	6 58.1	21 52.3	27 40.9	29 31.6
6 Th	18 54 53	13 42 29	19 06 20	26 33 50	1 02.7	19 26.3	23 41.7	27 16.8	3 56.1	10 07.7	6 56.3	21 54.8	27 40.8	29 30.3
7 F	18 58 49	14 39 40	3♓57 41	11♓17 05	0 55.6	21 32.1	24 12.8	27 53.1	4 13.9	10 17.5	6 54.5	21 57.2	27 40.6	29 28.9
8 Sa	19 02 46	15 36 52	18 31 29	25 40 29	0 50.9	23 36.3	24 42.4	28 29.4	4 31.7	10 27.2	6 52.7	21 59.6	27 40.4	29 27.5
9 Su	19 06 42	16 34 03	2♈43 51	9♈41 33	0 48.6	25 39.0	25 10.5	29 05.8	4 49.8	10 36.8	6 50.7	22 01.9	27 40.2	29 26.2
10 M	19 10 39	17 31 16	16 33 39	23 20 20	0D 48.0	27 40.0	25 37.1	29 42.2	5 08.0	10 46.2	6 48.6	22 04.2	27 39.9	29 24.8
11 Tu	19 14 35	18 28 28	0♉01 52	6♉38 33	0R 48.1	29 39.3	26 02.1	0♍18.7	5 26.4	10 55.6	6 46.4	22 06.5	27 39.6	29 23.4
12 W	19 18 32	19 25 41	13 10 45	19 38 49	0 47.7	1♌36.8	26 25.4	0 55.2	5 44.9	11 04.8	6 44.2	22 08.7	27 39.2	29 22.0
13 Th	19 22 29	20 22 55	26 03 07	2♊23 59	0 45.6	3 32.4	26 47.0	1 31.8	6 03.6	11 13.9	6 41.9	22 10.9	27 38.8	29 20.6
14 F	19 26 25	21 20 09	8♊41 44	14 56 40	0 41.1	5 26.3	27 06.9	2 08.4	6 22.5	11 22.9	6 39.4	22 13.1	27 38.4	29 19.2
15 Sa	19 30 22	22 17 24	21 09 02	27 19 03	0 33.7	7 18.2	27 24.9	2 45.0	6 41.5	11 31.7	6 36.9	22 15.2	27 38.0	29 17.8
16 Su	19 34 18	23 14 39	3♋26 54	9♋32 46	0 23.5	9 08.3	27 41.0	3 21.7	7 00.6	11 40.5	6 34.3	22 17.3	27 37.5	29 16.3
17 M	19 38 15	24 11 54	15 36 46	21 39 05	0 11.2	10 56.5	27 55.2	3 58.4	7 19.9	11 49.0	6 31.7	22 19.4	27 37.0	29 14.9
18 Tu	19 42 11	25 09 10	27 39 48	3♌39 06	29♈57.6	12 42.8	28 07.4	4 35.2	7 39.4	11 57.5	6 28.9	22 21.4	27 36.5	29 13.5
19 W	19 46 08	26 06 26	9♌37 06	15 33 59	29 43.8	14 27.3	28 17.5	5 12.0	7 59.0	12 05.8	6 26.1	22 23.3	27 36.0	29 12.1
20 Th	19 50 04	27 03 42	21 29 58	27 25 17	29 31.1	16 09.8	28 25.5	5 48.9	8 18.7	12 14.0	6 23.2	22 25.2	27 35.4	29 10.7
21 F	19 54 01	28 00 59	3♍20 12	9♍15 03	29 20.3	17 50.6	28 31.3	6 25.7	8 38.6	12 22.0	6 20.2	22 27.1	27 34.8	29 09.2
22 Sa	19 57 58	28 58 16	15 10 13	21 06 06	29 12.1	19 29.4	28 34.9	7 02.7	8 58.6	12 29.9	6 17.2	22 29.0	27 34.1	29 07.8
23 Su	20 01 54	29 55 34	27 03 10	3♎01 57	29 06.7	21 06.4	28R 36.2	7 39.6	9 18.7	12 37.7	6 14.0	22 30.8	27 33.4	29 06.4
24 M	20 05 51	0♌52 51	9♎03 00	15 06 53	29 03.9	22 41.5	28 35.2	8 16.6	9 38.9	12 45.3	6 10.8	22 32.5	27 32.7	29 04.9
25 Tu	20 09 47	1 50 09	21 14 15	27 25 42	29 02.9	24 14.7	28 31.8	8 53.7	9 59.3	12 52.8	6 07.5	22 34.2	27 32.0	29 03.5
26 W	20 13 44	2 47 28	3♏41 53	10♏03 26	29 02.8	25 46.1	28 26.1	9 30.8	10 19.8	13 00.1	6 04.2	22 35.9	27 31.2	29 02.1
27 Th	20 17 40	3 44 47	16 30 56	23 04 56	29 02.5	27 15.5	28 17.9	10 07.9	10 40.5	13 07.3	6 00.8	22 37.5	27 30.4	29 00.7
28 F	20 21 37	4 42 06	29 45 53	6♐34 07	29 00.8	28 43.1	28 07.4	10 45.0	11 01.2	13 14.3	5 57.3	22 39.1	27 29.6	28 59.2
29 Sa	20 25 33	5 39 26	13♐29 52	20 33 08	28 56.9	0♍08.7	27 54.4	11 22.2	11 22.1	13 21.2	5 53.8	22 40.6	27 28.8	28 57.8
30 Su	20 29 30	6 36 46	27 43 46	5♑01 23	28 50.6	1 32.4	27 39.1	11 59.5	11 43.0	13 27.9	5 50.2	22 42.1	27 27.9	28 56.4
31 M	20 33 27	7 34 07	12♑25 20	19 54 46	28 41.9	2 54.0	27 21.4	12 36.7	12 04.1	13 34.5	5 46.5	22 43.5	27 27.0	28 55.0

August 2023

LONGITUDE

Day	Sid.Time	☉	0 hr ☽	Noon☽	True☊	☿	♀	♂	⚳	♃	♄	♅	♆	♇
1 Tu	20 37 23	8♌31 28	27♑28 37	5♒05 37	28♈31.7	4♍13.7	27♌01.5	13♍14.1	12♎25.3	13♉40.9	5♓42.8	22♉44.9	27♓26.1	28♑53.6
2 W	20 41 20	9 28 51	12♒44 25	20 23 34	28R 21.2	5 31.3	26R 39.3	13 51.4	12 46.6	13 47.2	5R 39.0	22 46.3	27R 25.1	28R 52.2
3 Th	20 45 16	10 26 14	28 01 38	5♓37 15	28 11.5	6 46.7	26 15.0	14 28.8	13 08.0	13 53.3	5 35.2	22 47.6	27 24.1	28 50.8
4 F	20 49 13	11 23 38	13♓09 11	20 36 25	28 03.8	8 00.0	25 48.6	15 06.2	13 29.5	13 59.2	5 31.3	22 48.8	27 23.1	28 49.4
5 Sa	20 53 09	12 21 03	27 58 06	5♈13 37	27 58.6	9 11.0	25 20.3	15 43.7	13 51.2	14 05.0	5 27.3	22 50.1	27 22.1	28 48.0
6 Su	20 57 06	13 18 29	12♈22 34	19 24 47	27 55.9	10 19.8	24 50.3	16 21.2	14 12.9	14 10.6	5 23.3	22 51.2	27 21.0	28 46.7
7 M	21 01 02	14 15 56	26 20 13	3♉09 03	27D 55.2	11 26.1	24 18.6	16 58.7	14 34.7	14 16.1	5 19.3	22 52.3	27 19.9	28 45.3
8 Tu	21 04 59	15 13 25	9♉51 32	16 28 01	27R 55.3	12 29.9	23 45.5	17 36.3	14 56.6	14 21.4	5 15.2	22 53.4	27 18.8	28 43.9
9 W	21 08 56	16 10 55	22 58 57	29 24 46	27 55.2	13 31.1	23 11.2	18 14.0	15 18.6	14 26.5	5 11.1	22 54.4	27 17.7	28 42.6
10 Th	21 12 52	17 08 26	5♊45 58	12♊03 02	27 53.8	14 29.7	22 35.9	18 51.6	15 40.7	14 31.4	5 06.9	22 55.4	27 16.6	28 41.2
11 F	21 16 49	18 05 59	18 16 25	24 26 36	27 50.1	15 25.3	21 59.7	19 29.4	16 02.9	14 36.2	5 02.7	22 56.3	27 15.4	28 39.9
12 Sa	21 20 45	19 03 34	0♋33 58	6♋38 56	27 43.9	16 18.0	21 22.9	20 07.1	16 25.2	14 40.8	4 58.5	22 57.2	27 14.2	28 38.6
13 Su	21 24 42	20 01 09	12 41 50	18 42 59	27 35.1	17 07.6	20 45.7	20 44.9	16 47.6	14 45.2	4 54.2	22 58.0	27 13.0	28 37.3
14 M	21 28 38	20 58 46	24 42 39	0♌41 05	27 24.3	17 53.9	20 08.5	21 22.8	17 10.0	14 49.4	4 49.9	22 58.8	27 11.7	28 36.0
15 Tu	21 32 35	21 56 24	6♌38 31	12 35 08	27 12.2	18 36.7	19 31.3	22 00.7	17 32.6	14 53.5	4 45.5	22 59.5	27 10.5	28 34.7
16 W	21 36 31	22 54 04	18 31 08	24 26 42	27 00.1	19 15.9	18 54.5	22 38.6	17 55.2	14 57.4	4 41.1	23 00.2	27 09.2	28 33.4
17 Th	21 40 28	23 51 44	0♍22 02	6♍17 19	26 48.8	19 51.2	18 18.2	23 16.6	18 18.0	15 01.0	4 36.7	23 00.9	27 07.9	28 32.2
18 F	21 44 25	24 49 26	12 12 46	18 08 38	26 39.2	20 22.4	17 42.7	23 54.6	18 40.8	15 04.5	4 32.3	23 01.4	27 06.6	28 30.9
19 Sa	21 48 21	25 47 09	24 05 11	0♎02 44	26 32.1	20 49.3	17 08.2	24 32.6	19 03.7	15 07.9	4 27.8	23 02.0	27 05.2	28 29.7
20 Su	21 52 18	26 44 53	6♎01 37	12 02 13	26 27.5	21 11.7	16 35.0	25 10.7	19 26.6	15 11.0	4 23.3	23 02.4	27 03.8	28 28.4
21 M	21 56 14	27 42 39	18 04 59	24 10 21	26D 25.3	21 29.3	16 03.1	25 48.9	19 49.7	15 13.9	4 18.9	23 02.9	27 02.5	28 27.2
22 Tu	22 00 11	28 40 26	0♏18 50	6♏30 58	26 25.0	21 41.9	15 32.9	26 27.1	20 12.8	15 16.7	4 14.4	23 03.3	27 01.1	28 26.0
23 W	22 04 07	29 38 13	12 47 16	19 08 18	26 25.8	21R 49.2	15 04.3	27 05.3	20 36.0	15 19.3	4 09.8	23 03.6	26 59.7	28 24.9
24 Th	22 08 04	0♍36 02	25 34 37	2♐06 43	26R 26.5	21 51.0	14 37.7	27 43.6	20 59.3	15 21.6	4 05.3	23 03.9	26 58.2	28 23.7
25 F	22 12 00	1 33 53	8♐45 04	15 30 04	26 26.4	21 47.2	14 13.0	28 21.9	21 22.6	15 23.8	4 00.8	23 04.1	26 56.8	28 22.5
26 Sa	22 15 57	2 31 44	22 21 59	29 21 00	26 24.6	21 37.6	13 50.5	29 00.2	21 46.0	15 25.8	3 56.2	23 04.3	26 55.3	28 21.4
27 Su	22 19 54	3 29 37	6♑27 05	13♑40 03	26 20.8	21 22.0	13 30.1	29 38.6	22 09.5	15 27.6	3 51.7	23 04.4	26 53.8	28 20.3
28 M	22 23 50	4 27 31	20 59 30	28 24 48	26 15.1	21 00.5	13 12.0	0♎17.1	22 33.0	15 29.2	3 47.2	23 04.5	26 52.4	28 19.2
29 Tu	22 27 47	5 25 26	5♒55 08	13♒29 26	26 08.0	20 33.0	12 56.3	0 55.5	22 56.6	15 30.6	3 42.6	23R 04.5	26 50.8	28 18.1
30 W	22 31 43	6 23 23	21 06 31	28 45 03	26 00.5	19 59.6	12 42.9	1 34.0	23 20.3	15 31.8	3 38.1	23 04.5	26 49.3	28 17.1
31 Th	22 35 40	7 21 21	6♓23 40	14♓00 58	25 53.6	19 20.7	12 31.9	2 12.6	23 44.0	15 32.8	3 33.5	23 04.4	26 47.8	28 16.0

Astro Data	Planet Ingress	Last Aspect	☽ Ingress	Last Aspect	☽ Ingress	☽ Phases & Eclipses	Astro Data
Dy Hr Mn	Dy Hr Mn	Dy Hr Mn	Dy Hr Mn	Dy Hr Mn	Dy Hr Mn	Dy Hr Mn	
☽0N 9 4:01	♂ ♍ 10 11:41	2 13:34 ♆ □	♑ 2 17:21	1 2:14 ♇ ☌	♒ 1 3:59	3 11:40 ○ 11♑19	1 July 2023
☊D 10 1:58	☿ ♌ 11 4:12	4 16:47 ♇ ☌	♒ 4 17:31	2 21:17 ♀ ☍	♓ 3 3:07	10 1:49 ☾ 17♈36	Julian Day # 45107
☊R 11 1:23	☊ ♈R 17 19:47	6 13:43 ♂ ☍	♓ 6 17:34	5 1:22 ♇ ⚹	♈ 5 3:20	17 18:33 ● 24♋56	SVP 4♓56'02"
♃∠♆ 22 11:48	☉ ♌ 23 1:52	8 18:23 ♇ ⚹	♈ 8 19:20	7 4:14 ♇ □	♉ 7 6:26	25 22:08 ☽ 2♏43	GC 27♐10.0 ⚴ 25♌47.0
♀R 23 1:34	☿ ♍ 28 21:32	10 23:12 ☿ □	♉ 10 23:57	9 10:40 ♇ △	♊ 9 13:06		Eris 25♈13.2 ⚵ 4♋51.8
☽0S 23 15:31		13 6:12 ♇ △	♊ 13 7:27	11 17:28 ♆ □	♋ 11 22:53	1 18:33 ○ 9♒16	⚷ 19♈44.6 ⚶ 3♊24.6
☽0N 5 11:00	☉ ♍ 23 9:02	15 12:37 ♆ □	♋ 15 17:15	14 7:48 ♇ ☍	♌ 14 10:37	8 10:30 ☾ 15♉39	☽Mean ☊ 0♉37.1
☊D 7 2:48	♂ ♎ 27 13:21	18 3:07 ♇ ☍	♌ 18 4:41	16 9:39 ☉ ☌	♍ 16 23:15	16 9:39 ● 23♌17	
☊R 8 10:37		20 14:10 ♀ ☌	♍ 20 17:14	19 8:52 ♇ △	♎ 19 11:55	24 9:58 ☽ 1♐00	1 August 2023
⚳0S 9 20:31		23 4:07 ♇ △	♎ 23 5:55	21 20:32 ☉ ⚹	♏ 21 23:23	31 1:37 ○ 7♓25	Julian Day # 45138
☽0S 19 20:47		25 15:06 ♇ □	♏ 25 16:56	24 5:11 ♇ ⚹	♐ 24 8:09		SVP 4♓55'56"
☿0S 21 3:28		27 22:37 ♇ ⚹	♐ 28 0:25	26 11:57 ♂ □	♑ 26 13:06		GC 27♐10.1 ⚴ 9♍55.7
☊D 21 16:26	♅ R29 2:40	29 23:52 ♀ △	♑ 30 3:45	28 11:50 ♇ ☌	♒ 28 14:33		Eris 25♈15.1R ⚵ 22♋05.7
☿R 23 20:01	♂0S29 22:10			30 3:05 ♅ □	♓ 30 13:58		⚷ 19♈56.0R ⚶ 15♊37.9
☊R 24 9:49	☿0N30 18:51						☽Mean ☊ 28♈58.6

*Giving the positions of planets daily at midnight, Greenwich Mean Time (0:00 UT)
Each planet's retrograde period is shaded gray.

2023 Planetary Ephemeris

LONGITUDE — September 2023

Day	Sid.Time	☉	0 hr ☽	Noon ☽	True☊	☿	♀	♂	⚳	♃	♄	♅	♆	♇
1 F	22 39 36	8♍19 20	21♓35 37	29♓06 27	25♈48.2	18♍36.7	12♌23.4	2♎51.2	24♎07.8	15♉33.6	3♓29.0	23♉04.3	26♓46.3	28♑15.0
2 Sa	22 43 33	9 17 21	6♈32 25	13♈52 41	25R44.7	17R48.0	12R17.3	3 29.8	24 31.7	15 34.2	3R24.5	23R04.1	26R44.7	28R14.0
3 Su	22 47 29	10 15 24	21 06 36	28 13 46	25D43.2	16 55.5	12 13.6	4 08.5	24 55.6	15 34.7	3 20.0	23 03.9	26 43.1	28 13.0
4 M	22 51 26	11 13 29	5♉13 57	12♉07 06	25 43.4	15 59.9	12D12.2	4 47.2	25 19.5	15R34.9	3 15.5	23 03.6	26 41.6	28 12.1
5 Tu	22 55 23	12 11 36	18 53 20	25 32 55	25 44.6	15 02.4	12 13.3	5 26.0	25 43.6	15 34.9	3 11.1	23 03.3	26 40.0	28 11.1
6 W	22 59 19	13 09 45	2♊06 11	8♊33 34	25R45.9	14 04.0	12 16.6	6 04.8	26 07.6	15 34.7	3 06.6	23 03.0	26 38.4	28 10.2
7 Th	23 03 16	14 07 56	14 55 33	21 12 39	25 46.4	13 06.0	12 22.3	6 43.7	26 31.8	15 34.3	3 02.2	23 02.5	26 36.8	28 09.3
8 F	23 07 12	15 06 09	27 25 23	3♋34 19	25 45.5	12 09.6	12 30.2	7 22.6	26 56.0	15 33.8	2 57.8	23 02.1	26 35.2	28 08.4
9 Sa	23 11 09	16 04 24	9♋39 59	15 42 52	25 43.0	11 16.3	12 40.2	8 01.6	27 20.2	15 33.0	2 53.4	23 01.6	26 33.5	28 07.6
10 Su	23 15 05	17 02 41	21 43 28	27 42 14	25 38.7	10 27.3	12 52.4	8 40.6	27 44.5	15 32.0	2 49.1	23 01.0	26 31.9	28 06.7
11 M	23 19 02	18 01 00	3♌39 37	9♌35 58	25 33.0	9 43.8	13 06.7	9 19.6	28 08.9	15 30.8	2 44.8	23 00.4	26 30.3	28 05.9
12 Tu	23 22 58	18 59 21	15 31 41	21 27 04	25 26.5	9 06.8	13 22.9	9 58.7	28 33.3	15 29.4	2 40.5	22 59.7	26 28.7	28 05.2
13 W	23 26 55	19 57 44	27 22 24	3♍17 58	25 19.7	8 37.3	13 41.1	10 37.9	28 57.8	15 27.8	2 36.2	22 59.0	26 27.0	28 04.4
14 Th	23 30 52	20 56 09	9♍14 01	15 10 46	25 13.5	8 16.0	14 01.1	11 17.1	29 22.3	15 26.0	2 32.0	22 58.2	26 25.4	28 03.6
15 F	23 34 48	21 54 36	21 08 27	27 07 16	25 08.4	8D03.6	14 23.0	11 56.3	29 46.8	15 24.0	2 27.9	22 57.4	26 23.7	28 02.9
16 Sa	23 38 45	22 53 04	3♎07 26	9♎09 11	25 04.7	8 00.3	14 46.7	12 35.6	0♏11.4	15 21.8	2 23.7	22 56.6	26 22.1	28 02.2
17 Su	23 42 41	23 51 35	15 12 44	21 18 20	25D02.7	8 06.4	15 12.0	13 14.9	0 36.1	15 19.4	2 19.7	22 55.7	26 20.4	28 01.6
18 M	23 46 38	24 50 07	27 26 16	3♏36 49	25 02.3	8 22.0	15 38.9	13 54.3	1 00.8	15 16.8	2 15.6	22 54.7	26 18.7	28 00.9
19 Tu	23 50 34	25 48 41	9♏50 18	16 07 02	25 03.1	8 47.0	16 07.5	14 33.7	1 25.5	15 14.0	2 11.7	22 53.7	26 17.1	28 00.3
20 W	23 54 31	26 47 17	22 27 23	28 51 42	25 04.6	9 21.0	16 37.6	15 13.2	1 50.3	15 11.1	2 07.7	22 52.7	26 15.4	27 59.7
21 Th	23 58 27	27 45 54	5♐20 21	11♐53 40	25 06.2	10 03.8	17 09.1	15 52.7	2 15.1	15 07.9	2 03.9	22 51.6	26 13.8	27 59.1
22 F	0 02 24	28 44 34	18 32 00	25 15 37	25R07.4	10 54.9	17 42.1	16 32.2	2 40.0	15 04.5	2 00.1	22 50.5	26 12.1	27 58.6
23 Sa	0 06 21	29 43 14	2♑04 46	8♑59 33	25 07.7	11 53.7	18 16.4	17 11.8	3 04.8	15 01.0	1 56.3	22 49.3	26 10.4	27 58.1
24 Su	0 10 17	0♎41 57	16 00 03	23 06 11	25 07.0	12 59.7	18 52.0	17 51.5	3 29.8	14 57.3	1 52.6	22 48.1	26 08.8	27 57.6
25 M	0 14 14	1 40 41	0♒17 42	7♒34 15	25 05.1	14 12.2	19 28.9	18 31.2	3 54.7	14 53.3	1 49.0	22 46.8	26 07.1	27 57.1
26 Tu	0 18 10	2 39 27	14 55 18	22 20 09	25 02.6	15 30.5	20 07.1	19 10.9	4 19.8	14 49.2	1 45.4	22 45.5	26 05.5	27 56.7
27 W	0 22 07	3 38 15	29 47 59	7♓17 48	24 59.7	16 54.1	20 46.4	19 50.7	4 44.8	14 44.9	1 41.9	22 44.1	26 03.9	27 56.3
28 Th	0 26 03	4 37 04	14♓48 35	22 19 12	24 57.0	18 22.2	21 26.9	20 30.5	5 09.9	14 40.5	1 38.5	22 42.7	26 02.2	27 55.9
29 F	0 30 00	5 35 55	29 48 32	7♈15 30	24 54.9	19 54.3	22 08.5	21 10.4	5 34.9	14 35.8	1 35.1	22 41.3	26 00.6	27 55.6
30 Sa	0 33 56	6 34 49	14♈39 04	21 58 21	24D53.8	21 29.7	22 51.2	21 50.3	6 00.1	14 31.0	1 31.8	22 39.8	25 59.0	27 55.2

LONGITUDE — October 2023

Day	Sid.Time	☉	0 hr ☽	Noon ☽	True☊	☿	♀	♂	⚳	♃	♄	♅	♆	♇
1 Su	0 37 53	7♎33 44	29♈12 33	6♉21 05	24♈53.6	23♍07.9	23♌34.9	22♎30.3	6♏25.2	14♉26.1	1♓28.5	22♉38.3	25♓57.3	27♑54.9
2 M	0 41 50	8 32 41	13♉23 30	20 19 29	24 54.2	24 48.4	24 19.5	23 10.3	6 50.4	14R20.9	1R25.4	22R36.8	25R55.7	27R54.7
3 Tu	0 45 46	9 31 41	27 08 56	3♊51 51	24 55.3	26 30.7	25 05.2	23 50.3	7 15.7	14 15.6	1 22.3	22 35.2	25 54.1	27 54.4
4 W	0 49 43	10 30 43	10♊28 23	16 58 48	24 56.5	28 14.5	25 51.8	24 30.4	7 40.9	14 10.1	1 19.3	22 33.5	25 52.5	27 54.2
5 Th	0 53 39	11 29 47	23 23 27	29 42 46	24 57.6	29 59.3	26 39.3	25 10.6	8 06.2	14 04.5	1 16.4	22 31.9	25 50.9	27 54.0
6 F	0 57 36	12 28 54	5♋57 13	12♋07 19	24R58.2	1♎44.9	27 27.6	25 50.8	8 31.5	13 58.7	1 13.5	22 30.2	25 49.4	27 53.9
7 Sa	1 01 32	13 28 03	18 13 38	24 16 44	24 58.2	3 31.0	28 16.8	26 31.1	8 56.8	13 52.8	1 10.8	22 28.4	25 47.8	27 53.8
8 Su	1 05 29	14 27 14	0♌17 10	6♌15 31	24 57.7	5 17.3	29 06.7	27 11.4	9 22.2	13 46.7	1 08.1	22 26.6	25 46.2	27 53.7
9 M	1 09 25	15 26 28	12 12 19	18 08 05	24 56.8	7 03.8	29 57.4	27 51.7	9 47.6	13 40.4	1 05.5	22 24.8	25 44.7	27 53.6
10 Tu	1 13 22	16 25 43	24 03 21	29 58 34	24 55.7	8 50.2	0♍48.9	28 32.1	10 13.0	13 34.1	1 03.0	22 23.0	25 43.2	27 53.5
11 W	1 17 19	17 25 01	5♍54 11	11♍50 37	24 54.6	10 36.3	1 41.1	29 12.6	10 38.5	13 27.5	1 00.5	22 21.1	25 41.7	27D53.5
12 Th	1 21 15	18 24 22	17 48 13	23 47 21	24 53.6	12 22.2	2 34.0	29 53.1	11 03.9	13 20.9	0 58.2	22 19.2	25 40.1	27 53.5
13 F	1 25 12	19 23 44	29 48 18	5♎51 19	24 52.9	14 07.6	3 27.5	0♏33.7	11 29.4	13 14.1	0 55.9	22 17.2	25 38.7	27 53.6
14 Sa	1 29 08	20 23 08	11♎56 40	18 04 32	24 52.5	15 52.6	4 21.7	1 14.3	11 54.9	13 07.2	0 53.8	22 15.2	25 37.2	27 53.6
15 Su	1 33 05	21 22 35	24 15 06	0♏28 30	24D52.3	17 37.1	5 16.5	1 54.9	12 20.5	13 00.2	0 51.7	22 13.2	25 35.7	27 53.7
16 M	1 37 01	22 22 03	6♏44 53	13 04 22	24 52.4	19 21.0	6 11.9	2 35.6	12 46.0	12 53.1	0 49.7	22 11.1	25 34.3	27 53.9
17 Tu	1 40 58	23 21 34	19 27 02	25 52 59	24 52.5	21 04.3	7 07.8	3 16.4	13 11.6	12 45.9	0 47.8	22 09.1	25 32.8	27 54.0
18 W	1 44 54	24 21 07	2♐22 18	8♐55 05	24R52.6	22 47.0	8 04.4	3 57.2	13 37.2	12 38.5	0 46.1	22 07.0	25 31.4	27 54.2
19 Th	1 48 51	25 20 41	15 31 22	22 11 14	24 52.6	24 29.1	9 01.4	4 38.0	14 02.8	12 31.1	0 44.4	22 04.8	25 30.0	27 54.4
20 F	1 52 47	26 20 17	28 54 43	5♑41 53	24 52.5	26 10.5	9 59.0	5 18.9	14 28.4	12 23.6	0 42.8	22 02.7	25 28.7	27 54.7
21 Sa	1 56 44	27 19 56	12♑32 44	19 27 14	24 52.4	27 51.4	10 57.1	5 59.9	14 54.0	12 16.0	0 41.3	22 00.5	25 27.3	27 55.0
22 Su	2 00 41	28 19 35	26 25 21	3♒26 58	24D52.3	29 31.6	11 55.7	6 40.9	15 19.7	12 08.3	0 39.9	21 58.3	25 26.0	27 55.3
23 M	2 04 37	29 19 17	10♒31 55	17 40 00	24 52.4	1♏11.2	12 54.7	7 21.9	15 45.3	12 00.6	0 38.6	21 56.1	25 24.7	27 55.6
24 Tu	2 08 34	0♏19 00	24 50 52	2♓04 10	24 52.7	2 50.2	13 54.2	8 03.0	16 11.0	11 52.7	0 37.4	21 53.8	25 23.4	27 56.0
25 W	2 12 30	1 18 44	9♓19 26	16 36 08	24 53.2	4 28.6	14 54.2	8 44.2	16 36.7	11 44.9	0 36.3	21 51.6	25 22.1	27 56.4
26 Th	2 16 27	2 18 31	23 53 38	1♈11 16	24 53.8	6 06.4	15 54.5	9 25.3	17 02.4	11 36.9	0 35.3	21 49.3	25 20.8	27 56.8
27 F	2 20 23	3 18 19	8♈28 20	15 44 06	24 54.4	7 43.7	16 55.4	10 06.6	17 28.1	11 29.0	0 34.4	21 46.9	25 19.6	27 57.3
28 Sa	2 24 20	4 18 09	22 57 48	0♉08 44	24R54.7	9 20.4	17 56.6	10 47.9	17 53.8	11 20.9	0 33.6	21 44.6	25 18.4	27 57.7
29 Su	2 28 16	5 18 01	7♉16 13	14 19 38	24 54.5	10 56.6	18 58.2	11 29.2	18 19.5	11 12.9	0 32.9	21 42.3	25 17.2	27 58.2
30 M	2 32 13	6 17 54	21 18 29	28 12 19	24 53.7	12 32.3	20 00.2	12 10.6	18 45.2	11 04.8	0 32.3	21 39.9	25 16.1	27 58.8
31 Tu	2 36 10	7 17 50	5♊00 49	11♊43 47	24 52.3	14 07.5	21 02.6	12 52.0	19 10.9	10 56.7	0 31.8	21 37.5	25 14.9	27 59.3

Astro Data	Dy Hr Mn
☽0N	1 20:26
☊D	3 7:47
♀D	4 1:21
♃R	4 14:12
☊R	6 22:33
☿D	15 20:22
☽0S	16 2:18
☊D	17 19:21
☊R	22 19:31
☉0S	23 6:51
☽0N	29 7:12
☊D	30 16:53
☊R	6 14:11
☿0S	7 9:37
♇D	11 1:12

Planet Ingress	Dy Hr Mn
⚳ ♏	15 12:51
☉ ♎	23 6:51
☿ ♎	5 0:10
♀ ♍	9 1:12
♂ ♏	12 4:05
☿ ♏	22 6:50
☉ ♏	23 16:22
☽0S13	8:55
☊D15	1:26
☊R18	12:50
☊D22	2:44
☽0N26	17:08
☊R28	3:11

Last Aspect Dy Hr Mn		☽ Ingress	Dy Hr Mn
1 10:37	♇ ⚹	♈	1 13:26
3 11:58	♇ □	♉	3 15:01
5 16:47	♇ △	♊	5 20:08
7 22:23	♆ □	♋	8 5:01
10 12:48	♇ ☍	♌	10 16:37
12 15:07	♅ □	♍	13 5:19
15 13:51	♇ △	♎	15 17:46
18 1:07	♇ □	♏	18 4:59
20 10:23	♇ ⚹	♐	20 14:07
22 19:33	☉ □	♑	22 20:21
24 20:07	♇ ☌	♒	24 23:31
26 12:40	♅ □	♓	27 0:19
28 20:59	♇ ⚹	♈	29 0:18

Last Aspect Dy Hr Mn		☽ Ingress	Dy Hr Mn
30 21:51	♇ □	♉	1 1:19
3 1:21	♇ △	♊	3 5:04
5 6:36	♀ ⚹	♋	5 12:33
7 19:13	♇ ☍	♌	7 23:26
10 9:38	♂ ⚹	♍	10 12:03
12 20:12	♇ △	♎	13 0:23
15 7:02	♇ □	♏	15 11:05
17 15:45	♇ ⚹	♐	17 19:38
19 19:03	☉ ⚹	♑	20 1:56
22 6:02	☿ □	♒	22 6:07
23 19:05	♅ □	♓	24 8:34
26 6:40	♇ ⚹	♈	26 10:03
28 8:21	♇ □	♉	28 11:45
30 11:37	♇ △	♊	30 15:09

☽ Phases & Eclipses Dy Hr Mn	
6 22:22	☾ 14♊04
15 1:41	● 21♍59
22 19:33	☽ 29♐32
29 9:59	○ 6♈00
6 13:49	☾ 13♋03
14 17:56	● 21♎08
14 18:00:41	● A 05'17"
22 3:31	☽ 28♑28
28 20:25	○ 5♉09
28 20:15	● P 0.122

Astro Data

1 September 2023
Julian Day # 45169
SVP 4♓55'52"
GC 27♐10.2 ⚴ 24♍10.3
Eris 25♈07.2R ⚵ 8♌20.2
⚷ 19♈18.9R ⚶ 26♊15.8
☽ Mean ☊ 27♈20.1

1 October 2023
Julian Day # 45199
SVP 4♓55'49"
GC 27♐10.3 ⚴ 7♎55.0
Eris 24♈52.4R ⚵ 22♌45.6
⚷ 18♈08.6R ⚶ 3♋59.2
☽ Mean ☊ 25♈44.8

*Giving the positions of planets daily at midnight, Greenwich Mean Time (0:00 UT)
Each planet's retrograde period is shaded gray.

2023 PLANETARY EPHEMERIS

November 2023

LONGITUDE

Day	Sid.Time	☉	0 hr ☽	Noon ☽	True ☊	☿	♀	♂	⚳	♃	♄	♅	♆	♇
1 W	2 40 06	8♏17 48	18♊21 09	24♊52 56	24♈50.5	15♏42.2	22♍05.4	13♏33.5	19♏36.7	10♉48.5	0♓31.4	21♉35.1	25♓13.8	27♑59.9
2 Th	2 44 03	9 17 48	1♋19 16	7♋40 23	24R 48.6	17 16.4	23 08.5	14 15.0	20 02.4	10R 40.4	0R 31.1	21R 32.7	25R 12.7	28 00.6
3 F	2 47 59	10 17 50	13 56 36	20 08 19	24 46.7	18 50.3	24 11.9	14 56.6	20 28.2	10 32.2	0 30.9	21 30.3	25 11.7	28 01.2
4 Sa	2 51 56	11 17 55	26 16 00	2♌20 09	24 45.3	20 23.6	25 15.7	15 38.3	20 53.9	10 24.1	0D 30.8	21 27.8	25 10.6	28 01.9
5 Su	2 55 52	12 18 01	8♌21 20	14 20 07	24D 44.6	21 56.6	26 19.9	16 20.0	21 19.7	10 15.9	0 30.8	21 25.4	25 09.6	28 02.6
6 M	2 59 49	13 18 09	20 17 06	26 12 55	24 44.7	23 29.2	27 24.3	17 01.7	21 45.4	10 07.8	0 31.0	21 22.9	25 08.6	28 03.4
7 Tu	3 03 45	14 18 20	2♍08 08	8♍03 24	24 45.6	25 01.4	28 29.1	17 43.5	22 11.2	9 59.7	0 31.2	21 20.5	25 07.7	28 04.1
8 W	3 07 42	15 18 32	13 59 16	19 56 19	24 47.1	26 33.2	29 34.1	18 25.3	22 37.0	9 51.6	0 31.5	21 18.0	25 06.8	28 04.9
9 Th	3 11 39	16 18 47	25 55 05	1♎56 04	24 48.8	28 04.6	0♎39.4	19 07.2	23 02.7	9 43.5	0 32.0	21 15.5	25 05.9	28 05.7
10 F	3 15 35	17 19 03	7♎59 43	14 06 26	24 50.3	29 35.6	1 45.0	19 49.2	23 28.5	9 35.5	0 32.5	21 13.0	25 05.0	28 06.6
11 Sa	3 19 32	18 19 21	20 16 35	26 30 26	24R 51.2	1♐06.3	2 50.9	20 31.2	23 54.3	9 27.5	0 33.2	21 10.5	25 04.1	28 07.4
12 Su	3 23 28	19 19 41	2♏48 13	9♏10 05	24 51.0	2 36.6	3 57.0	21 13.2	24 20.0	9 19.5	0 33.9	21 08.1	25 03.3	28 08.3
13 M	3 27 25	20 20 03	15 36 07	22 06 19	24 49.6	4 06.6	5 03.4	21 55.3	24 45.8	9 11.7	0 34.8	21 05.6	25 02.5	28 09.3
14 Tu	3 31 21	21 20 27	28 40 38	5♐18 56	24 46.8	5 36.1	6 10.1	22 37.5	25 11.6	9 03.8	0 35.7	21 03.1	25 01.8	28 10.2
15 W	3 35 18	22 20 53	12♐01 02	18 46 42	24 42.9	7 05.3	7 16.9	23 19.7	25 37.3	8 56.1	0 36.8	21 00.6	25 01.1	28 11.2
16 Th	3 39 14	23 21 20	25 35 39	2♑27 33	24 38.3	8 34.0	8 24.0	24 02.0	26 03.1	8 48.4	0 38.0	20 58.1	25 00.4	28 12.2
17 F	3 43 11	24 21 48	9♑22 07	16 18 59	24 33.7	10 02.3	9 31.3	24 44.3	26 28.8	8 40.8	0 39.2	20 55.6	24 59.7	28 13.2
18 Sa	3 47 08	25 22 18	23 17 49	0♒18 20	24 29.7	11 30.1	10 38.9	25 26.6	26 54.6	8 33.3	0 40.6	20 53.1	24 59.1	28 14.3
19 Su	3 51 04	26 22 49	7♒20 12	14 23 11	24 26.8	12 57.5	11 46.6	26 09.0	27 20.3	8 25.9	0 42.1	20 50.6	24 58.5	28 15.4
20 M	3 55 01	27 23 22	21 26 59	28 31 24	24D 25.4	14 24.2	12 54.5	26 51.5	27 46.0	8 18.6	0 43.7	20 48.1	24 57.9	28 16.5
21 Tu	3 58 57	28 23 55	5♓36 13	12♓41 13	24 25.5	15 50.4	14 02.7	27 34.0	28 11.7	8 11.4	0 45.4	20 45.7	24 57.4	28 17.6
22 W	4 02 54	29 24 30	19 46 13	26 50 58	24 26.6	17 15.9	15 11.0	28 16.5	28 37.4	8 04.4	0 47.2	20 43.2	24 56.9	28 18.8
23 Th	4 06 50	0♐25 05	3♈55 16	10♈58 52	24 28.1	18 40.6	16 19.5	28 59.1	29 03.1	7 57.4	0 49.0	20 40.8	24 56.4	28 20.0
24 F	4 10 47	1 25 42	18 01 27	25 02 43	24R 29.2	20 04.5	17 28.2	29 41.7	29 28.7	7 50.5	0 51.0	20 38.3	24 56.0	28 21.2
25 Sa	4 14 44	2 26 20	2♉02 21	8♉59 56	24 29.1	21 27.4	18 37.1	0♐24.4	29 54.4	7 43.8	0 53.1	20 35.9	24 55.5	28 22.4
26 Su	4 18 40	3 27 00	15 55 08	22 47 31	24 27.3	22 49.3	19 46.2	1 07.2	0♐20.0	7 37.2	0 55.3	20 33.5	24 55.2	28 23.7
27 M	4 22 37	4 27 41	29 36 45	6♊22 26	24 23.4	24 10.0	20 55.4	1 50.0	0 45.7	7 30.7	0 57.6	20 31.1	24 54.8	28 24.9
28 Tu	4 26 33	5 28 23	13♊04 16	19 41 59	24 17.5	25 29.2	22 04.8	2 32.8	1 11.3	7 24.4	1 00.0	20 28.7	24 54.5	28 26.2
29 W	4 30 30	6 29 06	26 15 23	2♋44 20	24 10.2	26 46.9	23 14.4	3 15.7	1 36.9	7 18.2	1 02.5	20 26.3	24 54.3	28 27.5
30 Th	4 34 26	7 29 51	9♋08 49	15 28 50	24 02.2	28 02.7	24 24.2	3 58.6	2 02.4	7 12.2	1 05.0	20 23.9	24 54.0	28 28.9

December 2023

LONGITUDE

Day	Sid.Time	☉	0 hr ☽	Noon ☽	True ☊	☿	♀	♂	⚳	♃	♄	♅	♆	♇
1 F	4 38 23	8♐30 37	21♋44 33	27♋56 10	23♈54.4	29♐16.5	25♎34.0	4♐41.6	2♐28.0	7♉06.3	1♓07.7	20♉21.6	24♓53.8	28♑30.3
2 Sa	4 42 19	9 31 25	4♌03 59	10♌08 22	23R 47.6	0♑27.8	26 44.1	5 24.7	2 53.5	7R 00.6	1 10.5	20R 19.3	24R 53.6	28 31.6
3 Su	4 46 16	10 32 14	16 09 45	22 08 39	23 42.4	1 36.4	27 54.3	6 07.8	3 19.1	6 55.0	1 13.4	20 17.0	24 53.5	28 33.1
4 M	4 50 13	11 33 04	28 05 36	4♍01 13	23 39.2	2 41.7	29 04.6	6 50.9	3 44.6	6 49.6	1 16.3	20 14.7	24 53.4	28 34.5
5 Tu	4 54 09	12 33 56	9♍56 05	15 50 54	23D 37.9	3 43.5	0♏15.1	7 34.1	4 10.0	6 44.3	1 19.4	20 12.4	24 53.3	28 35.9
6 W	4 58 06	13 34 49	21 46 17	27 42 56	23 38.2	4 41.1	1 25.7	8 17.3	4 35.5	6 39.3	1 22.5	20 10.2	24D 53.3	28 37.4
7 Th	5 02 02	14 35 43	3♎41 30	9♎42 37	23 39.4	5 33.9	2 36.4	9 00.6	5 00.9	6 34.4	1 25.8	20 08.0	24 53.3	28 38.9
8 F	5 05 59	15 36 38	15 46 56	21 55 01	23R 40.6	6 21.2	3 47.3	9 44.0	5 26.4	6 29.6	1 29.1	20 05.8	24 53.3	28 40.4
9 Sa	5 09 55	16 37 35	28 07 24	4♏24 32	23 40.7	7 02.4	4 58.3	10 27.4	5 51.7	6 25.1	1 32.5	20 03.6	24 53.4	28 41.9
10 Su	5 13 52	17 38 33	10♏46 49	17 14 30	23 39.1	7 36.6	6 09.4	11 10.8	6 17.1	6 20.7	1 36.1	20 01.5	24 53.5	28 43.5
11 M	5 17 48	18 39 32	23 47 47	0♐26 43	23 35.2	8 03.0	7 20.6	11 54.3	6 42.4	6 16.5	1 39.7	19 59.4	24 53.6	28 45.0
12 Tu	5 21 45	19 40 33	7♐11 13	14 01 05	23 28.7	8 20.7	8 31.9	12 37.9	7 07.8	6 12.5	1 43.4	19 57.3	24 53.8	28 46.6
13 W	5 25 42	20 41 34	20 55 58	27 55 23	23 20.2	8R 28.9	9 43.4	13 21.5	7 33.0	6 08.7	1 47.2	19 55.3	24 54.0	28 48.2
14 Th	5 29 38	21 42 36	4♑58 46	12♑05 27	23 10.2	8 26.7	10 54.9	14 05.1	7 58.3	6 05.1	1 51.0	19 53.2	24 54.3	28 49.8
15 F	5 33 35	22 43 39	19 14 43	26 25 47	23 00.1	8 13.5	12 06.5	14 48.8	8 23.5	6 01.7	1 55.0	19 51.2	24 54.6	28 51.5
16 Sa	5 37 31	23 44 42	3♒37 54	10♒50 20	22 50.8	7 48.9	13 18.3	15 32.5	8 48.7	5 58.5	1 59.1	19 49.3	24 54.9	28 53.1
17 Su	5 41 28	24 45 46	18 02 27	25 13 38	22 43.5	7 12.6	14 30.1	16 16.3	9 13.9	5 55.5	2 03.2	19 47.4	24 55.2	28 54.8
18 M	5 45 24	25 46 50	2♓23 25	9♓31 24	22 38.8	6 25.0	15 42.0	17 00.1	9 39.0	5 52.7	2 07.4	19 45.5	24 55.6	28 56.5
19 Tu	5 49 21	26 47 54	16 37 17	23 40 54	22D 36.5	5 26.8	16 54.0	17 44.0	10 04.1	5 50.1	2 11.7	19 43.6	24 56.0	28 58.2
20 W	5 53 17	27 48 59	0♈42 06	7♈40 52	22 36.1	4 19.3	18 06.0	18 27.9	10 29.1	5 47.7	2 16.1	19 41.8	24 56.5	28 59.9
21 Th	5 57 14	28 50 04	14 37 10	21 31 01	22R 36.5	3 04.4	19 18.2	19 11.9	10 54.1	5 45.5	2 20.5	19 40.0	24 57.0	29 01.6
22 F	6 01 11	29 51 09	28 22 29	5♉11 35	22 36.5	1 44.3	20 30.4	19 55.9	11 19.1	5 43.5	2 25.1	19 38.3	24 57.5	29 03.4
23 Sa	6 05 07	0♑52 15	11♉58 19	18 42 40	22 34.9	0 21.8	21 42.7	20 39.9	11 44.0	5 41.7	2 29.7	19 36.6	24 58.0	29 05.1
24 Su	6 09 04	1 53 21	25 24 37	2♊04 04	22 30.8	28♐59.5	22 55.1	21 24.0	12 08.9	5 40.1	2 34.4	19 34.9	24 58.6	29 06.9
25 M	6 13 00	2 54 27	8♊40 56	15 15 05	22 23.7	27 40.3	24 07.5	22 08.2	12 33.8	5 38.7	2 39.2	19 33.3	24 59.3	29 08.7
26 Tu	6 16 57	3 55 33	21 46 22	28 14 39	22 13.7	26 26.6	25 20.1	22 52.4	12 58.6	5 37.6	2 44.0	19 31.7	24 59.9	29 10.5
27 W	6 20 53	4 56 40	4♋39 49	11♋01 44	22 01.5	25 20.3	26 32.7	23 36.6	13 23.3	5 36.6	2 48.9	19 30.1	25 00.6	29 12.3
28 Th	6 24 50	5 57 47	17 20 20	23 35 36	21 48.0	24 23.1	27 45.3	24 20.9	13 48.1	5 35.9	2 53.9	19 28.6	25 01.3	29 14.1
29 F	6 28 47	6 58 54	29 47 32	5♌56 14	21 34.5	23 35.8	28 58.1	25 05.2	14 12.7	5 35.3	2 59.0	19 27.2	25 02.1	29 15.9
30 Sa	6 32 43	8 00 01	12♌01 51	18 04 36	21 22.2	22 59.0	0♐10.9	25 49.6	14 37.4	5 35.0	3 04.1	19 25.8	25 02.9	29 17.8
31 Su	6 36 40	9 01 09	24 04 48	0♍02 46	21 12.0	22 32.8	1 23.8	26 34.0	15 02.0	5D 34.9	3 09.3	19 24.4	25 03.7	29 19.6

Astro Data	Dy Hr Mn
♄ D	4 7:04
☊ D	5 8:47
♃∠♆	5 21:05
☽ 0S	9 16:38
♀0S	11 5:22
☊ R	11 8:49
☊ D	20 10:45
☽ 0N	23 0:26
☊ R	24 11:03
☊ D	5 6:03
♆ D	6 13:23
☽ 0S	7 0:37
☊ R	8 15:25
☿ R	13 7:10
☊ D	19 18:34

Planet Ingress	Dy Hr Mn
♀ ♎	8 9:32
☿ ♐	10 6:26
☉ ♐	22 14:04
♂ ♐	24 10:16
⚳ ♐	25 5:15
☿ ♑	1 14:33
♀ ♏	4 18:52
☉ ♑	22 3:28
☿ ♐R	23 6:19
♀ ♐	29 20:25
☽ 0N20	5:18
☊ R21	13:54
♃ D31	2:42

Last Aspect Dy Hr Mn		☽ Ingress	Dy Hr Mn
1 12:38	♆ □	♋	1 21:31
4 3:29	♇ ☍	♌	4 7:22
6 7:26	☿ □	♍	6 19:40
9 4:56	☿ ⚹	♎	9 8:09
11 15:07	♇ □	♏	11 18:40
13 23:05	♇ ⚹	♐	14 2:24
15 22:58	♆ □	♑	16 7:43
18 8:29	♇ ☌	♒	18 11:29
20 10:51	☉ □	♓	20 14:30
22 15:11	♂ △	♈	22 17:21
24 17:42	♇ □	♉	24 20:30
26 21:53	♇ △	♊	27 0:41
29 1:04	☿ ☍	♋	29 6:55

Last Aspect Dy Hr Mn		☽ Ingress	Dy Hr Mn
1 13:08	♇ ☍	♌	1 16:02
4 2:12	♀ ⚹	♍	4 3:51
6 13:51	♇ △	♎	6 16:36
9 1:06	♇ □	♏	9 3:36
11 8:58	♇ ⚹	♐	11 11:12
13 6:50	♆ □	♑	13 15:33
15 16:05	♇ ☌	♒	15 17:57
17 12:05	☉ ⚹	♓	17 19:59
19 21:05	♇ ⚹	♈	19 22:48
22 2:48	☉ △	♉	22 2:51
24 6:41	♇ △	♊	24 8:16
26 7:57	☿ ☍	♋	26 15:16
28 22:58	♇ ☍	♌	29 0:24
31 5:19	♂ △	♍	31 11:54

☽ Phases & Eclipses Dy Hr Mn	
5 8:38	☾ 12♌40
13 9:29	● 20♏44
20 10:51	☽ 27♒51
27 9:17	○ 4♊51
5 5:50	☾ 12♍49
12 23:33	● 20♐40
19 18:40	☽ 27♓35
27 0:34	○ 4♋58

Astro Data

1 November 2023
Julian Day # 45230
SVP 4♓55'45"
GC 27♐10.3 ⚴ 21♎54.6
Eris 24♈34.1R ⚵ 5♍46.1
⚷ 16♈45.8R ⚶ 7♋29.2
☽ Mean ☊ 24♈06.3

1 December 2023
Julian Day # 45260
SVP 4♓55'40"
GC 27♐10.4 ⚴ 4♏59.4
Eris 24♈18.6R ⚵ 15♍36.2
⚷ 15♈45.7R ⚶ 4♋39.3R
☽ Mean ☊ 22♈31.0

*Giving the positions of planets daily at midnight, Greenwich Mean Time (0:00 UT)
Each planet's retrograde period is shaded gray.

2023 ASTEROID EPHEMERIS

Ceres, Pallas, Juno, Vesta

2023	Ceres	Pallas	Juno	Vesta
JAN 1	3♎09.3	20R49.6	24♓34.1	14♓01.2
JAN 11	5 01.0	17S28.8	28 57.5	18 01.1
JAN 21	6 17.9	14 20.5	3♈38.8	22 09.9
JAN 31	6 55.3	11 58.2	8 35.5	26 25.9
FEB 10	6R50.0	10 49.3	13 44.9	0♉47.4
FEB 20	6 01.1	10D29.5	19 05.1	5 13.2
MAR 2	4 32.1	11 20.6	24 34.4	9 42.2
MAR 12	2 32.3	13 03.2	0♊10.9	14 13.3
MAR 22	0 16.1	15 27.0	5 53.3	18 45.6
APR 1	28♍00.1	18 23.1	11 40.4	23 18.8
APR 11	26 05.3	21 44.3	17 30.8	27 51.6
APR 21	24 40.9	25 24.2	23 23.4	2♋23.8
MAY 1	23 55.9	29 23.3	29 17.4	6 54.6
MAY 11	23D55.2	3♏23.9	5♊11.3	11 23.5
MAY 21	24 28.9	7 37.4	11 05.0	15 50.0
MAY 31	25 41.8	11 57.2	16 57.2	20 13.5
JUN 10	27 26.5	16 21.5	22 47.1	24 33.6
JUN 20	29 38.4	20 49.3	28 34.2	28♋49.8
JUN 30	2♎13.6	25 19.8	4♋17.7	2♌59.8
JUL 10	5 08.0	29 52.1	9 56.9	7 04.7
JUL 20	8 18.7	4♐25.8	15 31.5	11 02.8
AUG 9	11 43.0	9 00.6	21 00.6	14 52.2
AUG 19	15 18.6	13 35.6	26 23.6	18 33.7
AUG 29	19 03.6	18 11.7	1♌40.0	22 03.4
SEP 8	22 56.6	22 47.6	6 49.0	25 19.8
SEP 18	26 56.0	27 23.2	11 49.9	28 20.6
SEP 28	1♏00.7	1♑58.4	16 41.1	1♍02.7
OCT 8	5 09.8	6 32.8	21 23.3	3 22.3
OCT 18	9 22.2	11 06.1	25 53.5	5 15.4
OCT 28	13 37.1	15 37.8	0♍11.1	6 37.1
NOV 7	17 53.2	20 07.4	4 13.6	7 22.3
NOV 17	22 11.2	24 34.3	7 59.5	7R26.8
NOV 27	26 28.8	28 57.9	11 25.9	6 47.2
DEC 7	0♐45.6	3♒17.1	14 29.7	5 23.8
DEC 17	5 00.9	7 31.0	17 07.4	3 22.6
DEC 27	9 13.8	11 38.5	19 14.8	0 53.9
JAN 6	13 23.3	15 37.9	20 47.3	28♌16.1

2023	Ceres	Pallas	Juno	Vesta
JAN 1	09N39.5	32S02.6	08S26.4	12S09.0
JAN 21	09 56.1	29 01.1	05 21.7	08 33.9
FEB 10	11 16.3	22 46.7	01 50.0	04 49.3
MAR 2	13 21.9	15 00.7	01N52.1	01 02.8
MAR 22	15 21.9	07 07.2	05 28.9	02N38.4
APR 11	16 14.7	01 07.8	08 45.5	06 07.9
MAY 1	15 34.2	03N33.1	11 28.8	09 19.6
MAY 21	13 35.9	06 37.4	13 28.0	12 08.4
JUN 10	10 46.8	08 17.1	14 36.3	14 30.2
JUN 30	07 27.7	08 47.4	15 01.9	16 22.2
JUL 20	03 52.2	08 25.8	14 51.1	17 43.2
AUG 9	00 09.6	07 26.0	14 18.3	18 34.3
AUG 29	03S33.0	06 02.4	13 33.7	18 59.1
SEP 18	07 09.0	04 27.8	12 46.5	19 04.4
OCT 8	10 32.6	02 54.4	11 59.9	19 00.4
OCT 28	13 38.2	01 34.1	11 17.3	19 00.3
NOV 17	16 20.7	00 38.5	10 40.9	18 46.9
DEC 7	18 36.1	00 19.1	10 09.9	19 55.4
DEC 27	20S22.0	00N46.6	09S49.7	21S15.8

Psyche, Eros, Lilith, Toro

2023	Psyche	Eros	Lilith	Toro
JAN 1	13♍58.8	9♐34.5	23♏56.9	22♏26.3
JAN 11	16 40.4	16 26.0	24 43.7	27 01.7
JAN 21	19 08.5	23 05.1	24R49.8	1♐26.8
JAN 31	21 20.0	29 31.6	24 12.8	5 40.0
FEB 10	23 12.4	5♑45.5	22 54.8	9 39.7
FEB 20	24 42.6	11 46.9	21 02.1	13 24.1
MAR 2	25 47.2	17 35.3	18 46.1	16 49.7
MAR 12	26 24.3	23 10.4	16 22.6	19 55.2
MAR 22	26R28.4	28 31.7	14 07.9	22 39.8
APR 1	26 00.9	3♒38.0	12 16.6	24 57.1
APR 11	25 01.8	8 28.2	10 58.5	26 44.2
APR 21	23 36.2	13 00.8	10 17.9	27 56.9
MAY 1	21 44.6	17 13.1	10D15.6	28R31.7
MAY 11	19 43.0	21 02.3	10 49.0	28 26.0
MAY 21	17 40.5	24 24.4	11 54.3	27 36.1
MAY 31	15 49.1	27 13.8	13 27.7	26 06.8
JUN 10	14 18.6	29 24.2	15 24.7	24 07.3
JUN 20	13 15.7	0♓47.1	17 41.8	21 50.9
JUN 30	12 44.3	1♓12.7	20 15.7	20 03.7 (?)
JUL 10	12D45.1	0 32.2	23 03.6	27♏51.5
JUL 20	13 17.0	28♒38.5	26 03.2	25 50.1
AUG 9	15 44.9	21 35.9	2♐29.7	25D58.8
AUG 19	17 35.1	17 15.9	5 53.6	27 48.6
AUG 29	19 45.7	13 15.4	9 22.8	0♐36.2
SEP 8	22 13.8	10 09.2	12 56.1	4 13.1
SEP 18	24 57.4	8 16.4	16 32.8	8 34.2
SEP 28	27 54.4	7D42.0	20 11.7	13 35.7
OCT 8	1♎02.8	8 20.0	23 52.0	19 14.3
OCT 18	4 21.0	10 01.4	27 32.9	25 28.3
OCT 28	7 47.7	12 36.8	1♑13.4	2♑15.2
NOV 7	11 21.5	15 57.3	4 52.7	9 30.7
NOV 17	15 01.3	19 56.1	8 29.8	17 09.8
NOV 27	18 45.9	24 27.8	12 03.6	25 06.5
DEC 7	22 34.0	29 26.2	15 32.8	3♒09.0
DEC 17	26 25.6	4♓53.6	18 56.7	11 08.9
DEC 27	0♍18.5	10 42.3	22 13.2	22 29.8 (?)
JAN 6	4♍12.3	16♓52.0	25♑21.0	7♓17.9

2023	Psyche	Eros	Lilith	Toro
JAN 1	13S47.5	28S44.2	03S29.7	24S50.9
JAN 21	15 00.2	30 08.2	04 42.7	27 15.6
FEB 10	15 45.1	30 00.8	04 44.3	29 06.1
MAR 2	16 00.7	28 37.8	03 33.3	30 20.6
MAR 22	15 46.4	26 18.0	01 40.4	31 21.5
APR 11	15 03.6	23 23.1	00N04.5	32 01.1
MAY 1	13 59.6	20 08.7	01 05.8	32 22.8
MAY 21	12 51.8	16 51.9	01 13.7	32 04.4 (?)
JUN 10	12 04.4	13 48.8	00S12.8	29 21.0
JUN 30	11 54.4	11 14.1	00S47.4	24 42.8
JUL 20	12 24.3	09 25.1	02 37.9	20 23.0
AUG 9	13 26.5	08 29.1	04 50.2	17 46.1
AUG 29	14 49.6	08 11.5	07 17.0	16 33.3
SEP 18	16 22.3	08 22.1	09 50.1	16 21.6
OCT 8	17 54.4	07 34.6	12 27.1	15 12.7 (?)
OCT 28	20 23.0	04 41.1	17 20.0	11 05.3
NOV 17	21 06.3	01 59.0	19 27.0	13 18.1
DEC 7	21S23.1	01N51.5	21S15.8	07S36.2

Saffo, Amor, Pandora, Icarus

2023	Saffo	Amor	Pandora	Icarus
JAN 1	2R38.3	3♈26.0	17♏22.2	5♍12.8
JAN 11	1♍42.4	11 23.2	21 47.4	10 57.9
JAN 21	0 02.4	18 56.7	26 14.9	17 22.7
JAN 31	27♌46.0	25 55.9	0♐48.9	24 40.0
FEB 10	25 07.5	2♉55.6	5 13.4	3♎11.1
FEB 20	22 24.8	9 23.1	9 42.9	13 41.4
MAR 2	19 57.1	15 30.1	14 11.7	27 44.2
MAR 12	17 59.5	21 18.6	18 37.7	13♏29.6
MAR 22	16 41.2	26 48.0	23 01.4	29♏56.0
APR 1	16 05.8	1♊59.4	27 21.4	26 27.7
APR 11	16D12.3	6 52.5	1♑36.5	25 30.1
APR 21	16 56.1	11 27.3	5 45.8	25 51.0
MAY 1	18 14.9	15 43.2	9 47.6	24 37.9
MAY 11	20 01.7	19 39.2	13 40.8	23 21.9
MAY 21	22 12.6	23 14.2	17 22.8	20 54.0
MAY 31	24 43.3	26 25.9	20 52.0	19 48.2
JUN 10	27 32.1	29 12.0	24 05.8	10 41.2 (?)
JUN 20	0♍34.4	1♋29.3	27 01.0	2 33.1
JUN 30	3 48.6	3 13.8	29 33.9	23♍06.4
JUL 10	7 12.6	4 21.3	1♒40.5	13 49.4
JUL 20	10 44.9	4 46.9	3 16.1	5 49.4
JUL 30	14 24.3	4R26.2	4 15.7	0 00.1
AUG 9	18 09.4	3 16.9	4R35.6	26♌15.4
AUG 19	21 59.5	1 19.9	4 12.8	24 14.7
AUG 29	25 53.6	28♊40.6	3 08.0	23 35.9
SEP 8	29 51.0	25 33.5	1 27.3	23♍59.0
SEP 18	3♎51.1	22 16.4	29♑22.2	25 10.1
SEP 28	7 53.2	19 10.4	27 09.8	26 58.3
OCT 8	11 56.0	16 33.3	25 08.9	29 15.7
OCT 18	16 01.1	14 36.8	23 35.7	1♎57.7
OCT 28	20 05.1	13 24.4	22 42.1	4 58.7
NOV 7	24 05.7	13 01.6	22D32.9	8 17.5
NOV 17	28 06.5	13 30.0	23 08.2	11 51.9
NOV 27	2♏04.5	14 44.0	24 25.5	15 40.6
DEC 7	5 58.6	16 37.2	26 19.8	19 42.8
DEC 17	9 48.3	19 00.9	28 46.3	23 57.2
DEC 27	13 30.4	21 52.3	1♓40.0	28 23.0
JAN 6	17♏04.0	25♊07.6	4♓56.5	3♏15.0

2023	Saffo	Amor	Pandora	Icarus
JAN 1	00S38.9	16S31.5	27S28.0	30S26.0
JAN 21	00 44.7	15 20.5	25 53.8	26 13.5
FEB 10	00N33.2	13 06.1	23 49.5	19 11.0
MAR 2	02 07.1	09 17.9	21 19.7	04 21.2
MAR 22	04 56.6	03 57.9	18 31.2	25N04.8
APR 11	07 12.1	03N57.9	15 31.6	29 35.0
MAY 1	07 57.6	11 00.5	12 09.0	08 00.9 (?)
JUN 10	06 56.4	23 04.8	05 54.8	27 48.4
JUN 30	05 37.0	30 04.1	03 10.6	36 07.0
JUL 20	03 42.8	30 23.6	01 02.2	39 13.1
AUG 9	01 55.1	09 09.6	00S07.6	37 32.7
SEP 18	06 04.4	08 22.3	04 34.5	26 31.3
OCT 8	08 28.7	08 50.8	06 02.3	23 46.7
NOV 17	12 56.4	09 23.3	05 55.4	18 45.1
DEC 7	15S22.6	09S25.7	02N33.7	31S05.7

Diana, Hidalgo, Urania, Chiron

2023	Diana	Hidalgo	Urania	Chiron
JAN 1	23♓40.5	24♏56.1	1♈03.5	11♈58.1
JAN 11	26 35.8	25 53.9	0♉50.1	12♈05.6
JAN 21	29 41.6	26 45.1	1♈22.3	12 36.1
JAN 31	3♈17.6	27 22.2	2 50.6	13 24.1
FEB 10	6 59.3	27 50.2	4 53.4	14 28.3
FEB 20	10 52.3	28 05.9	7 29.1	15 45.3
MAR 2	14 55.0	28R08.5	10 33.2	17 12.6
MAR 12	19 05.9	27 57.7	13 56.8	18 45.7
MAR 22	23 24.1	27 33.4	17 39.0	20 22.6
APR 1	27 48.6	26 56.2	21 35.5	21 59.4
APR 11	2♉18.1	26 07.3	25 43.9	23 34.5
APR 21	6 52.5	25 08.9	29 59.4	25 04.3
MAY 1	11 30.9	24 03.7	4♉22.5	26 27.3
MAY 11	16 12.5	22 54.2	8 51.3	27 40.8
MAY 21	20 57.1	21 43.9	13 24.0	28 43.2
MAY 31	25 44.4	20 34.2	18 00.3	29 32.4
JUN 10	0♊33.3	19 30.0	22 38.4	0♉07.0
JUN 20	5 22.9	18 40.2	27 18.1	0 25.1
JUN 30	10 12.2	17 57.9	1♊58.5	0R25.3
JUL 10	15 00.9	17 26.0	6 38.7	0 07.3
JUL 20	19 58.6	17 05.7	11 20.3	29♈31.3
AUG 9	24 48.5	16 59.3	16 00.5	28 38.7
AUG 19	29 38.0	17D05.3	20 39.6	27 48.1
AUG 29	4♋28.7	17 22.9	25 16.4	27 09.9
SEP 8	9 13.7	18 31.0	4♋58.7	26 18.5 (?)
SEP 18	18 19.7	19 20.3	8 57.9	26 00.5
SEP 28	22 48.2	20 16.6	13 46.6	25 48.3
OCT 8	0♌53.5	22 40.4	18 33.3	25 44.8
OCT 18	4 34.1	23 40.4	26 13.5	25 49.6
OCT 28	7 52.8	24 56.5	4♌14.6	26 09.8
NOV 7	10 44.0	26 18.0	7 59.4	26 40.4
NOV 17	13 02.1	27 42.7	11 31.4	27 20.3
NOV 27	14 40.4	29 07.9	14 49.6	28 07.1
DEC 7	15 32.0	0♐29.5	17 49.6	29 06.4
DEC 17	15R33.5	1♐50.5	20 27.0	0♉01.1
JAN 6	14♌40.9	4♐24.7	20♋28.9	15♈29.3

2023	Diana	Hidalgo	Urania	Chiron
JAN 1	02N28.8	3♐54.7	22N59.1	06N21.4
JAN 21	04 52.1	41 18.6	22 40.1	06 39.3
FEB 10	07 25.4	42 41.2	22 40.6	06 53.8 (?)
MAR 2	10 52.1	43 58.9	23 13.3	07 20.3
MAR 22	13 11.6	44 00.0	24 58.4	07 48.1
APR 11	14 41.0	43 22.1	22 57.4	08 13.7
MAY 1	15 41.2	42 08.1	25 38.4	08 34.7
MAY 21	15 45.6	40 21.5	22 50.6	08 49.1
JUN 10	15 32.2	38 14.0	24 30.0	08 55.1
JUN 30	14 44.4	36 41.0	22 12.6	08 51.6
JUL 20	13 48.9	34 32.4	23 59.4	08 38.4
AUG 9	12 48.7	32 12.1	22 37.5	08 16.1
AUG 29	11 52.6	30 34.6	25 10.4	07 47.1
SEP 18	11 04.9	30 34.7	22 57.4	07 13.8
OCT 8	10 29.1	30 59.6	24 59.0	06 40.6
OCT 28	10 06.6	32 34.3	23 24.5	06 11.4
NOV 17	09 56.9	34 47.7	25 38.4	05 50.3
DEC 7	09 45.6	41 44.5	20S15.4	05 40.8
DEC 27	09S44.3	42 10.5	20S15.4	07N20.8

Giving the positions of asteroids every ten days in LONGITUDE at 00:00 GMT

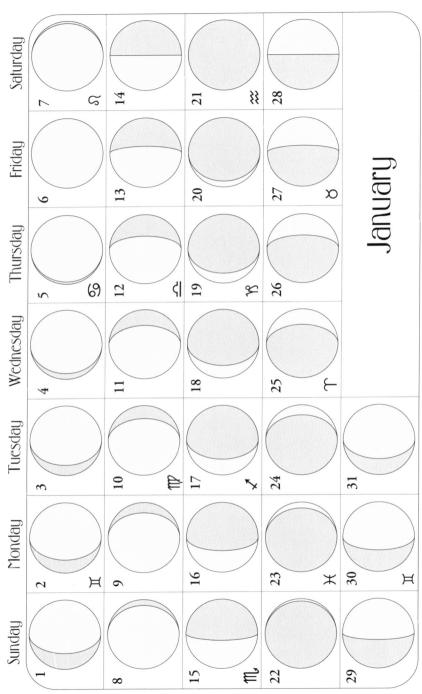

January

214

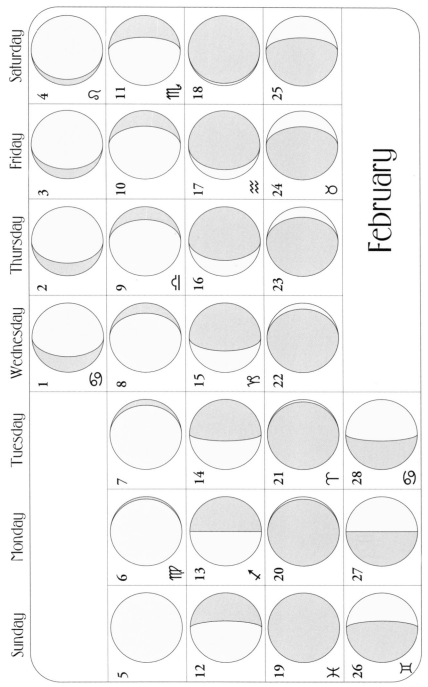

February

215

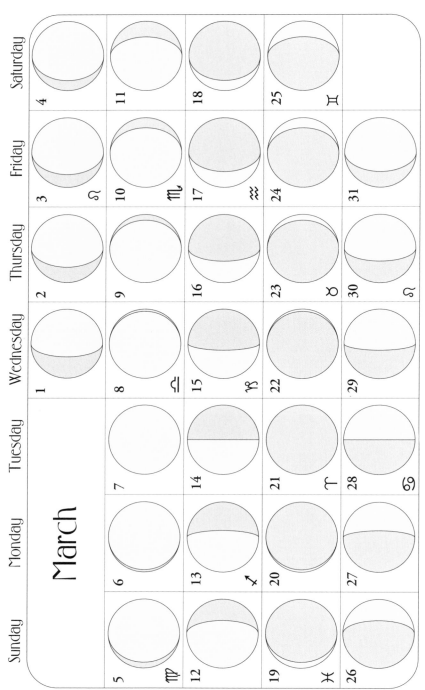

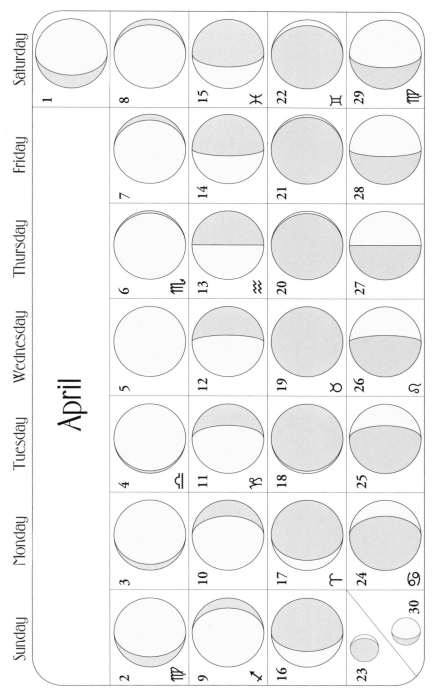
217

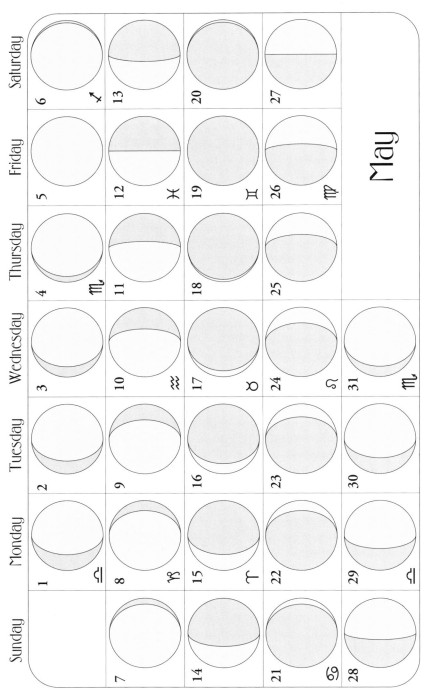

May

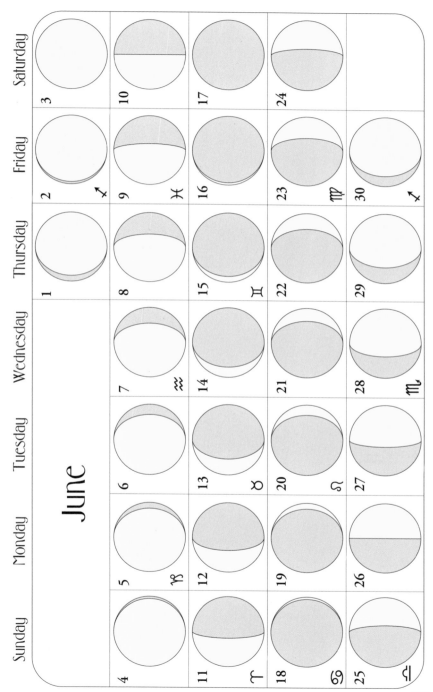

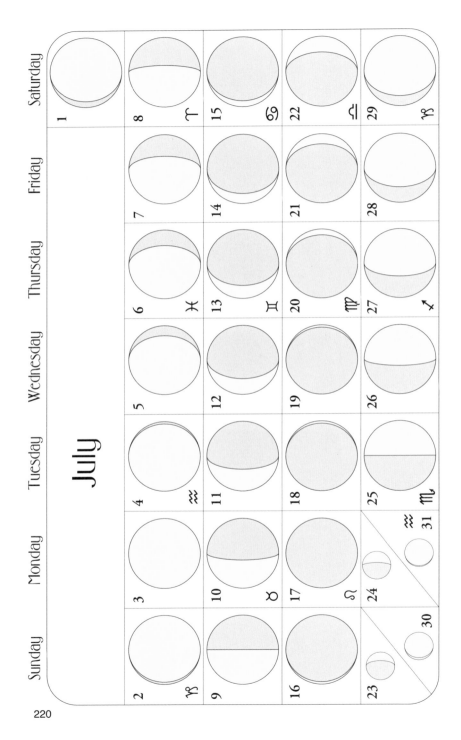

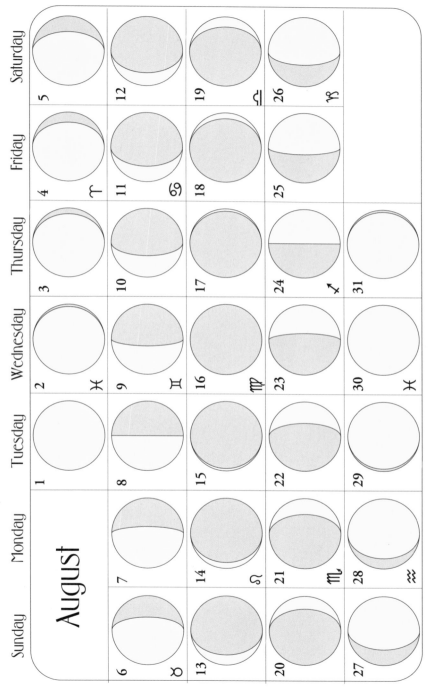

August

Sunday	Monday	Tuesday	Wednesday	Thursday	Friday	Saturday
		1	2 ♓	3	4 ♈	5
6 ♉	7	8	9 ♊	10	11 ♋	12
13	14 ♌	15	16 ♍	17	18	19 ♎
20	21 ♏	22	23	24 ♐	25	26 ♑
27	28 ♒	29	30 ♓	31		

221

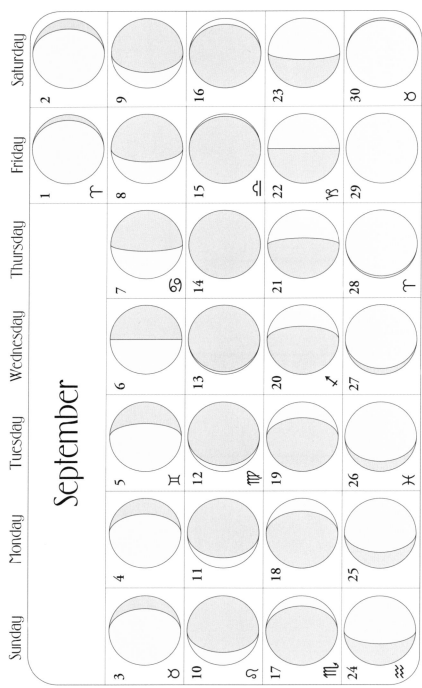

September

222

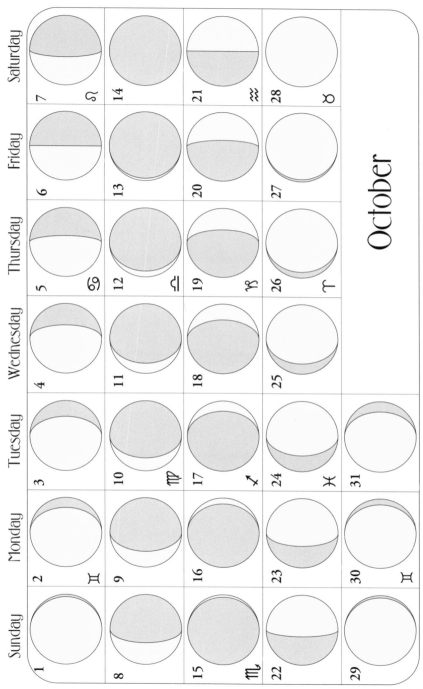

October

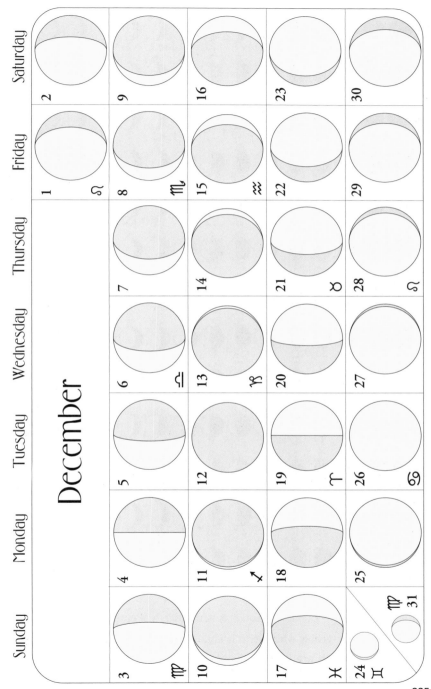

December

Sunday	Monday	Tuesday	Wednesday	Thursday	Friday	Saturday
					1 ♌	2
3 ♍	4	5	6 ♎	7	8 ♏	9
10	11 ♐	12	13 ♑	14	15 ♒	16
17 ♓	18	19 ♈	20	21 ♉	22	23
24 ♊	25	26 ♋	27	28 ♌	29	30
31 ♍						

225

Eclipse Key:

☽ = Solar ☾ = Lunar **T** = Total **A** = Annular *n* = Penumbral **P** = Partial

Lunar Eclipses are visible wherever it is night and cloud free during full moon time.

Times on this page are in EST (Eastern Standard Time -5 from GMT)
or DST, Daylight Saving Time (Mar 12 - Nov 5, 2023)

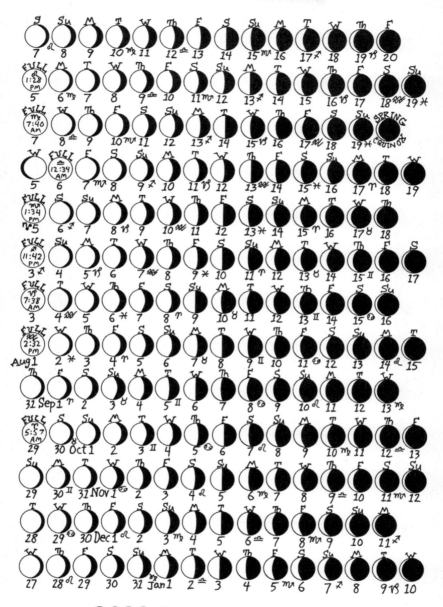

2023 Lunar Phases

This format available on cards from: **http://snakeandsnake.com**

Snake and Snake Productions 3037 Dixon Rd Durham, NC 27707

Conventional Holidays 2023

January 1	New Years Day*
January 16	Martin Luther King Jr. Day
January 22	Tibetan & Chinese New Year
February 14	Valentine's Day*
February 20	President's Day
February 22	Ash Wednesday
March 8	International Women's Day*
March 12	Mexika (Aztec) New Year*
March 12	Daylight Saving Time Begins
March 17	St. Patrick's Day*
March 23–April 21	Ramadan
April 2	Palm Sunday
April 6–April 13	Passover
April 7	Good Friday
April 9	Easter
April 22	Earth Day*
May 5	Cinco de Mayo*
May 14	Mother's Day
May 29	Memorial Day
June 18	Father's Day
June 19	Juneteenth*
July 4	Independence Day*
September 4	Labor Day
September 16–17	Rosh Hashanah
September 25	Yom Kippur
October 9	Indigenous Peoples' Day
October 31	Halloween*
November 1	All Saints' Day*
November 2	Day of the Dead*
November 5	Daylight Saving Time Ends
November 11	Veteran's Day*
November 23	Thanksgiving Day
December 8–15	Chanukah/Hanukkah
December 25	Christmas Day*
December 26	Boxing Day*
Dec. 26–Jan. 1	Kwanzaa*
December 31	New Years Eve*
	* Same date every year

WORLD TIME ZONES

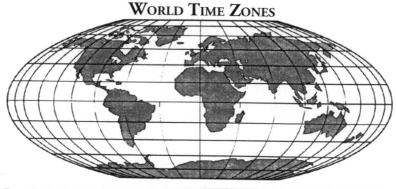

ID LW	NT BT	CA HT	YST	PST	MST	CST	EST	AST	BST	AT	WAT	GMT	CET	EET	BT	USSR Z3	USSR Z4	USSR Z5	SST	CCT	JST	GST	USSR Z10	ID LE
-12	-11	-10	-9	-8	-7	-6	-5	-4	-3	-2	-1	**0**	+1	+2	+3	+4	+5	+6	+7	+8	+9	+10	+11	+12
-4	-3	-2	-1	**0**	+1	+2	+3	+4	+5	+6	+7	+8	+9	+10	+11	+12	+13	+14	+15	+16	+17	+18	+19	+20

STANDARD TIME ZONES FROM WEST TO EAST CALCULATED FROM PST AS ZERO POINT:

IDLW:	International Date Line West	-4
NT/BT:	Nome Time/Bering Time	-3
CA/HT:	Central Alaska & Hawaiian Time	-2
YST:	Yukon Standard Time	-1
PST:	Pacific Standard Time	0
MST:	Mountain Standard Time	+1
CST:	Central Standard Time	+2
EST:	Eastern Standard Time	+3
AST:	Atlantic Standard Time	+4
NFT:	Newfoundland Time	+4 1/2
BST:	Brazil Standard Time	+5
AT:	Azores Time	+6
WAT:	West African Time	+7
GMT:	Greenwich Mean Time	+8
WET:	Western European Time (England)	+8
CET:	Central European Time	+9
EET:	Eastern European Time	+10

BT:	Bagdhad Time	+11
IT:	Iran Time	+11 1/2
USSR	Zone 3	+12
USSR	Zone 4	+13
IST:	Indian Standard Time	+13 1/2
USSR	Zone 5	+14
NST:	North Sumatra Time	+14 1/2
SST:	South Sumatra Time & USSR Zone 6	+15
JT:	Java Time	+15 1/2
CCT:	China Coast Time	+16
MT:	Moluccas Time	+16 1/2
JST:	Japanese Standard Time	+17
SAST:	South Australian Standard Time	+17 1/2
GST:	Guam Standard Time	+18
USSR	Zone 10	+19
IDLE:	International Date Line East	+20

HOW TO CALCULATE TIME ZONE CORRECTIONS IN YOUR AREA:

ADD if you are **east** of PST (Pacific Standard Time); **SUBTRACT** if you are **west** of PST on this map (see right-hand column of chart above).

All times in this calendar are calculated from the West Coast of North America where We'Moon is made. Pacific Standard Time (PST Zone 8) is zero point for this calendar, except during Daylight Saving Time (March 12–November 5, 2023, during which times are given for PDT Zone 7). If your time zone does not use Daylight Saving Time, add one hour to the standard correction during this time. At the bottom of each page, EST/EDT (Eastern Standard or Daylight Time) and GMT (Greenwich Mean Time) times are also given. For all other time zones, calculate your time zone correction(s) from this map and write it on the inside cover for easy reference.

2024

JANUARY
S	M	T	W	T	F	S
	1	2	3	4	5	6
7	8	9	10	**11**	12	13
14	15	16	17	18	19	20
21	22	23	24	○25	26	27
28	29	30	31			

FEBRUARY
S	M	T	W	T	F	S
				1	2	3
4	5	6	7	8	**9**	10
11	12	13	14	15	16	17
18	19	20	21	22	23	○24
25	26	27	28	29		

MARCH
S	M	T	W	T	F	S
					1	2
3	4	5	6	7	8	9
10	11	12	13	14	15	16
17	18	19	20	21	22	23
24	○25	26	27	28	29	30
31						

APRIL
S	M	T	W	T	F	S
	1	2	3	4	5	6
7	**8**	9	10	11	12	13
14	15	16	17	18	19	20
21	22	○23	24	25	26	27
28	29	30				

MAY
S	M	T	W	T	F	S
			1	2	3	4
5	6	**7**	8	9	10	11
12	13	14	15	16	17	18
19	20	21	22	○23	24	25
26	27	28	29	30	31	

JUNE
S	M	T	W	T	F	S
						1
2	3	4	5	**6**	7	8
9	10	11	12	13	14	15
16	17	18	19	20	○21	22
23	24	25	26	27	28	29
30						

JULY
S	M	T	W	T	F	S
	1	2	3	4	**5**	6
7	8	9	10	11	12	13
14	15	16	17	18	19	20
○21	22	23	24	25	26	27
28	29	30	31			

AUGUST
S	M	T	W	T	F	S
				1	2	3
4	5	6	7	8	9	10
11	12	13	14	15	16	17
18	○19	20	21	22	23	24
25	26	27	28	29	30	31

SEPTEMBER
S	M	T	W	T	F	S
1	**2**	3	4	5	6	7
8	9	10	11	12	13	14
15	16	○17	18	19	20	21
22	23	24	25	26	27	28
29	30					

OCTOBER
S	M	T	W	T	F	S
		1	**2**	3	4	5
6	7	8	9	10	11	12
13	14	15	16	○17	18	19
20	21	22	23	24	25	26
27	28	29	30	31		

NOVEMBER
S	M	T	W	T	F	S
					1	2
3	4	5	6	7	8	9
10	11	12	13	14	○15	16
17	18	19	20	21	22	23
24	25	26	27	28	29	**30**

DECEMBER
S	M	T	W	T	F	S
1	2	3	4	5	6	7
8	9	10	11	12	13	14
○15	16	17	18	19	20	21
22	23	24	25	26	27	28
29	**30**	31				

Owning My Story
□ *Suzanne Grace Michell 2016*

● = NEW MOON, PST/PDT

○ = FULL MOON, PST/PDT

230

WE'MOON 2023:
SILVER LINING

• **Datebook** The best-selling astrological moon calendar, earth-spirited handbook in natural rhythms, and visionary collection of women's creative work. Week-at-a-glance format. Choice of 3 bindings: Spiral, Sturdy Paperback Binding or Unbound. We proudly offer a full translation of the classic datebook, in Spanish, too! 8x5¼, 240 pages, $22.95

• **Cover Poster** featuring "*Ancient Angel,*" by Cathy McClelland—a meditation on infinite possibilities and inner divinity. 11x17, $10

• **We'Moon on the Wall** A beautiful full color wall calendar featuring inspired art and writing from *We'Moon 2023,* with key astrological information, interpretive articles, lunar phases and signs. 12x12, $17.95

• **We'Moon Totes** made with organic cotton, proudly displaying the cover of We'Moon. Perfect for stowing all of your goodies in style. Sm: 13x14x3", $13 & Lg: 18x13x6", $15

232

• Greeting Cards An assortment of six gorgeous note cards featuring art from *We'Moon 2023*, with writings from each artist on the back. Wonderful to send for any occasion: Holy Day, Birthday, Anniversary, Sympathy, or just to say hello. Each pack is wrapped in biodegradable cellophane. Blank inside. 5x7, $13.95

Check out page 231 for details on these offerings:

• *The Last Wild Witch* by Starhawk, illustrated by Lindy Kehoe.

• *In the Spirit of We'Moon ~ Celebrating 30 Years: An Anthology of We'Moon Art and Writing*

• *Preacher Woman for the Goddess: Poems, Invocations, Plays and Other Holy Writ* by We'Moon Special Editor Bethroot Gwynn.

All products printed in full color on recycled paper with low VOC soy-based ink.

Become a We'Moon Contributor!
Send submissions for
We'Moon 2025
the 44th edition!

Call for Contributions: Available in the spring of 2023
Postmark-by Date for all art and writing: August 1, 2023
Note: It is too late to contribute to
We'Moon 2024

We'Moon is made up by writers and artists like you! We welcome creative work by women from around the world. We'Moon is dedicated to amplifying images and writing from women with diverse perspectives, and is committed to minority inclusion. We seek to hold welcoming, celebratory space for all women, and are eager to publish more works depicting Black, Brown, Indigenous, Asian, Latine, and all voices from the margins, *created by* women who share these lived experiences. By nurturing space for all women to share their gifts, we unleash insight and wisdom upon the world—a blessing to us all.

> **We invite you to send in your art and writing for the next edition of We'Moon!**

Here's how:

Step 1: Visit wemoon.ws to download a Call for Contributions or send your request for one with a SASE (legal size) to **We'Moon Submissions, PO Box 187, Wolf Creek, OR 97497.** (If you are not within the US, you do not need to include postage.) The Call contains current information about the theme, specifications about how to submit your art and writing, and terms of compensation. There are no jury fees. The Call comes out in the early Spring every year.

Step 2: Fill in the accompanying Contributor's License, giving all the requested information, and return it with your art/writing by the due date. *No work will be accepted without a signed license!* We now accept email submissions, too. See our website for details.

Step 3: Plan ahead! To assure your work is considered for ***We'Moon 2025***, get your submissions postmarked by August 1, 2023.

NOTES

Esperanza
© Koco Collab 2021

Diosa de la Luna
© Kay Kemp 2018

Michif
Horse Women
© *Leah Marie Dorion*
2012

Stardust
◻ *D. Woodring—*
Portrait Priestess 2020

Promise of Spring
© *Lindy Kehoe 2020*

Passage Between Worlds
© LorrieArt 2019